COLLECTED POEMS AND
OTHER VERSE

STÉPHANE MALLARMÉ, the ~~~~~~~~~~~~~~~~~~~~~~~
'an uninterrupted succession ~~~~~~~~~~~~~~~~~~~
in 1842. His life was quiet and ~~~~~~~~~~~~~~~~~
1863 and taught English from t~~~~~~~~~~~~~~~~~~~
French provincial schools, and ~~~~~~~~~~~~~~~~~~
Geneviève (1864–1919) and ~~~~~~~~~~~~~~~~~~~~~
collected as *Poésies* (*Poetical Work*~~~~~~~~~ limited edition
(1887) and then, more fully, in 1899; his prose poems appeared in
Divagations (*Diversions*, 1897). The definitive text of *Un coup de dés
jamais n'abolira le hasard* (*A Dice Throw At Any Time Never Will
Abolish Chance*) was not published until 1913. He died at Valvins
in 1898, little known to the general public but greatly admired by
his literary colleagues, who had elected him Prince of Poets (in
succession to Verlaine) in 1896.

E. H. and A. M. BLACKMORE have edited and translated eleven
volumes of French literature, including *Six French Poets of the
Nineteenth Century* and *The Essential Victor Hugo* (both in Oxford
World's Classics). Their work has been awarded the American
Literary Translators' Association Prize and the Modern Language
Association Scaglione Prize for Literary Translation.

ELIZABETH MCCOMBIE is a Junior Research Fellow in French at
St John's College, University of Oxford. She is the author of
Mallarmé and Debussy: Unheard Music, Unseen Text (Oxford, 2003).
She lives in London with her husband and daughter.

OXFORD WORLD'S CLASSICS

For over 100 years Oxford World's Classic have brought readers closer to the world's great literature. Now with over 700 titles—from the 4,000-year-old myths of Mesopotamia to the twentieth century's greatest novels—the series makes available lesser-known as well as celebrated writing.

The pocket-sized hardbacks of the early years contained introductions by Virginia Woolf, T.S. Eliot, Graham Greene, and other literary figures which enriched the experience of reading. Today the series is recognized for its fine scholarship and reliability in texts that span world literature, drama and poetry, religion, philosophy and politics. Each edition includes perceptive commentary and essential background information to meet the changing needs of readers.

OXFORD WORLD'S CLASSICS

STÉPHANE MALLARMÉ

Collected Poems and Other Verse

Translated with Notes by
E. H. and A. M. BLACKMORE

With an Introduction by
ELIZABETH McCOMBIE

OXFORD
UNIVERSITY PRESS

OXFORD
UNIVERSITY PRESS

Great Clarendon Street, Oxford OX2 6DP

Oxford University Press is a department of the University of Oxford.
It furthers the University's objective of excellence in research, scholarship,
and education by publishing worldwide in

Oxford New York

Auckland Cape Town Dar es Salaam Hong Kong Karachi
Kuala Lumpur Madrid Melbourne Mexico City Nairobi
New Delhi Shanghai Taipei Toronto

With offices in

Argentina Austria Brazil Chile Czech Republic France Greece
Guatemala Hungary Italy Japan Poland Portugal Singapore
South Korea Switzerland Thailand Turkey Ukraine Vietnam

Oxford is a registered trade mark of Oxford University Press
in the UK and in certain other countries

Published in the United States
by Oxford University Press Inc., New York

First published as an Oxford World's Classics paperback 2006

British Library Cataloguing in Publication Data

Data available

Library of Congress Cataloging in Publication Data

Data available

Typeset in Ehrhardt
by RefineCatch Limited, Bungay, Suffolk
Printed in Great Britain by
Clays Ltd., St. Ives plc

ISBN 0-19-280362-X 978-0-19-280362-7

CONTENTS

COLLECTED POEMS AND OTHER VERSE

Poésies / Poetical Works

Anecdotes ou Poèmes/*Anecdotes or Poems*

APPENDIX 2 *Vers de circonstances/Occasional Verses*

INTRODUCTION

Stéphane Mallarmé (1842–98) is renowned as a radical innovator of verse and has achieved monumental status in his field due not least to the extraordinary intellectual and artistic influence of his work. His modernity is still striking today, even when put next to avant-garde poets such as Henri Michaux and Paul Eluard. He poses the questions that have become central to twentieth- and twenty-first-century literary criticism. Though an apparent aesthete, he even became for Jean-Paul Sartre a model of the 'committed' writer, admirable for the way he defamiliarized language.

But probably the best-known feature of Mallarmé's verse is its exceptional difficulty. Today's reader might feel sympathy with Paul Valéry's description in 1933 of his earliest encounter with some of the poems:

There were certain sonnets that reduced me to a state of stupor; poems in which I could find a combination of clarity, brightness, movement, the fullest sound, but strange difficulties as well: associations that were impossible to solve, a syntax that was sometimes strange, thought itself arrested at each stanza; in a word, the most surprising contrast was evident between what one might call the *appearance* of these lines, their *physical* presence, and the resistance they offered to immediate understanding. [. . .] I was confronting the problem of Mallarmé.[1]

The 'problem' that Valéry describes stems from Mallarmé's extraordinary reinvention of poetic expression. The reader has to grapple with great metaphysical questions, existential doubt, strangeness, and uncertainty; with rhythms of fragmentation and silence; dislocated syntax; the rapid formation, transmutation, and evaporation of images; and thoughts that seem to escape being fixed into any one interpretation. Valéry is outlining one of the fundamental tensions that mark out Mallarméan verse: the pull between the structural function of a poem's form, rhymes, and rich phonetic patterning, which can overwhelmingly suggest that there is or ought to be an

---

[1] Trans. M. Cowley and J. R. Lawler, in *Leonardo, Poe, Mallarmé* (London: Routledge, 1972), 258. All translations of Mallarmé's verse in this Introduction are by E. H. and A. M. Blackmore. Unless otherwise noted, all other translations are my own.

order of sense, a semantic completion produced from the poem's whole; and the concurrent, conflicting story of fragmentation and discontinuity, of syntactical and textual interruption, and affronts to semantic coherence.

Not all of Mallarmé's contemporary critics felt as generous about the 'problem' of his verse as Valéry. Paul Verlaine's 1883 study of Mallarmé in his article 'Damned Poets' reveals that many of Mallarmé's reviewers considered him a madman: 'In *Parnassus* he furnished verse of a novelty that caused a scandal in the newpapers. [. . .] In the civilized pages, in "the bosom" of the serious Reviews, everywhere or nearly so, it became fashionable to laugh, to recall to the tongue the accomplished writer, to the feelings of the beautiful the sure artist. Among the most influential, fools treated the man as a madman!'[2] Others accused him of deliberately mystifying credulous readers, his verse merely a display of linguistic preciosity that concealed triviality. In 1896 Marcel Proust attacked Symbolist poets, above all Mallarmé: 'The poet renounces that irresistible power of waking so many Sleeping Beauties dormant in us, if he speaks a language that we do not know.'[3]

Mallarmé replied later that year in the essay 'The Mystery in Letters': 'My preferred response to aggression is to retort that some contemporaries do not know how to read—except newspapers, that is.'[4] For him, and indeed for many of his Symbolist peers, the vital role of poetry was to purge language of its everyday setting. He expresses contempt for base, ordinary language, such as that used in journalism, which offers no resistance to understanding and forgoes its proper magic by referring simply to fact. He consciously distinguishes two effects of expression, transmitting a fact and evoking an emotion, and sees a clear divide between the latter and ease of comprehension. Verse should conjure up an atmosphere of strangeness, its function to express 'the mysterious sense of the aspects of existence'. This attachment to the oblique, suggestive utterance owes a clear debt to Gérard de Nerval's doubt in the possibility of a

---

[2] 'Les Poètes maudits', *Œuvres en prose complètes*, ed. Jacques Borel, Bibliothèque de la Pléiade (Paris: Gallimard, 1972), 657–8.

[3] In a short article, 'Contre l'obscurité', *La Revue blanche*, 15 July 1896 (republished in *Chroniques*, 1927).

[4] 'Le Mystère dans les lettres' appeared in *La Revue blanche* on 1 September 1896. *Œuvres complètes*, ii, ed. B. Marchal, Bibliothèque de la Pléiade (Paris: Gallimard, 2003), 234 (hereafter *OCii*).

coherent poetic voice and to Charles Baudelaire's aesthetic of 'evocative sorcery'. Mallarmé depicts the poet as high priest, necessarily set apart from the mundane political process in order to learn and reveal the mysterious truth. In a letter to Edmund Gosse (1893) he writes: 'Only the Poets have the right to speak.'[5] It is as such an isolated figure that J.-K. Huysmans paints Mallarmé in the novel *Against Nature* (1884), where the protagonist des Esseintes reads and admires his work:

He loved these lines, as he loved all the works of this poet who, in an age of universal suffrage and a period when money reigned supreme, lived apart from the world of letters, protected by his contempt from the stupidity surrounding him, taking pleasure, far from society, in the revelations of the intellect, in the fantasies of his brain, further refining already specious ideas, grafting on to them thoughts of exaggerated subtlety, perpetuating them in deductions barely hinted at and tenuously linked by an imperceptible thread [. . .] The result was a literary distillate, a concentrated essence, a sublimate of art.[6]

This depiction as one of the period's strange new decadent writers would push Mallarmé into the literary limelight. Its linkage between retreat from the world and linguistic distillation is corroborated by a line from 'The Tomb of Edgar Allan Poe': 'Bestow purer sense on the phrases of the crowd.' But in spite of his distance from society, the modern artist's search to reveal 'truth' was in Mallarmé's eyes not apolitical but, rather, radical and democratic. In an article extolling the modernity of his great friend Édouard Manet's painting, he writes: 'At this critical hour for the human race when Nature desires to work for herself, she requires certain lovers of hers—new and impersonal men placed directly in communion with the sentiment of their time—to loose the restraint of education, to let hand and eye do what they will, and thus through them, reveal herself.'[7] As with painting, the poet's task is to free linguistic units from their contingent relations through suggestion and to transpose them into a network of reciprocal relations—the 'essence' that

[5] *Œuvres complètes*, i, ed. B. Marchal, Bibliothèque de la Pléiade (Paris: Gallimard, 1998), 807 (hereafter *OCi*).

[6] *Against Nature* (*À Rebours*), trans. Margaret Mauldon (Oxford: Oxford University Press, 1998), 160.

[7] Trans. G. Millan in Gordon Millan, *Mallarmé: A Throw of the Dice* (London: Secker & Warburg, 1994), 220.

reflects and reveals the 'Idea'. Mallarmé endows this process with secular religiosity, calling it a 'divine transposition, for the accomplishment of which man exists, [which] goes from the fact to the ideal'.[8]

Mallarmé's mixture of Plato, Hegel, and a post-Romantic yearning for the mystical beyond cannot really be called a philosophy; but the concept of the Idea has a recurrent and strong structural function in his verse. In particular it gives legitimacy to the declared aim of truth-seeking, supporting the concept of the impersonal poet by rejecting the primacy of the personal in Romantic poetry. It also provides a framework for the central theme of Nothingness: non-meaning is not an absence of meaning but a potentiality of meaning that no specific meaning can exhaust. The shadow of the Idea drives Mallarmé constantly to test the limits and stability of knowledge.

Mallarmé and Prose

Mallarmé was not an unworldly poet. Alongside his relatively small output of verse he wrote much prose, including regular bulletins on the Paris literary and artistic scene for *The Athenaeum*, and theatrical reviews which he later called 'critical poems' and are assembled under the heading 'Theatre jottings' in his volume of collected prose, *Divagations* (*Diversions*). He translated into French Poe's *The Raven*, with Manet providing illustrations, and received several commissions, such as for an English-language textbook, *Les Mots anglais* (*English Words*), and a free adaptation of Cox's mythology, *Les Dieux antiques* (*The Ancient Gods*). Perhaps his most intriguing enterprise was the launch of a new magazine, *La Dernière Mode* (*The Latest Fashion*). Each number contained a fashion article signed 'Marguerite de Ponty', cooking tips, and a review of cultural events in Paris, all written by Mallarmé himself posing under various pseudonyms. This witty and ironic wordsmith of the everyday is a far cry from the reputedly obscure, sterile, and precious poet.

The short poems collected under the title 'Occasional Verses', presented in this volume in Appendix 2, and sometimes over-shadowed by the canonical poems, are gifts to mark a circumstance. They are displays of poetic dexterity, deftly interweaving proper

---

[8] 'Théodore de Banville', *OCii* 144.

names and allusion to their subjects' characteristics or situation in neat little rhyming kernels. Here we see a playful Mallarmé forging new linguistic relationships in order to establish connections between himself and others: he is a writer of rhymed addresses on letters to friends, a giver of fans and boxes of glacé fruit inscribed with verse. In a variation of 'divine transposition', occasions and objects become poetic acts, the quotidian becomes textual performance.

Mallarmé's range of verse form bears witness to this desire to build a bridge between the everyday and the absolute. He covers the spectrum: Petrarchan sonnets (two quatrains followed by two tercets), Shakespearean sonnets (three quatrains and one couplet; see for example 'The hair flight of a flame . . .'), alexandrines (the standard French twelve-syllable line), octosyllables and hepta-syllables. Then there are the prose pieces and journal articles. Following the move, most prominent in Baudelaire and Arthur Rimbaud, towards making the distinction between poetry and prose more fluid, Mallarmé wants to abolish the distinction altogether: 'Verse is everywhere in language where there is rhythm, everywhere, except in notices and on page four of the papers. In the genre called prose, there are verses [. . .] of all rhythms. But in truth there is no prose: there is the alphabet, and then verses more or less tight, more or less diffuse.'[9] It is in the prose pieces, significantly entitled 'Anecdotes or Poems', that poetry and the everyday meet and fuse. They can be narrative or lyric, more or less elliptical, short or long. They are richly poetic and syntactically complex explorations of anecdotes ranging from the banal to the bizarre, based on reminis-cences, journeys, spectacles, and so on, with a strong flavour of the absurd and the uncanny inherited from Poe and Baudelaire. This daring vision of the shared identity of verse and prose would lead eventually to a spatialized form, the radical experiment of *A Dice Throw*.

New Rhythms of Verse

Coming out of the 'Parnassian' movement, which prized imper-sonality, craft, and formal perfection over Romanticism's lyrical

[9] 'Sur l'évolution littéraire' [Enquête de Jules Huret] ('On Literary Evolution' [Inquiry by Jules Huret]), *OCii* 698.

inspiration, late nineteenth-century poets sought a new order. From the 1860s onwards artists were engaged with the need to reinvent linguistic, visual, and musical forms of expression. The 'liberation' of verse was begun by Victor Hugo, Théodore de Banville, and Baudelaire, who placed great value on the rhythm of dramatic breaks in sense produced by the tension between scansion and accent. Verlaine moved away from the sonnet and frequently exploited the 'imparisyllabic' line, achieving a new kind of unhindered weightlessness and indeterminacy. He claimed that achieving such an exquisite, directionless ambivalence in verse is the principal aim of the poet. Through the *impair* (the line of an uneven number of syllables, in contrast to the traditional alexandrine), which divests verse of its traditional rhythms and patterns of signification, attention can be drawn first and foremost to the language itself. Verlaine was responsible for a change in the prevailing poetic mood. His young followers, Charles Morice, Stuart Merrill, Henri de Régnier, and Francis Vielé-Griffin, would be at the forefront of a further innovation, that of 'free verse'; but Mallarmé always remained opposed to this complete abandonment of versificatory constraints altogether.

The drive for artistic revolution was born of *ennui*, a sense that everything had been done, written, and felt. In 'Sea Breeze', a poem that retains strong traces of Baudelaire, Mallarmé writes: 'The flesh is sad | and I've read every book.' In 'A Season in Hell' Rimbaud declares: 'I no longer know how to talk.' New expressivity was required. In this spirit of invention Mallarmé developed his complex, unsettling palette of poetic textures, combining hesitation, discontinuity, mobility, and stasis. His expansion of the verse category to include any language in varying degrees of tightness or diffuseness indicates how important to him as poetic tools are the constraint and release of fluidity, air, and blank space. He delights in the new rhythms that tightening and loosening can bring—from fan-beating in 'Another Fan', suspended in the timeless, ecstatic inertia of a kiss that can neither explode into fulfilment nor subside, to the self-organizing and disorganizing asymmetries of 'A Dice Throw'.

Mallarmé and Music

The move to 'liberate' verse and search for new rhythms of meaning was in large part guided by poets who looked to music to provide a

model. Mallarmé's observations about music inform his poetics at the most fundamental level. He lived at a time of heightened mutual awareness between music and literature, and his work represents a particularly fertile moment of crossover in the histories of the two arts. The composer Paul Dukas comments: 'Verlaine, Mallarmé and Laforgue brought us new tones and sonorities. They projected on to words glimmers that had never before been seen and used procedures undreamt of by their predecessors; [. . .] above all, they conceived of verse or prose as though musicians.'[10]

The relationship of music and literature had reached fever pitch with Richard Wagner, whose controversial theory of the *Gesamtkunstwerk* ('total art work') provoked an uncomfortable, defensive response in Symbolist circles. Wagner's influence challenged writers to reclaim language as the supremely expressive medium to rival the power of music. René Ghil and Stuart Merrill, for example, known as the *Instrumentistes*, tried harnessing the colours and emotions of music to specific nuances of language in tables of correspondences between the sounds of the alphabet and tones of orchestral instruments. Verlaine's calculated rhythmic irregularity was intended to invest poetry with 'musicality', as he proclaims in his 'Art poétique': 'Music above everything else! | And to write it favour the *Impair* | It is more vague and soluble in air.' Mallarmé greatly admired this brand of musical poetry:

The precision of your hearing, both mental and otherwise, confounds me. You can boast of having made known to our rhythms an extraordinary destiny; and putting aside that you are an astonishingly sensitive man, it will never be possible to speak of Verse without coming from it to Verlaine. In the end, in fact, nothing resembles a caprice less than your nimble and sure guitarist's art: that exists; and imposes itself as the new poetic discovery.[11]

Much of the momentum for the crossover between the arts came from gatherings held by Mallarmé in his small flat on Tuesday evenings. These became known as the *mardis* ('Tuesdays'); here Mallarmé would hold forth on his aesthetics, projects, and poetic heroes.

---

[10] Quoted in Robert Brussel, 'Claude Debussy et Paul Dukas', *La Revue musicale*, 7 (1926), 101.

[11] Letter to Verlaine, 1884 (*Correspondance*, ed. Henri Mondor and L. J. Austin, vol. 2, *1871–85* (Paris: Gallimard, 1965), 276).

In the early 1880s when the *mardis* began just a few of Mallarmé's friends were present, among them Verlaine, Ghil, and Merrill. By the height of Mallarmé's fame in the 1890s the crowd had swollen to include just about every major figure from the literary and artistic world of Paris and beyond, not least Oscar Wilde, André Gide, Valéry, and Claude Debussy. Debussy's tone poem *Prélude à l'Après-Midi d'un Faune* was later made into a ballet. Between Mallarmé and Debussy's work there is a very rich area of aesthetic and structural overlap, which goes beyond the coincidence of their sharing a period style.)

Mallarmé stands out from his contemporaries as an extraordinary listener and for the extent to which he achieves his brilliantly conceived musico-poetic aesthetic in practice. In his seminal lecture 'Music and Letters', given in Oxford and Cambridge in 1894, he claims that music and literature are two sides of the same coin: 'Music and Letters are the alternate face here broadened towards the obscure.'[12] His vision is that music and letters should have a shared structural rhythm in the artwork. But it is not merely the surface phonetic sonority of the poem that he considers musical; it is also what he calls the 'rhythms between the relations' (set up between certain configurations of language in verse), which reflect the Idea and enact a silent, structural music. 'It is the same as an orchestra', he writes, 'only literary and silent.'

He describes the new energies produced from the fragmentation of language in (his) verse and draws a parallel with the sounds and structures he hears in music: 'Verse, I believe, was waiting out of respect until the giant who stamped it with his blacksmith's hand steady and ever firmer had passed on, so that it could fracture. All language, adjusted to metre, concealing there its vital caesurae, escapes, according to a free disjunction into a thousand simple elements; and, I would point out, not without similarity to the multiple cries of an orchestration, that remains verbal.'[13] The disjunctive, multiple verbal complexity of liberated verse has similar patterns and rhythms, Mallarmé argues, to orchestral music. But how might this be? Valéry notices how disjunctive verse behaves like music when he writes:

---

[12] *OCii* 69.
[13] 'Crise de vers' ('Crisis in verse'), *OCii* 205. The 'giant' is Victor Hugo.

If the meaning of these lines [of certain Mallarmé sonnets] appeared to me to be very difficult to decipher, if I did not always manage to resolve these words into a complete thought, I nevertheless observed that verse was never more *clear* as verse, poetry was never more plainly poetry, speech was never more decisively or luminously musical than I found in the poems I was contemplating. Their poetic quality was manifest. And I could not help thinking that even in the greatest poets, if the *meaning* in most cases leaves no room for doubt, there are lines which are *dubious poetry*, which *we can read with the diction of prose without being forced to raise our voices to the point of song*.[14]

In spite of the poetry's unresolved questions and elusive nature, there is an overriding impression of its musical rhythms and sonorities. Language assumes some of the non-referential quality of music. Removed from the world of objects associated with ordinary reference, words share music's signifying patterns. Mallarmé writes: 'I say: a flower! And, beyond the oblivion to which my voice banishes no contour, as something other than the familiar calyces, arises musically the fragrant idea itself, the absent flower of all bouquets.'[15] The word takes on a new and singular existence as a pure 'musical' form. Thus poetry is endowed with a new emotive intensity and potential, a quality of feeling no less extraordinary than the novel structures in play.

Like music, the 'rhythms between the relations' in poems create reflections, connections, silences, and hermeneutic gaps, revealed and concealed but never totally unveiled, according to language's own logic. As patterns of meaning appear and disappear in the reading of a Mallarmé poem, they create their own structure or rhythm. The form of meaning is as prominent a part of the poetry as the phonetic and metrical form. Language freed from conventional modes of denotation assumes material existence independent of what it might signify; yet at the same time the word experienced as word creates an immediate consciousness of the absence of identity between word and sign. The word points at once to a thrilling Nothingness, a referential failure, at the heart of language, and to the pure generative power of language itself. This musical poetics inevitably draws close attention to its own practice and to the ultimately arbitrary relationship of language to reality.

[14] Trans. Cowley and Lawler, in *Leonardo, Poe, Mallarmé*, 259; italics original.
[15] *OCii* 213.

Early Career

Mallarmé's early poetry develops and perfects established post-Romantic themes. 'Ill Fortune', for example (1862, largely rewritten in 1887), borrows its title from a Baudelaire poem. It compares two types of poet: 'heaven's mendicants', foregone poets of the Ideal who suckle the breast of sorrow; and 'a hundred brothers whom none admire, | vile martyrs of contorted chance'. The former group, probably representing Mallarmé's great Romantic predecessors, is happily sacrificed at the hands of a mighty angel. In one ironic image the crowd kneels before them when they rather too easily and extravagantly 'versify sensual lamentations'. The latter group, probably representing contemporary poets, is cursed by a grotesque dwarf, a vulgar and tawdry personification of 'Ill Fortune'. The poem ends with the cursed poets as martyrs: 'When everyone has spat scorn in their faces, | these mockery-glutted heroes [. . .] grotesquely | hang themselves from a gas lamp in the street.' The debt to Baudelaire is clear in the contrast between the sacred of the Romantic (genuflections, the mighty angel) and the secular and grotesque of the modern (the accursed grovel in mud and swamp, hounded by 'this skeleton, dwarf, booted, whose armpit | has worms for hairs').

The theme of art replacing religion, and the base and mundane replacing God and the Ideal as the poetic focus, forms a significant part of Mallarmé's ideological inheritance. It can be found in other of his early poems such as 'The Windows', 'The Blue', and 'The Flowers'. After a time spent in crisis, depression, and deliberation (1865–7), Mallarmé would push his agnosticism to its most adventurous extreme, an unshakeable faith in literature. But his respect for religion as a marvel of human invention remained, as a letter to his friend the poet Henri Cazalis (1866) suggests: 'Before the Nothingness which is the Truth, these glorious lies! Such is the outline for my volume of lyric poetry, and such will probably be its title: *The Glory of the Lie* or *The Glorious Lie*. I shall sing as a man without hope.'[16]

In 1863, returned from a stay in London to improve his English, and despite wanting to stay in Paris, Mallarmé was posted to a lycée

---

[16] *OCi* 696.

in Tournon. Over the years spent in the provinces (later Besançon, then Avignon) before his return to Paris in 1871, he juggled writing with an unhappy teaching career. The period was critical for Mallarmé and decisive in terms of his poetic development. On several occasions he reached the depths of despair. The turning-point in his thought came in October 1864, when he started work on his *Herodias*. 'As for me,' he writes famously, 'I am hard at work. I have at last begun my *Herodias*. I am terrified because I have to invent a language that will inevitably result from a very new poetics, which I could best describe in these words: "Paint not the thing itself, but the effect that it produces." '[17] Mallarmé saw himself as putting a new poetic theory into practice, replacing a Parnassian focus on objects with Poe's concern for effect. He probably also wrote the prose poem 'The Demon of Analogy' around this time, in which a man is pursued through the streets by a haunting and arbitrary phrase. It deals with a similar idea: that it is necessary to go beyond a traditional referential reading and instead listen to and observe the relations between words in a new way.

The years of 'crisis' seem to have led Mallarmé to a renewed and steady belief in literature, an ideal of impersonality for the role he ascribed himself as writer, and a total rejection of God. In 1866 he describes in a letter to the poet Théodore Aubanel, in some markedly Christian metaphors, his process of transformation: 'As for me, I have worked more this summer than in my entire life. I have laid the foundations of a magnificent work. [. . .] I am dead and resurrected with the jewelled key of the ultimate treasure chest in my mind.'[18] He intended the as yet unfinished *Herodias* as a central part of a huge work that he thought would take him twenty years. This huge theatre project, a sort of modern mystery play—his answer to Wagner—would incorporate mime, dance, music, and text. It consumed him, but was never completed. The 'Scene', written in 1865, was published largely unedited in 1871; but Mallarmé abandoned the 'Overture' and worked on the 'Prelude', of which the only completed part is the 'Canticle of John the Baptist', right up to his death in 1898.

Mallarmé's thought seems dominated also by the principle of a mythical, all-encompassing Book. Although the concept behind the

---

[17] Letter to Cazalis, 1864 (*OCi* 663).   [18] *OCi* 703.

Work or Book remained constant, its envisaged shape kept changing over his career. In 1885 he writes to Verlaine: 'I have always dreamed of attempting something else, with the patience of an alchemist. [. . .] A book, quite simply, in many volumes, a book that is truly a book, structured and premeditated. [. . .] I will go further. I will say: the Book, persuaded that there is only one. [. . .] The Orphic explanation of the Earth that is the sole task of the poet and the supreme literary game.'[19] The Book would be a system of all thought in language. A year later he was reported as saying: 'I believe that Literature, rediscovering its origins that are a combination of Art and Science, will provide us with a Theatre of which the performances will be the truly modern religious celebration.'[20] His grand, totalizing ambition would never bear its final fruit. He conceived of the Book more as a guiding light in his search for secular Truth than as a realizable goal: he proved 'by the parts that have been written that such a book exists and that I have knowledge of what I have not been able to accomplish'.[21] It lends a beguiling cosmic dimension of incomparable grandeur and scope to the theatres of reading, to the performative and permutational structures of his 'supreme literary game'.

'Sonnet Allegorical of Itself'

It has been argued that *Herodias*, in its various forms, allegorically represents the emergence of a new kind of writing that explores the reflexivity of language, that is to say the self-reflecting, self-enacting power of language freed from its representational function. The icy virgin in the 'Scene' (1865) says: 'I love the horror of being virgin. [. . .] For myself alone I bloom, in isolation.' 'Gift of the Poem' and 'Saint', written in the same year, also offer examples.

'With her pure nails offering their onyx' is overloaded with such reflexivity. Written in 1868 after the 'crisis' period, under the title 'Sonnet Allegorical of Itself', then revised in 1887, the verse seems born of language itself. In the second stanza, for example, commentators have devoted much ink to pondering the possible referents of 'ptyx'. The debate highlights very well the relative inadequacy

[19] *OCi* 788.
[20] Trans. Millan, *Mallarmé: A Throw of the Dice*, 253.
[21] Ibid.

of traditional attempts to recuperate Mallarmé's difficult poems as 'intentional' representations of the real world (which is not by any means to say that all attempts to find a degree of coherence in Mallarmé's work are fruitless). For, cut free from immediate semantic reference, 'ptyx' asserts first and foremost its pure rhyming sonority. 'On the empty room's credences: no ptyx.' The space left by the ptyx's absence is filled by the material sound of the word itself. 'Abolished bauble, sonorous inanity': rhyme used for arbitrary ornamental effect has been abolished. The true representation of an object is achieved when the sound is reflected in and of itself. The stanza's '-yx' rhyme proliferates across the poem, carrying in its letter 'x' the symbol of its own reflexivity. Sound is literally born of the poem and gives rise to the poem.

The sonnet's ambiguous syntax creates different semantic discontinuities. Although the first and third lines of the first stanza have recognizable syntactical structure, the second line, even after several rereadings, is likely to be puzzling. Its rhythm and sound pattern give it a certain authority, but its four elements are cut off from one another. The critic Malcolm Bowie writes: 'The four ideas do not form part of a continuous syntactic sequence, but are free to develop new relationships of affinity or contrast among themselves.'[22] Equally, the line begins a proposition that will not be completed until the fifth line.

Reading such verse requires a constant switching between waves of pure sonority and of sense that emanate from the multi-contoured texture of the verse surface. Valéry evokes the fluctuation inherent in modern verse as 'that prolonged hesitation between the sound and the sense'.[23] Mallarmé's reader is pulled between those two simultaneously interwoven elements. The unfamiliar music arising from the unusual juxtaposition of words disorientates the ear: words dipped in and out of sound and sense prevent it from picking out immediate meanings.

Existence becomes both empty and yet resoundingly beautiful. Mallarmé's verse explores a paradoxical, shifting world of speculation and uncertainty, setting up a new kind of contract with the

---

[22] *Mallarmé and the Art of Being Difficult* (Cambridge: Cambridge University Press, 1978), 7.
[23] *Cahiers* (Paris: CNRS, 1957–61), iv. 782.

reader. Productive reading entails that conflicting patterns be made, simultaneously held, tested, revised, and allowed to falter.

Reading Mallarmé

The opening poem or dedication of the verse collected by Mallarmé in 1894 launches the reader on a labyrinthine journey that will conceal and constantly defer its destination. 'Toast' is at once a giant, overarching metaphor for this journey, which is about travelling and exploring rather than arriving, and an enactment of it. There will be moments of illumination, where patterns of coherence, local and large-scale, seem to crystallize, and moments where those patterns evaporate and we feel utterly lost. What we face ultimately are the limits of knowledge and the limitations of language for expressing the world. 'Toast' was written in 1893 as a special sonnet for one of a series of banquets organized by the literary magazine *La Plume*, at which Mallarmé was the guest of honour. By this time Mallarmé had a very busy social life in Paris and was looked to as the undisputed leader of French Symbolist poetry. As such, this sonnet can be read as an occasional toast in honour of his younger poet friends: 'We all, my various friends, we sail | with myself on the poop-deck now | while you as the majestic prow | cleave wintry seas of blast and gale.' He has retired to the poop-deck to oversee the younger generation, who are now leading poetry through hostile waters. 'I stand and offer you this toast | solitude, star, or rocky coast | to things of any kind deserving | of our sail's white preoccupation.' Mallarmé toasts these things worthy of the poet's attention, naming verse metaphorically as the sail of the poetry ship. The metaphor for the poet and poetry, then, grows out of the occasion: the champagne foaming in the cup suggests the foam whipped up by the sea, from which comes the image of the sirens; the white tablecloth of the banquet hall suggests the sail. The verse itself is the foam, is produced out of a 'Nothing', an insignificant toast: 'this foam, this virgin verse | designating the cup, no more.' In spite of the drunken pitching and tossing of the boat, the poet heroically stands firm to toast the poetic act. Mallarmé paints himself with a delicate blend of self-irony, wit, and seriousness. He is 'spurred by a fine intoxication', but steadfastly 'fearless'. This is pure frivolity based on nothing (but) foam; but it is a frivolity that produces lasting poetry saluting the heroism of the artist.

Mallarmé put this poem first in italic type as a kind of epigraph. He stressed its ambiguity by changing its title from 'Toast' (the same in French as in English) to 'Salut', a pun on the French greeting 'Hello there' and noun 'Salvation'. In this new role the poem has the added dimensions of note to the reader, an *au lecteur* and dedication. It invites the reader to make a precarious, but perhaps redemptive, voyage through the collection, while 'Nothingness', lurking everywhere behind, is dedicated as a treacherous sea—a sea that will appear in other poems, such as 'Stilled beneath the oppressive cloud . . .' and 'For the sole task of travelling . . .'. The nautical image will reach its climax in *A Dice Throw*, where the risk that 'NOTHING | WILL HAVE TAKEN PLACE | OTHER THAN THE PLACE' is terrifyingly dramatized.

Mallarmé's work is remarkable for its sheer variety and degree of experimentation. 'A Faun in the Afternoon' is an early and radical example. An extraordinary hymn to the undefinable, unlocatable moment of intense eroticism, it lingers and hovers on the edge of illusion. We cannot be sure whether or not the scene takes place: the faun muses, 'Did I love a dream?' Syntactic patterns are left incomplete ('Let me reflect . . .'), creating sudden breaks in sense that dramatize the ebb and flow of doubt and certainty, of the struggle to rekindle memories of intoxicating desire. Such incomplete propositions throw up unresolved possibilities that resonate and hover in the blank spaces on the page; italic type is used to suggest a shift in mood or tone of voice. Both these techniques foreshadow the orchestration of the acoustic drama in the yet more innovative *A Dice Throw*. *Faun* creates unprecedented rhythmical asymmetry and new possibilities of sound, which may be what attracted Debussy to base his tone poem on it.

Broken syntax and semantic discontinuity occur throughout Mallarmé's poems, of course, but within the constraints laid down by sonnet form and, in most cases, punctuation. (Poems that appear later in the volume, such as 'To introduce myself into your tale . . .' and 'Stilled beneath the oppressive cloud . . .', abandon punctuation.) From the grammatical ambiguities produced by the syntactical interruptions a whole host of possible senses and connections arises. The reader is stripped of the usual guidelines for reading; she cannot follow the expected thread of continuous syntax. Line phrases are interrupted by parenthetical propositions or by phrases

whose grammatical status cannot be established until several lines later. Add to this the pushes and pulls created by the conflicting frameworks of metre and rhyme and one can sense the enormous complexity. The process of reading injects intellectual doubt into traditional poetic structures. In 'Little Ditty I', for example, the ruptured texture prevents us ever quite knowing where to start or how to get a grip on the poem. The Shakespearean sonnet form draws attention immediately to the final couplet, which stands summatively alone: 'your naked bliss should plumb | the wave that you become.' It asserts the prospect of an imminent dramatic climax and forms a focal point towards which the poem should progress. The rhyme scheme is rich and symmetrical (solitude/desuetude; pier/here // high/sky; hold/gold; and so on). But from the very first instant the reader's progress is hindered by the textual forces exerted.

But this is not to say that the experience of reading Mallarmé is one of feeling perpetually lost, or that no meaning can be reached, leaving us with nothing much more than superior nonsense. There are poems in which there is a coherent set of concerns; in which uncertainties can form a kind of simplicity, though they draw attention to their own frailty. And the poetry demands of the reader an active participation. The structured hesitation and mobile stasis in the texts initiate a self-conscious signifying and interpretative practice. Some texts yield to pressure: from some of the multiple available meanings, the sense of a goal is strong enough for other meanings to be discarded or to linger in the background. But the poems vary in difficulty, intensity, and open-endedness. Some sonnets have difficulty at their very heart and never settle into any one pattern; the questions they pose are left unresolved. To try to constrain them is seriously to reduce their intellectual subtlety. One such is 'Prose (For des Esseintes)', linguistically and conceptually a most taxing poem: it constantly opens out, proposing change and new directions.

Yet faced with the semantic and phonetic overloading of such a difficult poem it is easy to want to fix an interpretation. For 'This virginal long-living lovely day', many commentators have done so using the allegory of its swan. Indeed, the swan is rich with imagery and a standard symbol of the Parnassian aesthetic. Baudelaire's swan signifies his view of himself as artist, impersonal, exiled, a stranger

to the world. In the Mallarmé poem we could read an extended metaphor of the swan as poet: his body is trapped in the ice as he reaches for the sky (the artist's sense of impotence), the new day offers the chance of longed-for inspiration, and so on. But if we allow the allegory to take hold, many paradoxical elements have to be overlooked. For example, the swan's relationship to the 'horror of earth that traps his wings' is rather ambivalent. The 'lost hard lake' beneath the ice is haunted by 'ice-flights'. The swan has a close affinity with his holder: flights that have not been flown, turned to ice. Similarly, the dawning day that might release the swan is in some way co-substantial with him: it is expected to act like a swan, 'with a wing's wild blow'. This question of coexistence, of separation from and identification with the surroundings, is unsolved in the poem. Then, the swan's attitude towards his captivity can be read in two conflicting ways. Does he struggle against his winter entrapment but then become resigned to his failure to sing? Or is he magnificent and defiant in a splendid prison that allows him to achieve purity far from the practical world? With these concurrent but opposing positions, we do not know whether the 'futile things' to which the swan-poet is condemned in the last line are empty and lifeless or a happy release. Playing with the apparent completion and stillness of the allegory is a conflicting set of contradictory suggestions.

Much Mallarmé criticism has been dogged by an erroneous belief that such completion is recoverable. But the richness of the poems lies in allowing Mallarmé's carefully engineered discontinuities to breathe. And these 'rhythms between the relations', or reflections of the Idea, do not become a loose, nonsensical haze: the reader is guided by a strong framework of oppositions, reflections, and analogies that helps to impose an order—or many orders. All the same, there are never grounds for saying what the poem is 'really' about. In disappointing our familiar notions of intelligibility, Mallarmé opens up a performance and exploration of awesome, intractable metaphysical dilemmas.

'*A Dice Throw At Any Time Never Will Abolish Chance*': *The Musical Score*

In 'A Dice Throw' now-familiar themes—terrible Nothingness, the contingency of knowledge, the frailty of language—are writ large at a sharply experiential level. Written towards the end of Mallarmé's life and published in 1897, it is arguably his culminating work, the ultimate dramatic expression of his ideas and techniques. It tests our most fundamental notions of intelligibility. At the poem's centre is metaphysical crisis, the constant threat of collapse into incoherence. It is a thoroughgoing investigation of chance as an aesthetic principle; its tension resides in the enactment of the principal statement, 'A Dice Throw At Any Time Never Will Abolish Chance'.

Mallarmé had experimented with the removal of normal punctuation in some earlier sonnets. Here it is again abandoned in favour of what might be called a spatialized variety. Unusually large blank spaces interrupt the phrases across the double page, at times threatening to engulf it completely. The drama occurs between the instant and the space that reabsorbs it; the extremely mobile text has a fluctuating, rubato-driven reading tempo. In a preface to the poem's first publication, Mallarmé writes that the spatially separated groups of words are akin to a musical score:

Let me add that, for anyone who would read it aloud, a musical score results from this stripped-down form of thought (with retreats, prolongations, flights) or from its very layout. The difference in type-face between the principal theme, a secondary one, and adjacent ones, dictates the level of importance when uttered orally, and the position on the stave, intermediate, high or low on the page, will indicate how the intonation rises and falls.[24]

It is the irregular rhythm, at once fluid and restrained, of sonorous and semantic traits interwoven with silence, leading and deflecting potential connections and meanings, that gives the poem its musical qualities. The layout is a new verse form, the shape assumed by the mixture of 'free verse' and the prose poem expanded in time and space, akin to symphonic structure. The result is what Mallarmé describes as 'a simultaneous vision of the Page', organized around

---

[24] Trans. E. H. and A. M. Blackmore in Stéphane Mallarmé, *Collected Poems and Other Verse*, 263.

the principal sentence that runs through the text in large upper-case letters as a reminder that every statement is provisional. The different typefaces construct an acoustic presentation of simultaneous events running at intervals through the multi-layered text.

The reader is given certain structural clues that can then be applied elsewhere in the poem. But even as she develops these keys, they dissolve, to be replaced by a different possibility. Just as a glimmer of sense is offered, it retreats from her grasp again. For example, as the dice land in the final line they seem to offer a certainty ('Every Thought emits a Dice Throw'), but the niggling doubt that 'NOTHING | WILL HAVE TAKEN PLACE | OTHER THAN THE PLACE' hovers from the preceding page. The descent to the final line appears balanced by 'A CONSTELLATION', an immobile cluster on the middle right of the eleventh double page; but that is offset by the downwards pull of 'keeping watch | wondering | rolling on' and the vast blank space on the left-hand side. And the last line provides not a point of repose but only a brief staging post: together with the principal statement, it provides an overarching framework for the poem as a whole, an 'all-at-once' perception rather than a real-time encounter. The text plunges back into the hypothetical. 'A Dice Throw' does not follow a single course. It does not offer itself as a single object of contemplation with a fixable reading position. The imagery of sea, shipwreck, and gambling is enacted in the violence and risk of reading as the poem swirls and surges over a background of simultaneous blankness and multiplicity. Like Joyce's *Finnegans Wake*, which ends so that the next word could be the first word of the book, the ending of 'A Dice Throw' appears to promise conclusion but in fact points back into what seems infinite possibility. The work is a journey, but not one that moves from a beginning towards an end.

NOTE ON THE TEXT AND TRANSLATION

The main body of this book contains all the works finally collected by Mallarmé himself under the heading 'poems': the verse *Poésies* prepared for publication in 1894, the prose 'Poèmes' issued in 1897 as part of his volume *Divagations* (*Diversions*), and the unclassifiable 'Poème' *Un coup de dés jamais n'abolira le hasard* (*A Dice Throw At Any Time Never Will Abolish Chance*), set up in proof for separate publication in 1898. (The *Poésies* and *Un coup de dés ...* did not actually pass through the press until after his death—in 1899 and 1914 respectively.)

Divagations includes all of Mallarmé's prose poems, but the 1894 collection of *Poésies* does not contain all his verse. The two appendices to the present edition supply the other significant verse works.

Appendix 1 contains all the verse that has been added posthumously to the body of Mallarmé's *Poésies* (apart from juvenilia—we have arbitrarily defined that category as ending in 1861, the year before he began publishing poems—and fragments). Most of these pieces were interpolated among the *Poésies* by the poet's daughter Geneviève, either in the 1899 Deman edition or in the 1913 Gallimard edition; others were inserted by Henri Mondor and Georges Jean-Aubry in the 1945 Pléiade edition. It is occasionally suggested that Geneviève may have had verbal authorization from her father for the general principle of inserting extra poems among his *Poésies*, or even for some or all of the specific additions made in 1899 and 1913. This is possible, but there is no evidence to support it. (Nor is there any evidence that Mallarmé authorized the posthumous removal of 'Conflit' from his prose poems and placement of 'La Gloire' at the end of the series. Prior to the composition of 'Conflit', he ended editions of his prose poems sometimes with 'Le Nénuphar blanc', sometimes with 'L'Ecclésiastique', but never with 'La Gloire'.) Moreover, there is widespread agreement that some at least of Geneviève's interpolations significantly disturb the 1894 architecture. Therefore, the present edition preserves—apparently for the first time in any language—the 1894 arrangement, the last known to have been approved by the poet himself, and relegates all posthumous additions to an appendix.

In his final instructions to his wife and daughter (written the day before his death), Mallarmé also authorized the publication of a selection of what he called *vers de circonstances* ('occasional verses'). Appendix 2 contains all the verse of this kind that he himself had ever released for publication (in some cases only after repeated entreaties from his friends). He never made any attempt to include such *vers de circonstances* among his *poésies* (even though many of the latter are also, in a sense, 'occasional' pieces), and all subsequent editors have respected this policy.

Original spelling and punctuation have been preserved. Spellings such as *évènement* were perfectly normal in nineteenth-century French and were not, as non-French readers sometimes imagine, devised by Mallarmé himself for special esoteric purposes. In the prose poems and the *Faune*, the French texts also reproduce the original variations in space between stanzas or paragraphs (though the English translations do not always match these). Titles or subtitles in round brackets (thus) are Mallarmé's own; those in square brackets [thus] are editorial. Each item is printed in its final state; earlier drafts, where they differ significantly, are cited and translated in the Explanatory Notes.

French originals and English translations are presented on facing pages, with one inevitable exception. *Un coup de dés* . . . can make its proper impression only if it is allowed to occupy both sides of each page; in this case, therefore, the French text is printed on pp. 139–59, and the English translation on pp. 161–81.

Further information about the composition and publication of Mallarmé's various volumes, and comments on individual poems, can be found in the Explanatory Notes.

Mallarmé is commonly regarded as the most untranslatable of all French poets, and different translators have advocated very different strategies for dealing with his work. (The more incurable the disease, the greater the diversity of treatments offered for it.) Henry Weinfeld (1994) declares 'with absolute certainty' that it is 'essential to work in rhyme and meter . . . If we take rhyme away from Mallarmé, we take away the *poetry* of his poetry.' Daisy Aldan (1999) agrees that the translations 'must themselves be poetry' but maintains that they 'must avoid that fallacy which attempts to recreate the rhyme schemes'. Charles Chadwick (1996), by contrast, advocates prose, arguing that 'any attempt at a verse translation

merely adds to the difficulties'. We ourselves have learnt from all three of these translators, and from many others. Perhaps the search for a best method of translating Mallarmé is as illusory as the search for a best method of depicting a cube in two dimensions. Different representations will illustrate different aspects of the original; no one representation will encompass it fully.

Mallarmé himself permitted a diversity of translatorial strategies. Like many writers of his generation, he was wary of free verse; but he, and other translators working with his approval, rendered poems into rhythmical prose, prose divided into separate lines, and rhymed verse. The present volume is similarly eclectic in approach, and contains translations of all those kinds. We have paid close attention to the English poems that he singled out for special praise, or in which he discerned a kinship with his own work—and we have studied them with particular care when, as is often the case, they do not conform to conventional ideas of what is Mallarméan. In a volume that aims to present the French texts in a form as close to the author's wishes as the Oxford World's Classics format will permit, it seems logical to adopt a similar approach to translations. Nevertheless, we fully recognize that renderings that departed further from Mallarmé's own literary preferences would be equally legitimate.

Many techniques available to French poets cannot be accurately imitated in English. We have sometimes been forced to use more punctuation than Mallarmé himself does. In French, details of gender and word-ending are often enough to show the syntactic relationships between words; but English is a less highly inflected language, and cannot always indicate syntax without some help from punctuation. Again, English verse is more heavily accented than French, and therefore requires more diversity in scansion and rhyme-schemes, and more generous use of run-on lines, if it is not to sound inflexible. Furthermore, English seems to be somewhat less tolerant of *rime riche* than French (though there is no obvious linguistic reason why this should be so; perhaps it is merely a matter of arbitrary convention). In preliminary experiments, we also discovered that readers found our translations easier to follow if most of the lines started with lower-case letters, so that the beginnings of sentences could be identified more readily. This policy (which is traditional in editions of Latin verse) was used within Mallarmé's own lifetime by at least one of his English-language disciples.

The translations and annotations attempt to incorporate, for the first time in a volume of this type, the results of the last six decades of Mallarmé research. Virtually all previous English versions—even the most recent ones—were based on the 1945 Pléiade edition or its precursors, which were issued before the bulk of Mallarmé's manuscripts had been published or even thoroughly examined. Therefore (to take two examples among many) the translators used an unintelligible text of lines 26–7 of the *Hérodiade* Overture (the 1945 edition unwittingly printed the third-person form of line 26 but the first-person form of line 27) and gave erroneous interpretations of the first four lines of the Wagner 'Hommage' (Mallarmé's own explanation was not available to the 1945 editors).

Dr Francine Giguère and Oxford University Press's anonymous pre-publication readers provided valuable assistance with the translations in this volume. We feel deeply privileged that our work has been supervised by Judith Luna of Oxford University Press and introduced by Dr Elizabeth McCombie. *Un coup de dés . . .* was typeset by Claire Dickinson, student at the Department of Typography & Graphic Communication, The University of Reading; she has managed to reproduce the layout of Mallarmé's corrected proofs more closely (especially on the poem's fourth page) than even the new Pléiade edition was able to do. We would also like to thank the copy-editor, Jeff New, the proofreader, Judith Colleran, and the book's designer, Bob Elliott, for their meticulous attention to detail. To Dr and Mrs H. J. Blackmore and Drs Warner and Erica Quarles de Quarles we are indebted in many ways that no acknowledgement could adequately summarize.

SELECT BIBLIOGRAPHY

Editions

Œuvres complètes, vol. 1, *Poésies*, ed. Carl Paul Barbier and Charles Gordon Millan (Paris, 1983). The projected second and third volumes were never published.

Œuvres, ed. Yves-Alain Favre (Paris, 1985).

Poésies, ed. Pierre Citron (Paris, 1987).

Poésies, ed. Lloyd James Austin (Paris, 1989).

Œuvres complètes, ed. Bertrand Marchal, 2 vols. (Paris, 1998–2003).

Biographical Studies

Dujardin, Édouard, *Mallarmé par un des siens* (Paris, 1936).

Gill, Austin, *The Early Mallarmé*, 2 vols. (Oxford, 1979–86).

Millan, Gordon, *Mallarmé: A Throw of the Dice* (London, 1994).

Mondor, Henri, *Vie de Mallarmé* (Paris, 1941).

Steinmetz, Jean-Luc, *Mallarmé: L'Absolu au jour le jour* (Paris, 1998).

Critical Studies

Abastado, Claude, *Expérience et théorie de la creation poétique chez Mallarmé* (Paris, 1970).

Bernard, Suzanne, *Mallarmé et la musique* (Paris, 1959).

Bersani, Leo, *The Death of Stéphane Mallarmé* (Cambridge, 1982).

Blanchot, Maurice, *L'Espace littéraire* (Paris, 1955).

Bowie, Malcolm, *Mallarmé and the Art of Being Difficult* (Cambridge, 1978).

Chadwick, Charles, *Mallarmé, sa pensée dans sa poésie* (Paris, 1962).

Cohn, Robert Greer, *Mallarmé's Masterwork: New Findings* (The Hague, 1966).

—— *Mallarmé's Prose Poems: A Critical Study* (Cambridge, 1987).

—— *Toward the Poems of Mallarmé* (Berkeley, Calif., 1965).

Davies, Gardner, *Mallarmé et le drame solaire* (Paris, 1959).

—— *Mallarmé et la rêve d' 'Hérodiade'* (Paris, 1978).

Dayan, Peter, *Mallarmé's 'Divine Transposition': Real and Apparent Sources of Literary Value* (Oxford, 1986).

Derrida, Jacques, *La Dissémination* (Paris: Seuil, 1972).

Florence, Penny, *Mallarmé, Manet and Redon: Visual and Aural Signs and the Generation of Meaning* (Cambridge, 1986).

Fowlie, Wallace, *Mallarmé* (Chicago, 1953).

Franklin, Ursula, *An Anatomy of Poesis: The Prose Poems of Stéphane Mallarmé* (Chapel Hill, NC, 1976).

Kravis, Judy, *The Prose of Mallarmé: The Evolution of a Literary Language* (Cambridge, 1976).

Kristeva, Julia, *La Révolution du langage poétique: l'avant-garde à la fin du XIXe siècle: Lautréamont et Mallarmé* (Paris, 1974).

Lloyd, Rosemary, *Mallarmé: Poésies* (London, 1984).

—— *Mallarmé: The Poet and His Circle* (Ithaca, NY, 1999).

McCombie, Elizabeth, *Mallarmé and Debussy: Unheard Music, Unseen Text* (Oxford, 2003).

Marchal, Bernard, *La Religion de Mallarmé* (Paris, 1988).

Paxton, Norman, *The Development of Mallarmé's Prose Style* (Geneva, 1968).

Pearson, Roger, *Unfolding Mallarmé: The Development of a Poetic Art* (Oxford, 1996).

—— *Mallarmé and Circumstance: The Translation of Silence* (Oxford, 2004).

St Aubyn, F. C., *Stéphane Mallarmé*, 2nd edn. (New York, 1989).

Sartre, Jean-Paul, *Mallarmé: La Lucidité et sa face d'ombre* (Paris, 1986).

Williams, Thomas A., *Mallarmé and the Language of Mysticism* (Athens, Ga., 1978).

Further Reading in Oxford World's Classics

Baudelaire, Charles, *The Flowers of Evil*, ed. and trans. James McGowan (Oxford, 1993).

Huysmans, Joris-Karl, *Against Nature*, trans. Margaret Mauldon (Oxford, 1998).

Rimbaud, Arthur, *Collected Poems*, ed. and trans. Martin Sorrell (Oxford, 2001).

Verlaine, Paul, *Selected Poems*, ed. and trans. Martin Sorrell (Oxford, 1999).

A CHRONOLOGY OF
STÉPHANE MALLARMÉ

1842   18 March: in Paris, birth of Étienne (Stéphane) Mallarmé, son of the civil servant Numa Mallarmé (born 1805) and his wife Élisabeth Desmolins (born 1819).

1844   25 March: birth of his sister Marie (Maria).

1847   2 April: death of his mother.

1848   27 October: his father marries Anne-Hubertine Mathieu (born 1829); by this marriage three daughters and a son are born between 1850 and 1854.

1854   Mallarmé's earliest surviving writings (school exercises).

1857   31 August: death of his sister Maria (commemorated in 'Autumn Lament' and probably elsewhere in his poems).

1862   Writes 'Ill Fortune', 'Futile Petition', 'The Bell-Ringer', 'Renewal', 'Summer Sadness', 'Alms', 'Autumn Lament', 'The Prodigal Son', '. . . In the Mystical Shadows', 'Often the Poet catches my gaze . . .', 'Winter Sun', 'Hatred of the Poor', and 'Because a bit of roast . . .'.

     25 February: his first published poem, 'Futile Petition', appears in *Le Papillon*.

     June: begins courting his future wife, the German-born governess Christina (Maria) Gerhard (born 1835).

     8 November: leaves for London, mainly to improve his knowledge of English; during the next few months he moves back and forth between France and England, sometimes accompanied by Maria Gerhard, sometimes alone.

1863   Writes 'The Castle of Hope', 'The Windows', 'Apparition', and possibly 'The Blue'.

     12 April: death of his father.

     10 August: in London, marries Maria Gerhard.

     5 November: appointed English teacher at a provincial secondary school in Tournon.

1864   Writes 'Anguish', 'A Punishment for the Clown', 'The Flowers', 'Poor Pale Child', 'A negress aroused by the devil . . .', 'Sigh', 'Weary of bitter rest . . .', 'Winter Shivers', 'The Pipe', 'Reminiscence', and probably 'The Demon of Analogy'.

2 July: his first published prose poems, 'Poor Pale Child' and 'Autumn Lament', appear in *La Semaine de Cusset et de Vichy*.

19 November: birth of his daughter Geneviève.

1865 Writes 'The Future Phenomenon', 'Sea Breeze', *A Faun in the Afternoon*, 'Gift of the Poem', 'Saint', and the *Herodias* Scene.

September: submits an early draft of his *Faun* for performance by France's leading theatrical company, the Comédie française; the proposal is rejected.

1866 Writes the *Herodias* Overture.

26 October: appointed English teacher at a secondary school in Besançon.

1867 6 October: appointed English teacher at a secondary school in Avignon.

1868 Writes 'With her pure nails offering their onyx high . . .' and 'What silk with balm from advancing days . . .'.

1871 Writes 'In the Garden'.

16 July: birth of his son Anatole.

25 October: appointed to teach at a secondary school in Paris.

1873 Writes 'Funerary Toast'.

April: meets the painter Édouard Manet and subsequently (at an unknown date) Manet's mistress Méry Laurent, to whom Mallarmé will dedicate a number of poems.

1874 6 September: founds a short-lived fashion journal, *La Dernière Mode* (*The Latest Fashion*), edited and substantially written by himself.

1876 Writes 'The Tomb of Edgar Allan Poe'.

April: publication of *A Faun in the Afternoon*, with illustrations by Manet.

1877 Writes 'When sombre winter sweeps over the forgotten woods . . .'.

1878 January: publication of his prose volume *Les Mots anglais* (*English Words*), a school text.

1879 8 October: death of his son Anatole, after an illness of some months.

December: publication of *Les Dieux antiques* (*The Ancient Gods*), Mallarmé's translation of a book on mythology by G. W. Cox.

1883 November–December: Paul Verlaine publishes an influential essay on Mallarmé, later collected in his volume *Les Poètes maudits*.

1884 Writes 'Another Fan (Belonging to Mademoiselle Mallarmé)'.

May: publication of J.-K. Huysmans' novel *A rebours* (*Against Nature*), which contains an influential discussion of Mallarmé's poetry.

1885   Writes 'Nothing on waking . . .', 'The White Water Lily', 'Homage' ('Already mourning . . .'), and 'The fine suicide fled victoriously . . .'.

1886   Writes 'Glory' and probably 'The Ecclesiastic', 'My old tomes closed upon the name Paphos . . .', and 'O so dear from afar . . .'.

1887   Writes 'The hair flight of a flame . . .' and 'Lady Without too much passion . . .'.

      October: publication of a de-luxe limited edition of his *Poésies* (*Poetical Works*).

      December: publication of his *Album de vers et de prose* (*Selected Verse and Prose*).

1888   Writes 'Invitation to the Inaugural Soirée of the *Revue indépendante*', 'Street Folk', 'The Cobbler', 'The Seller of Scented Herbs', and possibly 'If you wish we shall make love . . .'.

      July: publication of his collected translations of the poems of Edgar Allan Poe.

1890   Writes 'Album Leaf', 'Note', 'Fan (Belonging to Madame Mallarmé)', and 'Fan (Belonging to Méry Laurent)'.

1892   15 November: publication of his *Vers et prose*.

1893   Writes 'Toast' ('Nothing, this foam . . .') and 'Remembering Belgian Friends'.

      4 November: retires from teaching.

1894   Writes 'The Tomb of Charles Baudelaire', 'Little Ditty I', 'Homage' ('Every Dawn however numb . . .'), and possibly 'Little Ditty II' and 'Little Ditty (Warlike)'.

      12 November: sends his publisher Deman the manuscript of his collected *Poésies* (not published until 1899).

1895   Writes 'Toast' ('As a man sought . . .') and 'All the soul that we evoke . . .'.

1896   Writes *A Dice Throw At Any Time Never Will Abolish Chance* and 'Tomb' ('The black rock, cross . . .').

1897   15 January: publication of *Divagations* (*Diversions*), including his collected prose poems.

      2 July: receives the proofs of the definitive edition of *A Dice Throw* (not issued until 1913).

1898 Writes 'For the sole task of travelling . . .' and works on the
      proposed new Prelude to *Herodias* (including the 'Canticle of John
      the Baptist', possibly written earlier).

      9 September: death of Mallarmé, at Valvins.

COLLECTED POEMS
AND OTHER VERSE

Poésies

Salut

Rien, cette écume, vierge vers
A ne désigner que la coupe;
Telle loin se noie une troupe
De sirènes mainte à l'envers.

Nous naviguons, ô mes divers
Amis, moi déjà sur la poupe
Vous l'avant fastueux qui coupe
Le flot de foudres et d'hivers;

Une ivresse belle m'engage
Sans craindre même son tangage
De porter debout ce salut

Solitude, récif, étoile
A n'importe ce qui valut
Le blanc souci de notre toile.

Le Guignon

Au dessus du bétail ahuri des humains
Bondissaient en clartés les sauvages crinières
Des mendieurs d'azur le pied dans nos chemins.

Un noir vent sur leur marche éployé pour bannières
La flagellait de froid tel jusque dans la chair,
Qu'il y creusait aussi d'irritables ornières.

Toujours avec l'espoir de recontrer la mer,
Ils voyageaient sans pain, sans bâtons et sans urnes,
Mordant au citron d'or de l'idéal amer.

Poetical Works

Toast

Nothing, this foam, this virgin verse
designating the cup, no more;
so plunges far away a corps
of sirens, many in reverse.

We all, my various friends, we sail   5
with myself on the poop-deck now
while you as the majestic prow
cleave wintry seas of blast and gale;

spurred by a fine intoxication
and fearless even of its swerving   10
I stand and offer you this toast

solitude, star, or rocky coast
to things of any kind deserving
of our sail's white preoccupation.

Ill Fortune

Above the awestruck herd of human beings
    bounded resplendent the wild tousled manes
of heaven's mendicants treading our pathways.

    Dark gales, unfurled like flags for their campaigns,
lashed them with cold into the very marrow   5
    and gashed deep scratches there with harrowing pains.

They travelled without canes or bread or vessels,
    hoping for the sea that they always seek,
gnawing the sour Ideal's golden lemon.

La plupart râla dans les défilés nocturnes,
S'enivrant du bonheur de voir couler son sang,
O Mort le seul baiser aux bouches taciturnes!

Leur défaite, c'est par un ange très puissant
Debout à l'horizon dans le nu de son glaive:
Une pourpre se caille au sein reconnaissant.

Ils tettent la douleur comme ils tétaient le rêve
Et quand ils vont rythmant des pleurs voluptueux
Le peuple s'agenouille et leur mère se lève.

Ceux-là sont consolés, sûrs et majestueux;
Mais traînent à leurs pas cent frères qu'on bafoue,
Dérisoires martyrs de hasards tortueux.

Le sel pareil des pleurs ronge leur douce joue,
Ils mangent de la cendre avec le même amour,
Mais vulgaire ou bouffon le destin qui les roue.

Ils pouvaient exciter aussi comme un tambour
La servile pitié des races à voix ternes,
Égaux de Prométhée à qui manque un vautour!

Non, vils et fréquentant les déserts sans citerne,
Ils courent sous le fouet d'un monarque rageur,
Le Guignon, dont le rire inouï les prosterne.

Amants, il saute en croupe à trois, le partageur!
Puis le torrent franchi, vous plonge en une mare
Et laisse un bloc boueux du blanc couple nageur.

Grâce à lui, si l'un souffle à son buccin bizarre,
Des enfants nous tordront en un rire obstiné
Qui, le poing à leur cul, singeront sa fanfare.

Grâce a lui, si l'une orne à point un sein fané
Par une rose qui nubile le rallume,
De la bave luira sur son bouquet damné.

Most perished in the dark beneath the peak, 10
ravished with bliss to see their own blood spilling—
  ah, Death, sole kiss for mouths that cannot speak!

A mighty angel stands on the horizon
  with naked sword, and causes their defeat:
crimson blood clots within their grateful bosom. 15

  They suck Sorrow's teat after Fancy's teat
and when they versify sensual lamentations
  the crowd kneels, while their mother springs to her feet.

They are assured, comforted, and majestic,
  but drag a hundred brothers whom none admire, 20
vile martyrs of contorted chance, behind them.

  They devour ashes with the same desire,
The same salt tears ravage their gentle faces,
  yet they are racked by some doom coarse or dire.

These equals of Prometheus with no vulture 25
  could beat the drum in the same style, and so
arouse the drab-voiced tribes to abject pity!

  No; base, facing parched sands wherever they go,
they run beneath the lash of a rash tyrant,
  Ill Fortune, whose wild laughter lays them low. 30

He rides behind two lovers, and divides them;
  then dunks the pretty swimming pair, mud-worn
and lumpish, in a swamp beyond the torrent.

  Thanks to him, if some man blows his strange horn,
boys finger their behinds and ape his fanfare, 35
  so that we writhe in fits of rollicking scorn.

If the urn aptly decks a faded bosom
  and a rose in full bloom rekindles it,
he stains its damned bouquet with glistening mildew.

Et ce squelette nain, coiffé d'un feutre à plume
Et botté, dont l'aisselle a pour poils vrais des vers,
Est pour eux l'infini de la vaste amertume.

Vexés ne vont-ils pas provoquer le pervers,
Leur rapière grinçant suit le rayon de lune
Qui neige en sa carcasse et qui passe au travers.

Désolés sans l'orgueil qui sacre l'infortune,
Et tristes de venger leurs os de coups de bec,
Ils convoitent la haine, au lieu de la rancune.

Ils sont l'amusement des racleurs de rebec,
Des marmots, des putains et de la vieille engeance
Des loqueteux dansant quand le broc est à sec.

Les poëtes bons pour l'aumône ou la vengeance,
Ne connaissant le mal de ces dieux effacés,
Les disent ennuyeux et sans intelligence.

« Ils peuvent fuir ayant de chaque exploit assez,
» Comme un vierge cheval écume de tempête
» Plutôt que de partir en galops cuirassés.

» Nous soûlerons d'encens le vainqueur dans la fête:
» Mais eux, pourquoi n'endosser pas, ces baladins,
» D'écarlate haillon hurlant que l'on s'arrête! »

Quand en face tous leur ont craché les dédains,
Nuls et la barbe à mots bas priant le tonnerre,
Ces héros excédés de malaises badins

Vont ridiculement se pendre au réverbère.

Apparition

La lune s'attristait. Des séraphins en pleurs
Rêvant, l'archet aux doigts, dans le calme des fleurs

This skeleton, dwarf, booted, whose armpit 40
has worms for hairs, who wears a plumed felt hat,
   is for them the vast bitter infinite.

If angered, they must challenge evildoers;
   their scratchy foil follows the moonlight straight
into the corpse like snow, and passes through it. 45

   Desolate, with no pride to consecrate
misfortune, and grieved to avenge their pecked bones,
   they itch not for resentment but for hate.

They are the butt of brats and fiddle-scrapers
   and common harlots and the age-old brood 50
of ragamuffins dancing when the jug is empty.

   Poets who favour vengeance or free food,
unaware of the ailment of these spent gods,
   say they are wearisome and far from shrewd.

'Now let them flee, sated with every exploit, 55
   as virgin horses skim the tempest's roar
rather than ride off at an armoured gallop.

   'Intoxicate the feasting conqueror
with incense! As for those clowns, why not deck them
   in scarlet rags until they howl, "No more!" ' 60

When everyone has spat scorn in their faces,
   these mockery-glutted heroes, who entreat
the thunder quietly through their beards, grotesquely

   hang themselves from a gas lamp in the street.

Apparition

The moon grew sad. Seraphim in tears, dreaming,
bows poised, amid the stillness of the steaming

Vaporeuses, tiraient de mourantes violes
De blancs sanglots glissant sur l'azur des corolles
—C'etait le jour béni de ton premier baiser.
Ma songerie aimant à me martyriser
S'enivrait savamment du parfum de tristesse
Que même sans regret et sans déboire laisse
La cueillaison d'un Rêve au cœur qui l'a cuelli.
J'errais donc, l'œil rivé sur le pavé vieilli
Quand avec du soleil aux cheveux, dans la rue
Et dans le soir, tu m'es en riant apparue
Et j'ai cru voir la fée au chapeau de clarté
Qui jadis sur mes beaux sommeils d'enfant gâté
Passait, laissant toujours de ses mains mal fermées
Neiger de blancs bouquets d'étoiles parfumées.

Placet futile

Princesse! à jalouser le destin d'une Hébé
Qui poind sur cette tasse au baiser de vos lèvres,
J'use mes feux mais n'ai rang discret que d'abbé
Et ne figurerai même nu sur le Sèvres.

Comme je ne suis pas ton bichon embarbé,
Ni la pastille ni du rouge, ni Jeux mièvres
Et que sur moi je sais ton regard clos tombé,
Blonde dont les coiffeurs divins sont des orfèvres!

Nommez nous . . . toi de qui tant de ris framboisés
Se joignent en troupeau d'agneaux apprivoisés
Chez tous broutant les vœux et bêlant aux délires,

Nommez nous . . . pour qu'Amour ailé d'un éventail
M'y peigne flûte aux doigts endormant ce bercail,
Princesse, nommez nous berger de vos sourires.

blossoms, derived from moribund violas
white sobs that slid across azure corollas—
it was the blessed day of your first kiss.   5
Daydreams that took delight tormenting me
grew wisely drunk on scents of sorrow, free
from pang or taste of anything amiss,
left for the reaping heart by the reaped Reverie.
My eyes stared down at the old pavement while   10
I roamed, when, with hair sunlit, with a smile
you appeared in the street and in the night;
I thought I saw the fairy capped with light
who through my spoiled-child's sleep in former days
used to pass, while her half-closed hands always   15
dropped snows of scented stars in white bouquets.

Futile Petition

Dear Princess, in my envy at a Hebe's fate
when she dawns on the Sèvres at your lips' kiss, I waste
my passion but have just an abbé's modest state;
on that cup, even naked, I shall never be placed.

Because I am not your bewhiskered lapdog, nor   5
lipstick nor lozenge, nor coquettish Revelries,
and since I know your gaze fell on me shut, therefore,
O blonde whose hair is dressed by goldsmith deities,

appoint us—you whose many pleasing brambled wiles
gather within a flock of little tame pet sheep   10
nibbling at all desires, bleating with no restraint,

appoint us—so that Love winged with a fan may paint
me there, flute in my hand, lulling the lambs to sleep,
dear Princess, do appoint us shepherd of your smiles.

Le Pitre châtié

Yeux, lacs avec ma simple ivresse de renaître
Autre que l'histrion qui du geste évoquais
Comme plume la suie ignoble des quinquets,
J'ai troué dans le mur de toile une fenêtre.

De ma jambe et des bras limpide nageur traître,
A bonds multipliés, reniant le mauvais
Hamlet! c'est comme si dans l'onde j'innovais
Mille sépulcres pour y vierge disparaître.

Hilare or de cymbale à des poings irrité,
Tout à coup le soleil frappe la nudité
Qui pure s'exhala de ma fraîcheur de nacre,

Rance nuit de la peau quand sur moi vous passiez,
Ne sachant pas, ingrat! que c'etait tout mon sacre,
Ce fard noyé dans l'eau perfide des glaciers.

Les Fenêtres

Las du triste hôpital, et de l'encens fètide
Qui monte en la blancheur banale des rideaux
Vers le grand crucifix ennuyé du mur vide,
Le moribond sournois y redresse un vieux dos,

Se traîne et va, moins pour chauffer sa pourriture
Que pour voir du soleil sur les pierres, coller
Les poils blancs et les os de la maigre figure
Aux fenêtres qu'un beau rayon clair veut hâler,

Et la bouche, fiévreuse et d'azur bleu vorace,
Telle, jeune, elle alla respirer son trésor,
Une peau virginale et de jadis! encrasse
D'un long baiser amer les tièdes carreaux d'or.

A Punishment for the Clown

Eyes, lakes with all my simple urge to be reborn
other than as the player whose gesture would recall
for a quill the ignoble lamp-soot, I have torn
a gaping window in the makeshift canvas wall.

With leg and arms, a limpid swimmer laying a snare,   5
leaping repeatedly, disavowing the bad
Hamlet! it seems as if within the wave I had
created countless tombs to vanish virgin there.

A joyous golden hand-clashed cymbal, suddenly
the sun buffets my nakedness—the exhalation   10
shed from my fresh mother-of-pearl in purity,

rancid night of the skin when you passed over me,
not knowing, wretch! that it was my whole consecration,
this rouge drowned in the glaciers' floods of perfidy.

The Windows

Sick of the dreary sickroom and the pall
of stale incense rising from drab white drapes
to the big crucifix tired of the blank wall,
the dying slyboots stiffens his old back, scrapes

along and, less to warm his gangrene than   5
to see a ray of sunshine on the stones,
presses his white hair and gaunt facial bones
against the glass that bright light longs to tan.

And his mouth, feverish, thirsting for blue skies
as, in its youth, it went to taste its bliss,   10
some virgin flesh now long gone, putrifies
the warm gold panes with a long bitter kiss.

Ivre, il vit, oubliant l'horreur des saintes huiles,
Les tisanes, l'horloge et le lit infligé,
La toux; et quand le soir saigne parmi les tuiles,
Son œil, à l'horizon de lumière gorgé,

Voit des galères d'or, belles comme des cygnes,
Sur un fleuve de pourpre et de parfums dormir
En berçant l'éclair fauve et riche de leurs lignes
Dans un grand nonchaloir chargé de souvenir!

Ainsi, pris du dégoût de l'homme à l'âme dure
Vautré dans le bonheur, où ses seuls appétits
Mangent, et qui s'entête à chercher cette ordure
Pour l'offrir à la femme allaitant ses petits,

Je fuis et je m'accroche à toutes les croisées
D'où l'on tourne l'épaule à la vie, et, béni,
Dans leur verre, lavé d'éternelles rosées,
Que dore le matin chaste de l'Infini

Je me mire et me vois ange! et je meurs, et j'aime
—Que la vitre soit l'art, soit la mysticité—
A renaître, portant mon rêve en diadème,
Au ciel antérieur où fleurit la Beauté!

Mais, hélas! Ici-bas est maître: sa hantise
Vient m'écœurer parfois jusqu'en cet abri sûr,
Et le vomissement impur de la Bêtise
Me force à me boucher le nez devant l'azur.

Est-il moyen, ô Moi qui connais l'amertume,
D'enfoncer le cristal par le monstre insulté
Et de m'enfuir, avec mes deux ailes sans plume
—Au risque de tomber pendant l'éternité?

Drunk, forgetting the horrible Last Rite,
the clock, the cough, bedrest prescribed, weak teas,
he lives; when dusk bleeds in the tiles, he sees   15
on the distant horizon gorged with light

some golden galleys beautiful as swans
sleeping on streams of purple redolence
rock their rich fulvid flashing echelons,
in memory-laden vast indifference.   20

So, holding coarse-souled man in detestation—
sprawled in pleasure where his mere appetites
feed; striving to gain that abomination
and give it to the wife suckling his mites—

I flee and cling to every casement through   25
which we can turn from life, and, blessedly,
in its glass bathed with everlasting dew
gold in the chaste dawn of Infinity

I see myself—an angel!—and I die;
the window may be art or mysticism, yet   30
I long for rebirth in the former sky
where Beauty blooms, my dream being my coronet!

But, alas, our low World is suzerain!
even in this retreat it can be too
loathsome—till the foul vomit of the Inane   35
drives me to stop my nose before the blue.

O Self familiar with these bitter things,
can the glass outraged by that monster be
shattered? can I flee with my featherless wings—
and risk falling through all eternity?   40

Les Fleurs

Des avalanches d'or du vieil azur, au jour
Premier et de la neige éternelle des astres
Jadis tu détachas les grands calices pour
La terre jeune encore et vierge de désastres,

Le glaïeul fauve, avec les cygnes au col fin,
Et ce divin laurier des âmes exilées
Vermeil comme le pur orteil du séraphin
Que rougit la pudeur des aurores foulées,

L'hyacinthe, le myrte à l'adorable éclair
Et, pareille à la chair de la femme, la rose
Cruelle, Hérodiade en fleur du jardin clair,
Celle qu'un sang farouche et radieux arrose!

Et tu fis la blancheur sanglotante des lys
Qui roulant sur des mers de soupirs qu'elle effleure
A travers l'encens bleu des horizons pâlis
Monte rêveusement vers la lune qui pleure!

Hosannah sur le cistre et dans les encensoirs,
Notre dame, hosannah du jardin de nos limbes!
Et finisse l'écho par les célestes soirs,
Extase des regards, scintillement des nimbes!

O Mère, qui créas en ton sein juste et fort,
Calices balançant la future fiole,
De grandes fleurs avec la balsamique Mort
Pour le poëte las que la vie étiole.

Renouveau

Le printemps maladif a chassé tristement
L'hiver, saison de l'art serein, l'hiver lucide,
Et dans mon être à qui le sang morne préside
L'impuissance s'étire en un long bâillement.

The Flowers

On the first day you plucked huge calyces
once from the stars that snow for evermore
and the old azure's golden rockfalls for
the still-young earth pure from catastrophes,

wild gladiolus with the slim-necked swans,   5
divine laurel of exiled spirits, red
as the spotless toe of a seraph spread
with scarlet by the shame of rumpled dawns,

hyacinth, myrtle with its lovely glows
and, like a woman's flesh, the parting bud   10
of that garden Herodias, the cruel rose
who is steeped in a savage radiant blood!

You made the sobbing white of lilies too,
tumbling lightly across a sea of sighs on
their dreamy way to weeping moonlight through   15
the azure incense of the pale horizon!

Hosanna in the censers, on the lute,
Lady, and in our limbo garden bed!
Let echoes through the heavenly dusk fall mute,
ecstatic glances, haloes brightly shed!   20

Mother who moulded in your strong just womb
blooms to sway phials waiting in the distance,
immense flowers offering the fragrant Tomb
for weary poets wilted by existence!

Renewal

The sickly spring has sadly driven away
winter, clear winter, season of calm art;
and impotence stretches inside my heart,
yawning a long yawn, while my doleful blood holds sway.

Des crépuscules blancs tiédissent sous le crâne
Qu'un cercle de fer serre ainsi qu'un vieux tombeau,
Et, triste, j'erre après un rêve vague et beau,
Par les champs où la sève immense se pavane

Puis je tombe énervé de parfums d'arbres, las,
Et creusant de ma face une fosse à mon rêve,
Mordant la terre chaude où poussent les lilas,

J'attends, en m'abîmant que mon ennui s'élève . . .
—Cependant l'Azur rit sur la haie et l'éveil
De tant d'oiseaux en fleur gazouillant au soleil.

Angoisse

Je ne viens pas ce soir vaincre ton corps, ô bête
En qui vont les péchés d'un peuple, ni creuser
Dans tes cheveux impurs une triste tempête
Sous l'incurable ennui que verse mon baiser:

Je demande à ton lit le lourd sommeil sans songes
Planant sous les rideaux inconnus du remords,
Et que tu peux goûter après tes noirs mensonges,
Toi qui sur le néant en sais plus que les morts:

Car le Vice, rongeant ma native noblesse,
M'a comme toi marqué de sa stérilité,
Mais tandis que ton sein de pierre est habité

Par un cœur que la dent d'aucun crime ne blesse,
Je fuis, pâle, défait, hanté par mon linceul,
Ayant peur de mourir lorsque je couche seul.

[« Las de l'amer repos . . . »]

Las de l'amer repos où ma paresse offense
Une gloire pour qui jadis j'ai fui l'enfance

White twilights grow lukewarm in my skull, bound   5
like an antique tomb by an iron band;
after a faint fair dream, I roam the land
sadly, where floods of sap parade around.

Then the scent of trees fells me, stunned, undone;
my face scoops out a grave for my reveries,   10
I gnaw the warm soil where the lilacs grow

and wait engulfed in rising tedium—though
the Blue smiles on the hedge, and quantities
of wakened birds bloom chirping in the sun.

Anguish

I have not come to tame your body, Beast
holding a people's sins, or plough sad thunder
tonight into your filthy tresses under
the fatal tedium my kiss released:

I want deep, dreamless slumber from your bed;   5
within remorse's unknown drapes it flies,
and you can taste it after your dark lies,
you who know the Void better than the dead.

For Vice, devouring my innate nobility
has stamped me like yourself with its sterility,   10
but while there dwells within your breast of stone

a heart unharmed by any evil's tooth,
I flee, pale, haunted by my shroud, uncouth,
afraid of dying when I sleep alone.

['Weary of bitter rest . . .']

Weary of bitter rest where my failure to act
insults a fame for which I once fled from the dear

Adorable des bois de roses sous l'azur
Naturel, et plus las sept fois du pacte dur
De creuser par veillée une fosse nouvelle
Dans le terrain avare et froid de ma cervelle,
Fossoyeur sans pitié pour la stérilité,
—Que dire à cette Aurore, ô Rêves, visité
Par les roses, quand, peur de ses roses livides,
Le vaste cimetière unira les trous vides?—
Je veux délaisser l'Art vorace d'un pays
Cruel, et, souriant aux reproches vieillis
Que me font mes amis, le passé, le génie,
Et ma lampe qui sait pourtant mon agonie,
Imiter le Chinois au cœur limpide et fin
De qui l'extase pure est de peindre la fin
Sur ses tasses de neige à la lune ravie
D'une bizarre fleur qui parfume sa vie
Transparente, la fleur qu'il a sentie, enfant,
Au filigrane bleu de l'âme se greffant.
Et, la mort telle avec le seul rêve du sage,
Serein, je vais choisir un jeune paysage
Que je peindrais encor sur les tasses, distrait.
Une ligne d'azur mince et pâle serait
Un lac, parmi le ciel de porcelaine nue,
Un clair croissant perdu par une blanche nue
Trempe sa corne calme en la glace des eaux,
Non loin de trois grands cils d'émeraude, roseaux.

Le Sonneur

Cependant que la cloche éveille sa voix claire
A l'air pur et limpide et profond du matin
Et passe sur l'enfant qui jette pour lui plaire
Un angélus parmi la lavande et le thym,

Le sonneur effleuré par l'oiseau qu'il éclaire,
Chevauchant tristement en geignant du latin
Sur la pierre qui tend la corde séculaire,
N'entend descendre à lui qu'un tintement lointain.

childhood of rose woods thriving under nature's sheer
blue, and still wearier seven times of my grim pact
to carve out nightly some new grave in the terrain 5
that lies penurious and cold within my brain,
a pitiless gravedigger of sterility—
what shall I tell that Dawn, as roses visit me,
O Dreams, when the immense cemetery imposes
unity on the void holes, fearing its livid roses?— 10
I want to leave the ravenous Art of cruel lands
and, smiling at the antiquated reprimands
cast at me by the past, genius, my every friend,
even my lamp—although it knows my agonies—
to imitate the limpid-souled refined Chinese 15
who finds unalloyed rapture as he paints the end
of a flower on his cups made of moon-ravished snow,
some unfamiliar flower whose scent he used to know
in childhood, and which still perfumes his crystalline
life, grafting itself on the soul's blue filigree. 20
And, because death is such, with the sole reverie
of the sage, I shall choose serenely to design
a youthful landscape idly on the cups again.
A slender line of azure blue, pale and precise,
would be a lake in skies of naked porcelain, 25
a lucid crescent lost behind white cloud proceeds
to steep its placid horn into the waters' ice,
not far from three great emerald eyelashes, the reeds.

The Bell-Ringer

While the bell is awaking its clear chime
within the morning air, clean, crisp, and bright,
passing the child who sends for its delight
an *Ave* through the lavender and thyme,

its ringer, brushed by a bird he enlightened, 5
mumbles some Latin, totters sadly round
the stone that keeps the secular rope tightened,
and hears merely a distant tinkling sound.

Je suis cet homme. Hélas! de la nuit désireuse,
J'ai beau tirer le câble à sonner l'Idéal,
De froids péchés s'ébat un plumage féal,

Et la voix ne me vient que par bribes et creuse!
Mais, un jour, fatigué d'avoir enfin tiré,
O Satan, j'ôterai la pierre et me pendrai.

Tristesse d'été

Le soleil, sur le sable, ô lutteuse endormie,
En l'or de tes cheveux chauffe un bain langoureux
Et, consumant l'encens sur ta joue ennemie,
Il mêle avec les pleurs un breuvage amoureux.

De ce blanc flamboiement l'immuable accalmie
T'a fait dire, attristée, ô mes baisers peureux
« Nous ne serons jamais une seule momie
Sous l'antique désert et les palmiers heureux! »

Mais la chevelure est une rivière tiède,
Où noyer sans frissons l'âme qui nous obsède
Et trouver ce Néant que tu ne connais pas.

Je goûterai le fard pleuré par tes paupières,
Pour voir s'il sait donner au cœur que tu frappas
L'insensibilité de l'azur et des pierres.

L'Azur

De l'éternel Azur la sereine ironie
Accable, belle indolemment comme les fleurs,
Le poëte impuissant qui maudit son génie
A travers un désert stérile de Douleurs.

I am that man. No matter how I strain
on ardent night's rope to ring the Ideal,   10
cold sins flaunt their safe wings without a care,

the sound comes only hollow and piecemeal!
But, Satan, tired of having tugged in vain,
some day, loosing the stone, I shall hang myself there.

Summer Sadness

The sunlight warms a languid bath on the sand
in your gold hair, wrestler asleep; it sears
the incense from your hostile visage, and
mingles an amorous potion with your tears.

The never-varied calm of this white glow   5
made you say, timid kisses, in distress:
'Never shall we become one corpse below
the pleasant palms and ancient wilderness!'

Yet that hair is a tepid river to
drown undisturbed the soul obsessing us   10
and find the Void that you have never known!

I shall taste kohl wept from your eyes, and thus
see if it gives this heart stricken by you
the impassivity of sky and stone.

The Blue

The timeless blue's clear irony oppresses,
as indolently beautiful as flowers,
the impotent poet cursing his powers
across a sterile desert of Distresses.

Fuyant, les yeux fermés, je le sens qui regarde
Avec l'intensité d'un remords atterrant,
Mon âme vide. Où fuir? Et quelle nuit hagarde
Jeter, lambeaux, jeter sur ce mépris navrant?

Brouillards, montez! Versez vos cendres monotones
Avec de longs haillons de brume dans les cieux
Que noiera le marais livide des automnes
Et bâtissez un grand plafond silencieux!

Et toi, sors des étangs léthéens et ramasse
En t'en venant la vase et les pâles roseaux,
Cher Ennui, pour boucher d'une main jamais lasse
Les grands trous bleus que font méchamment les oiseaux.

Encor! que sans répit les tristes cheminées
Fument, et que de suie une errante prison
Éteigne dans l'horreur de ses noires traînées
Le soleil se mourant jaunâtre à l'horizon!

—Le Ciel est mort.—Vers toi, j'accours! donne, ô matière,
L'oubli de l'Idéal cruel et du Péché
A ce martyr qui vient partager la litière
Où le bétail heureux des hommes est couché,

Car j'y veux, puisqu'enfin ma cervelle, vidée
Comme le pot de fard gisant au pied d'un mur,
N'a plus l'art d'attifer la sanglotante idée,
Lugubrement bâiller vers un trépas obscur.

En vain! l'Azur triomphe et je l'entends qui chante
Dans les cloches. Mon âme, il se fait voix pour plus
Nous faire peur avec sa victoire méchante,
Et du métal vivant sort en bleus angélus!

Il roule par la brume, ancien et traverse
Ta native agonie ainsi qu'un glaive sûr;
Où fuir dans la révolte inutile et perverse?
Je suis hanté. L'Azur! l'Azur! l'Azur! l'Azur!

Fleeing, eyes shut, I feel it contemplate   5
with the fierceness of a remorseful blight
my void soul. Flee—but where? And what wild night
can be tossed, tatters, on this crushing hate?

Fogs, ascend! Shed your ash in monotone masses
with ragged lengths of mist into the skies;   10
let it drown all the autumns' pale morasses
and make a silent immense ceiling rise!

Come from the Lethean ponds, and on your way,
dear Tedium, gather livid reeds and mire
to block up, with your hands that never tire,   15
the blue holes torn by birds in wicked play.

Still more! ceaselessly let sad chimneys smoke
and let a drifting prison made of soot
in the horror of its black straggles choke
the yellowed sun dying at heaven's foot!—   20

The Sky has died.—Matter, I need your aid!
Help this martyr who shares the litter in
which the contented human herd is laid
to lose all thought of cruel Ideal or Sin,

for there I long—since nowadays my mind,   25
void as a rouge pot dropped beside a wall,
can drape no sobbing thought of any kind—
to yawn, mourning, toward obscure downfall.

Useless! the Blue has triumphed, soul; it sings
through the bells, sounding out to frighten us   30
all the more with its evil gloryings
from live metal in some blue angelus!

It drifts with the mist, ancient, running through
your innate torment like a trusty sword;
in vain revolt, what can we flee toward?   35
Haunted I am. The Blue! The Blue! The Blue!

Brise marine

La chair est triste, hélas! et j'ai lu tous les livres.
Fuir! là-bas fuir! Je sens que des oiseaux sont ivres
D'être parmi l'écume inconnue et les cieux!
Rien, ni les vieux jardins reflétés par les yeux
Ne retiendra ce cœur qui dans la mer se trempe
O nuits! ni la clarté déserte de ma lampe
Sur le vide papier que la blancheur défend,
Et ni la jeune femme allaitant son enfant.
Je partirai! Steamer balançant ta mâture
Lève l'ancre pour une exotique nature!
Un Ennui, désolé par les cruels espoirs,
Croit encore à l'adieu suprême des mouchoirs!
Et, peut-être, les mâts, invitant les orages
Sont-ils de ceux qu'un vent penche sur les naufrages
Perdus, sans mâts, sans mâts, ni fertiles îlots . . .
Mais, ô mon cœur, entends le chant des matelots!

Soupir

Mon âme vers ton front où reve, ô calme sœur,
Un automne jonché de taches de rousseur,
Et vers le ciel errant de ton œil angélique,
Monte, comme dans un jardin mélancolique,
Fidèle, un blanc jet d'eau soupire vers l'Azur!
—Vers l'Azur attendri d'Octobre pâle et pur
Que mire aux grands bassins sa langueur infinie:
Et laisse, sur l'eau morte où la fauve agonie
Des feuilles erre au vent et creuse un froid sillon,
Se traîner le soleil jaune d'un long rayon.

Aumône

Prends ce sac, Mendiant! tu ne le cajolas
Sénile nourisson d'une tétine avare
Afin de pièce à pièce en égoutter ton glas.

Sea Breeze

The flesh is sad—and I've read every book.
O to escape—to get away! Birds look
as though they're drunk for unknown spray and skies.
No ancient gardens mirrored in the eyes,
nothing can hold this heart steeped in the sea—   5
not my lamp's desolate luminosity
nor the blank paper guarded by its white
nor the young wife feeding her child, O night!
Away! You steamer with your swaying helm,
raise anchor for some more exotic realm!   10
Ennui, crushed down by cruel hopes, still relies
on handkerchiefs' definitive goodbyes!
Is this the kind of squall-inviting mast
that storm-winds buckle above shipwrecks cast
away—no mast, no islets flourishing? . . .   15
Still, my soul, listen to the sailors sing!

Sigh

My soul rises toward your brow where autumn teeming
with russet tinges, my calm sister, lingers dreaming,
toward the wandering sky of your angelic eyes
where a fountain of white water faithfully sighs,
as in some mournful garden, reaching toward the Blue!—   5
toward October's pitying Blue, pale and true,
which mirrors in broad pools its endless lethargy
and on dead water where a fulvid agony
of leaves drifts windtossed and ploughs a chill furrow, may
let the yellow sun trail in a long lingering ray.   10

Alms

Have this purse, Beggar! you never pled for it
a senile nursling from a stingy nipple
to drain your death-knell from it bit by bit.

Tire du métal cher quelque péché bizarre
Et, vaste comme nous, les poings pleins, le baisons
Souffles-y qu'il se torde! une ardente fanfare.

Église avec l'encens que toutes ces maisons
Sur les murs quand berceur d'une bleue éclaircie
Le tabac sans parler roule les oraisons,

Et l'opium puissant brise la pharmacie!
Robes et peau, veux-tu lacérer le satin
Et boire en la salive heureuse l'inertie,

Par les cafés princiers attendre le matin?
Les plafonds enrichis de nymphes et de voiles,
On jette, au mendiant de la vitre, un festin.

Et quand tu sors, vieux dieu, grelottant sous tes toiles
D'emballage, l'aurore est un lac de vin d'or
Et tu jures avoir au gosier les étoiles!

Faute de supputer l'éclat de ton trésor,
Tu peux du moins t'orner d'une plume, à complies
Servir un cierge au saint en qui tu crois encor.

Ne t'imagine pas que je dis des folies.
La terre s'ouvre vieille à qui crève la faim.
Je hais une autre aumône et veux que tu m'oublies

Et surtout ne va pas, frère, acheter du pain.

Don du poème

Je t'apporte l'enfant d'une nuit d'Idumée!
Noire, à l'aile saignante et pâle, déplumée,
Par le verre brûlé d'aromates et d'or,
Par les carreaux glacés, hélas! mornes encor,
L'aurore se jeta sur la lampe angélique,
Palmes! et quand elle a montré cette relique

Draw some immense strange sin from the dear metal,
   blow blazing fanfares on it, twist it round!   5
just as we kiss and clutch it in our fingers.

   All these houses are fragrant holy ground
when on the walls, soothing a sky blue clearing,
   tobacco rolls out prayers without a sound

and potent opium shatters its seller!   10
   Skirts and skin—would you have those satins torn
and drink blissful inaction in saliva

   at princely cafés waiting for the morn?
To beggars looking in they toss a banquet
   from lofty halls that nymphs and veils adorn.   15

When you leave, old god shivering in your burlap,
   a lake of golden wine is break of day
and you swear that the stars are in your gullet!

   If you can count no hoards, at least you may
deck yourself with a plume and burn at compline   20
   a candle to the saint whom you still pray.

Do not imagine that my words are folly.
   The old earth parts for those who die unfed.
I hate all other handouts; please forget me.

   Above all, brother, don't go and buy bread.   25

Gift of the Poem

I bring you this child of an Idumaean night!
black, with featherless wings bleeding and nearly white,
through the glass burned with spices and with gold,
through the panes still, alas! dismal and icy cold,
the sunrise flung itself on the angelic   5
lamp, O you palms! and when it showed that relic

A ce père essayant un sourire ennemi,
La solitude bleue et stérile a frémi.
O la berceuse, avec ta fille et l'innocence
De vos pieds froids, accueille une horrible naissance:
Et ta voix rappelant viole et clavecin,
Avec le doigt fané presseras-tu le sein
Par qui coule en blancheur sibylline la femme
Pour des lèvres que l'air du vierge azur affame?

Hérodiade

Scène

LA NOURRICE—HÉRODIADE

N.

Tu vis! ou vois-je ici l'ombre d'une princesse?
A mes lèvres tes doigts et leurs bagues, et cesse
De marcher dans un âge ignoré . . .

H.

                              Reculez.
Le blond torrent de mes cheveux immaculés,
Quand il baigne mon corps solitaire le glace
D'horreur, et mes cheveux que la lumière enlace
Sont immortels. O femme, un baiser me tûrait
Si la beauté n'etait la mort . . .
                              Par quel attrait
Menée et quel matin oublié des prophètes
Verse, sur les lointains mourants, ses tristes fêtes,
Le sais-je? tu m'as vue, ô nourrice d'hiver,
Sous la lourde prison de pierres et de fer
Où de mes vieux lions traînent les siècles fauves
Entrer, et je marchais, fatale, les mains sauves,
Dans le parfum désert de ces anciens rois:
Mais encore as-tu vu quels furent mes effrois?
Je m'arrête rêvant aux exils, et j'effeuille,
Comme près d'un bassin dont le jet d'eau m'accueille,
Les pâles lys qui sont en moi, tandis qu'épris

to this father attempting an unfriendly smile,
the blue and sterile solitude shivered all the while.
Woman lulling your little daughter, greet
a cruel birth, with the innocence of your cold feet   10
and your voice which both viol and harpsichord invest,
will you with shrivelled fingers press the breast
from which flows woman, Sibylline and white,
for lips starved of the virgin azure light?

Herodias

Scene

THE NURSE *and* HERODIAS

N.

You are alive! or do I see the ghost of a princess?
Cease walking in some unknown era; let me press
your fingers and their rings to my lips . . .

H.

                                        Stand back there!
Even the strong blonde stream of my unspotted hair
bathing my solitary body freezes it   5
with terror, woman, and my hairs entwined and knit
with bright light are immortal. One kiss would kill me
if beauty were not death . . .
                              By what affinity
I am drawn, and what dawn unknown to prophets pours
its doleful festivals on distant dying shores,   10
do I know? winter nurse, you saw me pass alone
into the heavy prison built of iron and stone
where my old lions haul the savage bygone years,
and, fated, with my hands unscathed, onward I went
among those ancient kings and their deserted scent: 15
but did you also see the nature of my fears?
I pause, dreaming of exiles, and I strip away,
as if beside a pool whose fountain welcomes me,
the pale lilies within me, while, allured to stare

De suivre du regard les languides débris
Descendre, à travers ma rêverie en silence,
Les bêtes, de ma robe écartent l'indolence
Et regardent mes pieds qui calmeraient la mer.
Calme, toi, les frissons de ta sénile chair,
Viens et ma chevelure imitant les manières
Trop farouches qui font votre peur des crinières,
Aide-moi, puisqu'ainsi tu n'oses plus me voir,
A me peigner nonchalamment dans un miroir.

N.

Sinon la myrrhe gaie en ses bouteilles closes,
De l'essence ravie aux vieillesses de roses
Voulez-vous, mon enfant, essayer la vertu
Funèbre?

H.

Laisse là ces parfums! Ne sais-tu
Que je les hais, nourrice, et veux-tu que je sente
Leur ivresse noyer ma tête languissante?
Je veux que mes cheveux qui ne sont pas des fleurs
A répandre l'oubli des humaines douleurs,
Mais de l'or, à jamais vierge des aromates,
Dans leurs éclairs cruels et dans leurs pâleurs mates,
Observent la froideur stérile du métal,
Vous ayant reflétés, joyaux du mur natal,
Armes, vases, depuis ma solitaire enfance.

N.

Pardon! l'âge effaçait, reine, votre défense
De mon esprit pâli comme un vieux livre ou noir . . .

H.

Assez! Tiens devant moi ce miroir.
                                   O miroir!
Eau froide par l'ennui dans ton cadre gelée
Que de fois et pendant les heures, désolée
Des songes et cherchant mes souvenirs qui sont
Comme des feuilles sous ta glace au trou profond,
Je m'apparus en toi comme une ombre lointaine.

at the descent of all the languid disarray   20
dropping down, in the silence, through my reverie,
the lions part the indolence of the dress I wear
and gaze upon my feet that would appease the sea.
Appease the shudders of your senile flesh; come here,
and while my hair is imitating the too furious   25
habits of lions' manes that animate your fear,
help me, since you no longer dare to see me thus,
help me comb my hair idly in a looking-glass.

N.

If not gay myrrh in its sealed bottles, my dear lass,
then do you you wish to sample the funereal   30
power of the essence stolen from old roses?

H.

                                    No
such perfumes! Surely, nurse, you know I hate them all,
or would you have me feel their drunken rapture flow
in overwhelming floods that drown my languid head?
I want these hairs of mine—which are not flowers that spread   35
abroad oblivion of every human pain,
but gold, forever unsullied by any scent—
I want them to remain, in their cruel glint and plain
paleness, a sterile cold metallic element
reflecting you adornments of my natal wall,   40
armour and vases, since my lonely childhood days.

N.

O queen, forgive me! age was starting to erase
your ban from my mind faint as an old book or black . . .

H.

No more! Hold up the looking-glass before me.
                                    Looking-glass!
Cold water frozen by the boredom at your back,   45
how many times, and during what long hours, dismayed
by dreams and groping for my memories that pass
like leaves beneath your ice and its profound abyss,
I saw myself within you like some distant shade,

Mais, horreur! des soirs, dans ta sévère fontaine,
J'ai de mon rêve épars connu la nudité!

Nourrice, suis–je belle?

N.

                    Un astre, en vérité:
Mais cette tresse tombe . . .

H.

                    Arrête dans ton crime
Qui refroidit mon sang vers sa source, et réprime
Ce geste, impiété fameuse: ah! conte-moi
Quel sûr démon te jette en ce sinistre émoi,
Ce baiser, ce parfums offerts et, le dirai-je?
O mon cœur, cette main encore sacrilège,
Car tu voulais, je crois, me toucher, sont un jour
Que ne finira pas sans malheur sur la tour . . .
O tour qu'Hérodiade avec effroi regarde!

N.

Temps bizarre, en effet, de quoi le ciel vous garde!
Vous errez, ombre seule et nouvelle fureur,
Et regardant en vous précoce avec terreur;
Mais pourtant adorable autant qu'une immortelle,
O mon enfant, et belle affreusement et telle
Que . . .

H.

                    Mais n'allais-tu pas me toucher?

N.

                                        J'aimerais
Être à qui le Destin réserve vos secrets.

H.

Oh! tais-toi!

N.

                    Viendra-t-il parfois?

yet some nights, in your grim fountain—horrible, this!— 50
I knew the nakedness of my own scattered dream!

Nurse, am I beautiful?

N.

Truly, a starry gleam:
and yet this tress is falling . . .

H.

Stop your wickedness
which chills my blood right to its wellsprings, and repress
that gesture, that notorious blasphemy: tell me 55
what cunning demon stirs your sinister sensibility,
that kiss, those offerings of perfume, and, shall I say?
O heart of mine, that ever sacrilegious hand,
for you wished, I believe, to touch me, are a day
that will not end without misfortune on the tower . . . 60
and that Herodias contemplates with dismay!

N.

These are indeed strange times, from which may heaven's power
keep you! you stray, a solitary shadow and
new fury, gazing at your own precocity
in fear, yet always lovely as a goddess, O 65
my child, and dreadful in your beauty, so much so
that . . .

H.

Were you not about to touch me?

N.

O to be
the one for whom your secrets are reserved by fate!

H.

Be silent!

N.

Will he be here some time?

H.

Étoiles pures,

N'entendez pas!

N.

Comment, sinon parmi d'obscures
Épouvantes, songer plus implacable encor
Et comme suppliant le dieu que le trésor
De votre grâce attend! Et pour qui, dévorée
D'angoisse, gardez-vous la splendeur ignorée
Et le mystère vain de votre être?

H.

Pour moi.

N.

Triste fleur qui croît seule et n'a pas d'autre émoi
Que son ombre dans l'eau vue avec atonie.

H.

Va, garde ta pitié comme ton ironie.

N.

Toutefois expliquez: oh! non, naïve enfant,
Décroîtra, quelque jour, ce dédain triomphant . . .

H.

Mais qui me toucherait, des lions respectée?
Du reste, je ne veux rien d'humain et, sculptée,
Si tu me vois les yeux perdus aux paradis,
C'est quand je me souviens de ton lait bu jadis.

N.

Victime lamentable à son destin offerte!

H.

Oui, c'est pour moi, pour moi, que je fleuris, déserte!
Vous le savez, jardins d'améthyste, enfouis
Sans fin dans de savants abîmes éblouis,
Ors ignorés, gardant votre antique lumière

H.

O you pure
stars, do not listen!

N.

How, except among obscure   70
terrors, can we envisage the divinity
still more implacable and like a suppliant
whom all the treasures of your beauty must await!
For whom would you, consumed by pangs, keep the unknown
splendour and the vain mystery of your being?

H.

For myself alone.   75

N.

Sad lonely flower, emotionally ignorant
but for its shadow seen in the stream listlessly.

H.

Go, spare your pity and your irony.

N.

Yet tell me this: oh! no, your triumphal disdain,
you poor innocent child, will some day surely wane . . .   80

H.

But when lions respect me, who would dare touch me?
Besides, I long for nothing human; if you see
me like a statue with eyes lost in paradise,
that is when I recall the milk you gave me formerly.

N.

Victim facing her doom—pitiful sacrifice!   85

H.

Yes, for myself alone I bloom, in isolation!
You gardens blossoming amethyst, you know this,
endlessly buried in some dazzling deep abyss,
unknown golds that preserve your old illumination

Sous le sombre sommeil d'une terre première,
Vous, pierres où mes yeux comme de purs bijoux
Empruntent leur clarté mélodieuse, et vous,
Métaux qui donnez à ma jeune chevelure
Une splendeur fatale et sa massive allure!
Quant à toi, femme née en des siècles malins
Pour la méchanceté des antres sibyllins,
Qui parles d'un mortel! selon qui, des calices
De mes robes, arôme aux farouches délices,
Sortirait le frisson blanc de ma nudité,
Prophétise que si le tiède azur d'été,
Vers lui nativement la femme se dévoile,
Me voit dans ma pudeur grelottante d'étoile,
Je meurs!

      J'aime l'horreur d'être vierge et je veux
Vivre parmi l'effroi que me font mes cheveux
Pour, le soir, retirée en ma couche, reptile
Inviolé, sentir en la chair inutile
Le froid scintillement de ta pâle clarté,
Toi qui te meurs, toi qui brûles de chasteté,
Nuit blanche de glaçons et de neige cruelle!

Et ta sœur solitaire, ô ma sœur éternelle,
Mon rêve montera vers toi: telle déjà,
Rare limpidité d'un cœur qui le songea,
Je me crois seule en ma monotone patrie,
Et tout, autour de moi, vit dans l'idolâtrie
D'un miroir qui reflète en son calme dormant
Hérodiade au clair regard de diamant . . .
O charme dernier, oui! je le sens, je suis seule.

N.

Madame, allez-vous donc mourir?

H.

      Non, pauvre aïeule,
Sois calme et, t'éloignant, pardonne à ce cœur dur,
Mais avant, si tu veux, clos les volets: l'azur
Séraphique sourit dans les vitres profondes,

beneath the sombre sleep of earth's primeval days,   90
you precious stones from which these eyes of mine like pure
gems borrow their melodious and brilliant rays,
and all you metals that bestow the massed allure
and fatal splendour on my head of youthful hair!
As for you—woman born in crafty centuries   95
suiting the wickedness of some Sibylline lair,
who speaks about a man and says the calyces
of my skirts, fragrant with ferocious ecstasies,
would bring forth the white shudder of my nakedness—
now prophesy that if the warm blue summer sky,   100
toward which women naturally will undress,
should see me in my shame, shivering, starlike, I
shall die!

        I love the horror of being virgin and
wish to live with the terror that my hair gives me
so that, retiring to my bed at night,   105
inviolate reptile, in my useless flesh I might
feel the chill scintillation of your pallid glow,
you that die to yourself and burn with chastity,
white sleepless night of icicles and cruel snow!

Your lone sister, my dream will rise toward you, O   110
my everlasting sister: and already such
I feel alone in my monotonous fatherland
(the rare transparence of a heart that dreamed as much),
while everything lives in idolatry beyond
as a mirror reflecting in its slumbrous balm   115
Herodias with her clear gaze of diamond . . .
O final charm, O yes! I am alone, I know.

N.

Are you then going to die, Madame?

H.

             No; as you go,
forgive this hard heart, poor old creature, and be calm;
but first close all the shutters, if you please,   120
seraphic blue sky smiles in each deep windowpane,

Et je déteste, moi, le bel azur!

                  Des ondes
Se bercent et, là-bas, sais-tu pas un pays
Où le sinistre ciel ait les regards haïs
De Vénus qui, le soir, brûle dans le feuillage:
J'y partirais.

           Allume encore, enfantillage,
Dis-tu, ces flambeaux où la cire au feu léger
Pleure parmi l'or vain quelque pleur étranger
Et . . .

                N.

Maintenant?

                H.

           Adieu.

                Vous mentez, ô fleur nue
De mes lèvres!

           J'attends une chose inconnue
Ou, peut-être, ignorant le mystère et vos cris,
Jetez-vous les sanglots suprêmes et meurtris
D'une enfance sentant parmi les rêveries
Se séparer enfin ses froides pierreries.

L'Après-midi d'vn favne

Églogve

LE FAVNE

Ces nymphes, je les veux perpétuer.

                Si clair,
Leur incarnat léger, qu'il voltige dans l'air
Assoupi de sommeils touffus.

              Aimai-je un rêve?

Mon doute, amas de nuit ancienne, s'achève
En maint rameau subtil, qui, demeuré les vrais

and how I hate the beautiful blue sky!
Mild seas
are swaying and, beyond, you may know some terrain
where the sinister sky's glances are hated by
Venus who burns among the leaves at evening: 125
there I would go.
One more, childish you say, desire:
kindle those torches where the wax with its frail fire
weeps some alien tear in the midst of the vain
gold and . . .

N.

And now?

H.

Farewell.
You are speaking a lie,
naked flower of my lips.
I wait an unknown thing   130
or possibly, not knowing the mystery and your screams,
you may be flinging out the last and wounded groans
wept by a childhood feeling its cold precious stones
finally separate in the midst of the dreams.

A Favn in the Afternoon

Eclogve

THE FAVN *speaks:*

I'd love to make them linger on, those nymphs.
So fair,
their frail incarnate, that it flutters in the air
drowsy with tousled slumbers.
Did I love a dream?

My doubt, hoard of old darkness, ends in a whole stream
of subtle branches which, remaining as the true   5

Bois mêmes, prouve, hélas! que bien seul je m'offrais
Pour triomphe la faute idéale de roses—

Réfléchissons . . .

                        ou si les femmes dont tu gloses
Figurent un souhait de tes sens fabuleux!
Faune, l'illusion s'échappe des yeux bleus
Et froids, comme une source en pleurs, de la plus chaste:
Mais, l'autre tout soupirs, dis-tu qu'elle contraste
Comme brise du jour chaude dans ta toison?
Que non! par l'immobile et lasse pâmoison
Suffoquant de chaleurs le matin frais s'il lutte,
Ne murmure point d'eau que ne verse ma flûte
Au bosquet arrosé d'accords; et le seul vent
Hors des deux tuyaux prompt à s'exhaler avant
Qu'il disperse le son dans une pluie aride,
C'est, à l'horizon pas remué d'une ride,
Le visible et serein souffle artificiel
De l'inspiration, qui regagne le ciel.

O bords siciliens d'un calme marécage
Qu'à l'envi des soleils ma vanité saccage,
Tacites sous les fleurs d'étincelles, CONTEZ
» *Que je coupais ici les creux roseaux domptés*
» *Par le talent; quand, sur l'or glauque de lointaines*
» *Verdures dédiant leur vigne à des fontaines,*
» *Ondoie une blancheur animale au repos:*
» *Et qu'au prélude lent où naissent les pipeaux,*
» *Ce vol de cygnes, non! de naïades se sauve*
» *Ou plonge . . .*
                        Inerte, tout brûle dans l'heure fauve
Sans marquer par quel art ensemble détala
Trop d'hymen souhaité de qui cherche le *la*:
Alors m'éveillerais-je à la ferveur première,
Droit et seul, sous un flot antique de lumière,
Lys! et l'un de vous tous pour l'ingénuité.

forests, show that I've offered myself (quite alone, too)
the roses' ideal failing as something glorious—

Let me reflect . . .

　　　　　　　　what if these women you discuss,
faun, represent desires of your own fabulous
senses! Illusion flows out of the chilly blue　　　　　　　10
eyes of the chaster one, like a fountain in tears:
the other, though, all sighs—do you think she appears
in contrast like a day's warm breeze across your fleece?
Not at all: through the lazy languishing release
stifling with heat the cool dawn's struggles, not a sound　　　15
of water but my flute's outpourings murmurs round
the thicket steeped in music; and the one stir of air
my dual pipes are swiftly shedding everywhere
and then dispersing in a sonorous arid sleet,
is, over the horizon that no ripples pleat,　　　　　　　20
the visible, serene and artificial sigh
of inspiration reascending to the sky.

O fringes of a placid mere in Sicily
thus plundered by my sun-rivalling vanity,
silent beneath the blooms of brilliant light, PROCLAIM　　25
'how I was cropping here the hollow reeds made tame
by talent, when, across the blue-green gold of things
far off—verdures devoting their vines to the springs—
came shimmering to rest a pallid animal glow;
and when the pipes were brought to birth, how at their slow　　30
prelude this flight of swans—no! naiads—fled away
or dived . . .

　　　　　　All things burn in the fulvid time of day,
inert, failing to show by what art it dispersed,
that nuptial excess craved by someone seeking A
natural; and then I must waken to the first　　　　　　　35
passion, erect, alone, beneath an age-old light,
lilies! and one among you, a simple neophyte.

Autre que ce doux rien par leur lèvre ébruité,
Le baiser, qui tout bas des perfides assure,
Mon sein, vierge de preuve, atteste une morsure
Mystérieuse, due à quelque auguste dent;
Mais, bast! arcane tel élut pour confident
Le jonc vaste et jumeau dont sous l'azur on joue,
Qui, détournant à soi le trouble de la joue
Rêve, dans un solo long, que nous amusions
La beauté d'alentour par des confusions
Fausses entre elle-même et notre chant crédule;
Et de faire aussi haut que l'amour se module
Évanouir du songe ordinaire de dos
Ou de flanc pur suivis avec mes regards clos,
Une sonore, vaine et monotone ligne.

Tâche donc, instrument des fuites, ô maligne
Syrinx, de refleurir aux lacs où tu m'attends!
Moi, de ma rumeur fier, je vais parler longtemps
Des déesses; et par d'idolâtres peintures,
A leur ombre enlever encore des ceintures:
Ainsi, quand des raisins j'ai sucé la clarté,
Pour bannir un regret par ma feinte écarté,
Rieur, j'élève au ciel d'été la grappe vide
Et, soufflant dans ses peaux lumineuses, avide
D'ivresse, jusqu'au soir je regarde au travers.

O nymphes, regonflons des SOUVENIRS divers.
» *Mon œil, trouant les joncs, dardait chaque encolure*
» *Immortelle, qui noie en l'onde sa brûlure*
» *Avec un cri de rage au ciel de la forêt;*
» *Et le splendide bain de cheveux disparaît*
» *Dans les clartés et les frissons, ô pierreries!*
» *J'accours; quand, à mes pieds, s'entrejoignent (meurtries*
» *De la langueur goûtée à ce mal d'être deux)*
» *Des dormeuses parmi leurs seuls bras hasardeux;*
» *Je les ravis, sans les désenlacer, et vole*
» *A ce massif, haï par l'ombrage frivole,*

Other than that sweet nothing voiced by their lip, the kiss
giving assurance softly of the faithless, this
virgin-proof breast of mine bears witness to some bite   40
of a mysterious kind from sacred teeth; but wait!
that certain esoteric something chose the great
twin reed played under heaven as its secret friend;
diverting the cheek's disturbances for its own end,
it dreams, in a long solo, that we have seduced   45
the beauties round about us by a false confusion
of them with the naive melody we've produced;
and dreams of, high as love itself can modulate,
evacuating from the commonplace illusion
of some pure loin or rear that my shut eyes create   50
a sonorous, monotonous and empty line.

Try, then, to flower again, organ of flights, malign
syrinx, across the lake-flats where you wait for me!
Proud of these sounds of mine, I'll speak perpetually
of goddesses; I'll lift more of the drapery   55
up from their shadows with idolatrous displays:
so, when I've sucked the gleam of grape-flesh, to erase
this disappointment that my sleight has scattered, I
raise the void cluster, laughing, to the summer sky;
avid for drunkenness, I blow into its light-   60
filled skins, and stare through them until the fall of night.

Nymphs, let's expand again various MEMORIES.
'My gaze delved through the reeds, darted on each of these
immortal throats plunging their heat into the flow
with cries of fury at the forest heavens; so   65
the glorious cascade of tresses slipped from view
in glitterings and shiverings—such jewelleries!
I sped there; at my feet lay linked (and wounded through
the languor tasted from this pain of being two)
a sleeping pair of nymphs in their lone careless braid   70
of limbs; I seized without unlacing them, and flew
here to this thicket hated by the frivolous shade

» *De roses tarissant tout parfum au soleil,*
» *Où notre ébat au jour consumé soit pareil.*
Je t'adore, courroux des vierges, ô délice
Farouche du sacré fardeau nu qui se glisse
Pour fuir ma lèvre en feu buvant, comme un éclair
Tressaille! la frayeur secrète de la chair:
Des pieds de l'inhumaine au cœur de la timide
Que délaisse à la fois une innocence, humide
De larmes folles ou de moins tristes vapeurs.
» *Mon crime, c'est d'avoir, gai de vaincre ces peurs*
» *Traîtresses, divisé la touffe échevelée*
» *De baisers que les dieux gardaient si bien mêlée;*
» *Car, à peine j'allais cacher un rire ardent*
» *Sous les replis heureux d'une seule (gardant*
» *Par un doigt simple, afin que sa candeur de plume*
» *Se teignît à l'émoi de sa sœur qui s'allume,*
» *La petite, naïve et ne rougissant pas:)*
» *Que de mes bras, défaits par de vagues trépas,*
» *Cette proie, à jamais ingrate se délivre*
» *Sans pitié du sanglot dont j'étais encore ivre.*

Tant pis! vers le bonheur d'autres m'entraîneront
Par leur tresse nouée aux cornes de mon front:
Tu sais, ma passion, que, pourpre et déjà mûre,
Chaque grenade éclate et d'abeilles murmure;
Et notre sang, épris de qui le va saisir,
Coule pour tout l'essaim éternel du désir.
A l'heure où ce bois d'or et de cendres se teinte
Une fête s'exalte en la feuillée éteinte:
Etna! c'est parmi toi visité de Vénus
Sur ta lave posant ses talons ingénus,
Quand tonne un somme triste ou s'épuise la flamme.
Je tiens la reine!

         O sûr châtiment . . .

                    Non, mais l'âme
De paroles vacante et ce corps alourdi
Tard succombent au fier silence de midi:
Sans plus il faut dormir en l'oubli du blasphème,

where roses dry up all their fragrance in the sun
and where our frolics may be squandered like the light.
I love these virgin angers, this untamed delight   75
of nude and sacred burdens slipping away to shun
my burning lips that drink in, as a lightning-sheet
quivers! the flesh's secret terror, from the feet
of the cruel girl to the heart of the timid one
simultaneously abandoned by an innocence, damp   80
with foolish tears or fluids of a less grim stamp.
'*My offence, in my joy at conquering these sly*
terrors, was that I prised apart the tousled wry
kisses the gods had kept so deftly mingled: I
no sooner strove to hide this ecstasy of mine   85
within one girl's happy recesses (with a fine
fingerhold on the other one—naive and slight,
not blushing in the least—so that her feathery white
might be tinged as her sister's passion caught alight),
than from my arms, untwined by some vague perishings,   90
this everlastingly ungrateful captive springs
free, careless of my still-intoxicated sighs.

No matter! Other nymphs will draw me nonetheless,
their tresses tangled on my horns, to happiness:
how, purple, freshly ripe, the pomegranates rise   95
and burst and murmur with the bees, my passion knows;
our blood, allured by what may seize its fancy, flows
for the swarm of desires eternally released.
Among the dead leaves, at times when the forest glows
with gold and ashen tints, there rises up a feast: 100
Etna! across your very slopes, then, Venus goes,
and on your laval ground she rests her artless toes
when sad slumbers are sounding and the flame has ceased.
I've seized the queen!
                    The punishment is certain . . .
                                        No,
but the soul void of words and heavy body slow-   105
ly fall before noon's haughty calm. No more ado;
must sleep now, must forget the blasphemy and blame,

Sur le sable altéré gisant et comme j'aime
Ouvrir ma bouche à l'astre efficace des vins!

Couple, adieu; je vais voir l'ombre que tu devins.

[« La chevelure vol . . . »]

La chevelure vol d'une flamme à l'extrême
Occident de désirs pour la tout déployer
Se pose (je dirais mourir un diadème)
Vers le front couronné son ancien foyer

Mais sans or soupirer que cette vive nue
L'ignition du feu toujours intérieur
Originellement la seule continue
Dans le joyau de l'œil véridique ou rieur

Une nudité de héros tendre diffame
Celle qui ne mouvant astre ni feux au doigt
Rien qu'à simplifier avec gloire la femme
Accomplit par son chef fulgurante l'exploit

De semer de rubis le doute qu'elle écorche
Ainsi qu'une joyeuse et tutélaire torche

Sainte

A la fenêtre recélant
Le santal vieux qui se dédore
De sa viole étincelant
Jadis avec flûte ou mandore,

Est la Sainte pâle, étalant
Le livre vieux qui se déplie
Du Magnificat ruisselant
Jadis selon vêpre et complie:

spread on the thirsty sand; and as I love to do
open my mouth to the wines' potent star!

                                    Both of you,
farewell; I'm going to see the shadow you became.   110

['The hair flight of a flame . . .']

The hair flight of a flame to the extreme
west of desire if it should all unlace
settles (a diadem dying it would seem)
near the crowned brow its former fireplace

but without sighing for more gold than this   5
live cloud kindling the fire ever within
at first the only one continues in
the jewel of the eye true or remiss

a tender naked hero would degrade
her who stirring no star or fire would   10
just condensing with glory womanhood
flashing with her head wreak the escapade

of strewing rubies on the doubt she would scorch
like a joyous and tutelary torch.

Saint

At the window that veils her old
sandalwood viol voiding gold
which used to cast its glitter in
the past with flute or mandolin

is the pale Saint displaying that   5
old volume the Magnificat
unfolded, from which compline or
vespersong used to stream before:

A ce vitrage d'ostensoir
Que frôle une harpe par l'Ange
Formée avec son vol du soir
Pour la délicate phalange

Du doigt que, sans le vieux santal
Ni le vieux livre, elle balance
Sur le plumage instrumental,
Musicienne du silence.

Toast funèbre

O de notre bonheur, toi, le fatal emblème!

Salut de la démence et libation blême,
Ne crois pas qu'au magique espoir du corridor
J'offre ma coupe vide où souffre un monstre d'or!
Ton apparition ne va pas me suffire:
Car je t'ai mis, moi-même, en un lieu de porphyre.
Le rite est pour les mains d'éteindre le flambeau
Contre le fer épais des portes du tombeau:
Et l'on ignore mal, élu pour notre fête
Très-simple de chanter l'absence du poëte,
Que ce beau monument l'enferme tout entier:
Si ce n'est que la gloire ardente du métier,
Jusqu'à l'heure commune et vile de la cendre,
Par le carreau qu'allume un soir fier d'y descendre,
Retourne vers les feux du pur soleil mortel!

Magnifique, total et solitaire, tel
Tremble de s'exhaler le faux orgueil des hommes.
Cette foule hagarde! elle annonce: Nous sommes
La triste opacité de nos spectres futurs.
Mais le blason des deuils épars sur de vains murs,
J'ai méprisé l'horreur lucide d'une larme,
Quand, sourd même à mon vers sacré qui ne l'alarme,
Quelqu'un de ces passants, fier, aveugle et muet,
Hôte de son linceul vague, se transmuait

at this ostensory pane draped
by a harp that the Angel shaped   10
in his flight through the evening shade
for the delicate finger-blade

as she is poising to caress,
neither old wood nor old edition,
but instrumental featheriness—   15
being the silence's musician.

Funerary Toast

You fatal emblem of our happiness!

A toast of lunacy, a wan libation,
not to the passage's magic aspiration
I raise my void cup bearing a gold monster in distress!
Your apparition is not enough for me: 5
I myself set you in the porphyry.
The rite requires that hands should quench the torch
against the strong iron gates at the tomb's porch:
chosen for our feast simply to declare
the poet's absence, we must be aware   10
that this fair monument holds all of him.
Unless the bright fame of what he has done,
until the ashes' hour so common and so grim,
through glass lit by a dusk proud to fall there
returns toward the fires of the pure mortal sun!   15

Sublime, total and solitary, then
he fears to breathe out the false pride of men.
'We are', declare these haggard teeming hosts,
'the sad opaque forms of our future ghosts.'
But with blazons of woe strewn across each vain wall   20
I scorn the lucid horror of a tear,
when, proud, mute, blind, the guest of his vague graveyard shawl,
one of those passers-by, failing to stir or hear
even my sacred verse, goes through a transformation

En le vierge héros de l'attente posthume.
Vaste gouffre apporté dans l'amas de la brume
Par l'irascible vent des mots qu'il n'a pas dits,
Le néant à cet Homme aboli de jadis:
« Souvenir d'horizons, qu'est-ce, ô toi, que la Terre? »
Hurle ce songe; et, voix dont la clarté s'altère,
L'espace a pour jouet le cri: « Je ne sais pas! »

Le Maître, par un œil profond, a, sur ses pas,
Apaisé de l'éden l'inquiète merveille
Dont le frisson final, dans sa voix seule, éveille,
Pour la Rose et le Lys, le mystère d'un nom.
Est-il de ce destin rien qui demeure, non?
O vous tous! oubliez une croyance sombre.
Le splendide génie éternel n'a pas d'ombre.
Moi, de votre désir soucieux, je veux voir,
A qui s'évanouit, hier, dans le devoir,
Idéal que nous font les jardins de cet astre,
Survivre pour l'honneur du tranquille désastre
Une agitation solennelle par l'air
De paroles, pourpre ivre et grand calice clair,
Que, pluie et diamant, le regard diaphane
Resté là sur ces fleurs dont nulle ne se fane,
Isole parmi l'heure et le rayon du jour!

C'est de nos vrais bosquets déjà tout le séjour,
Où le poëte pur a pour geste humble et large
De l'interdire au rêve, ennemi de sa charge:
Afin que le matin de son repos altier,
Quand la mort ancienne est comme pour Gautier
De n'ouvrir pas les yeux sacrés et de se taire,
Surgisse, de l'allée ornement tributaire,
Le sépulcre solide où gît tout ce qui nuit,
Et l'avare silence et la massive nuit.

into the virgin hero of posthumous expectation.   25
That dream the void, a massive chasm hurled
by the fierce wind of words he did not say
into the mist, howls at this Man dead long ago:
'Recalled horizons, speak, what is the World?'
and space, a voice whose clarity fades away,   30
toys with this cry: 'I do not know!'

The Master's keen eye, as he went, brought ease
to Eden's restless wonder, whose last throes
in his unique voice wake the mysteries
of a name for the Lily and the Rose.   35
Is none of this destiny enduring? none?
Forget so dark a credo, everyone.
Radiant eternal genius leaves no shade.
Mindful of your desires, I wish to see
in our task, the ideal that our star's parks have laid   40
upon us, for this man who vanished recently,
a solemn stir of words stay alive in the air
in honour of the calm catastrophe—
a huge clear bloom, a purple ecstasy,
which his diaphanous gaze remaining there,   45
rain and diamond, on these flowers that never fade away,
isolates in the hour and radiance of day!

Already within these true groves we stay,
where the true poet's broad and humble gesture must
keep them from dreams, those enemies of his trust: 50
so when he rests in pride at break of day,
when ancient death is as for Gautier
not to speak nor to open his consecrated eyes,
an ornamental tribute of the path may rise,
the solid tomb bedding all forms of blight,   55
and grudging silence and the massive night.

Prose

(pour des Esseintes)

Hyperbole! de ma mémoire
Triomphalement ne sais-tu
Te lever, aujourd'hui grimoire
Dans un livre de fer vêtu:

Car j'installe, par la science,
L'hymne des cœurs spirituels
En l'œuvre de ma patience,
Atlas, herbiers et rituels.

Nous promenions notre visage
(Nous fûmes deux, je le maintiens)
Sur maints charmes de paysage,
O sœur, y comparant les tiens.

L'ère d'autorité se trouble
Lorsque, sans nul motif, on dit
De ce midi que notre double
Inconscience approfondit

Que, sol des cent iris, son site,
Ils savent s'il a bien été,
Ne porte pas de nom que cite
L'or de la trompette d'Été.

Oui, dans une île que l'air charge
De vue et non de visions
Toute fleur s'étalait plus large
Sans que nous en devisions.

Telles, immenses, que chacune
Ordinairement se para
D'un lucide contour, lacune
Qui des jardins la sépara.

Prose

(For des Esseintes)

Hyperbole! can you not rise
from my memory triumph-crowned,
today a magic scrawl which lies
in a book that is iron-bound:

for by my science I instil   5
the hymn of spiritual hearts
in the work of my patient will,
atlases, herbals, sacred arts.

Sister, we strolled and set our faces
(we were two, so my mind declares)   10
toward various scenic places,
comparing your own charms with theirs.

The reign of confidence grows troubled
when, for no reason, it is stated
of this noon region, which our doubled   15
unconsciousness has penetrated,

that its site, soil of hundredfold
irises (was it real? how well
they know) bears no name that the gold
trumpet of Summertime can tell.   20

Yes, in an isle the air had charged
not with mere visions but with sight
every flower spread out enlarged
at no word that we could recite.

And so immense they were, that each   25
was usually garlanded
with a clear contour, and this breach
parted it from the garden bed.

Gloire du long désir, Idées
Tout en moi s'exaltait de voir
La famille des iridées
Surgir à ce nouveau devoir,

Mais cette sœur sensée et tendre
Ne porta son regard plus loin
Que sourire et, comme à l'entendre
J'occupe mon antique soin.

Oh! sache l'Esprit de litige,
A cette heure où nous nous taisons,
Que de lis multiples la tige
Grandissait trop pour nos raisons

Et non comme pleure la rive,
Quand son jeu monotone ment
A vouloir que l'ampleur arrive
Parmi mon jeune étonnement

D'ouïr tout le ciel et la carte
Sans fin attestés sur mes pas,
Par le flot même qui s'écarte,
Que ce pays n'exista pas.

L'enfant abdique son extase
Et docte déjà par chemins
Elle dit le mot: Anastase!
Né pour d'éternels parchemins,

Avant qu'un sépulcre ne rie
Sous aucun climat, son aïeul,
De porter ce nom: Pulchérie!
Caché par le trop grand glaïeul.

Ideas, glory of long desire,
all within me rejoiced to see 30
the irid family aspire
to this new responsibility,

but Sister, a wise comforter,
carried her glance no further than
a smile and, as if heeding her, 35
I labour on my ancient plan.

Let the litigious Spirit know,
as we are silent at this season,
the manifold lilies' stem would grow
to a size far beyond our reason 40

not as the shore in drearisome
sport weeps when it is fraudulent,
claiming abundance should have come
in my initial wonderment

hearing the heavens and map that gave 45
endless evidence close at hand,
by the very receding wave,
that there was never such a land.

The child, already dexterous
in the ways, sheds her ecstasy 50
and utters 'Anastasius!'
born for scrolls of eternity

before a sepulchre chuckles 'Ha!'
beneath its forebear any sky
to bear the name 'Pulcheria!' 55
veiled by too tall gladioli.

Éventail

(de Madame Mallarmé)

Avec comme pour langage
Rien qu'un battement aux cieux
Le futur vers se dégage
Du logis très précieux

Aile tout bas la courrière
Cet éventail si c'est lui
Le même par qui derrière
Toi quelque miroir a lui

Limpide (où va redescendre
Pourchassée en chaque grain
Un peu d'invisible cendre
Seule à me rendre chagrin)

Toujours tel il apparaisse
Entre tes mains sans paresse

Autre éventail

(de Mademoiselle Mallarmé)

O rêveuse, pour que je plonge
Au pur délice sans chemin,
Sache, par un subtil mensonge,
Garder mon aile dans ta main.

Une fraîcheur de crépuscule
Te vient à chaque battement
Dont le coup prisonnier recule
L'horizon délicatement.

Vertige! voici que frissonne
L'espace comme un grand baiser
Qui, fou de naître pour personne,
Ne peut jaillir ni s'apaiser.

Fan

(Belonging to Madame Mallarmé)

With no language but a trace
just a beating in the skies
so the future verse will rise
from its precious dwelling-place

thus the herald its wing low   5
this fan if it has become
that by which behind you some
looking-glass has shed its glow

limpidly (where grain by grain
some specks of invisible   10
scattered dust will surely fall
which is all that gives me pain)

like this may it always stand
in your never-idle hand

Another Fan

(Belonging to Mademoiselle Mallarmé)

Dreamer, that I may plunge in sweet
and pathless pleasure, understand
how, by ingenious deceit,
to keep my wing within your hand.

A coolness of the evening air   5
is reaching you at every beat;
its captive stroke with delicate care
drives the horizon to retreat.

Dizziness! space is quivering, see!
like one immense kiss which, insane   10
at being born for nobody,
can neither spurt up nor abstain.

Sens-tu le paradis farouche
Ainsi qu'un rire enseveli
Se couler du coin de ta bouche
Au fond de l'unanime pli!

Le sceptre des rivages roses
Stagnants sur les soirs d'or, ce l'est,
Ce blanc vol fermé que tu poses
Contre le feu d'un bracelet.

Feuillet d'album

Tout à coup et comme par jeu
Mademoiselle qui voulûtes
Ouïr se révéler un peu
Le bois de mes diverses flûtes

Il me semble que cet essai
Tenté devant un paysage
A du bon quand je le cessai
Pour vous regarder au visage

Oui ce vain souffle que j'exclus
Jusqu'à la dernière limite
Selon mes quelques doigts perclus
Manque de moyens s'il imite

Votre très naturel et clair
Rire d'enfant qui charme l'air

Remémoration d'amis belges

A des heures et sans que tel souffle l'émeuve
Toute la vétusté presque couleur encens
Comme furtive d'elle et visible je sens
Que se dévêt pli selon pli la pierre veuve

Feel how the untamed Eden slips
like a buried smile of caprice
down from the corner of your lips   15
deep into the unanimous crease.

The sceptre of shores tinged with rose
stagnant on golden waning days
is this, a white flight which you close
and set against a bracelet's blaze.   20

Album Leaf

Suddenly and as if in play
Mademoiselle who wished to hear
some of the wood of my array
of varied flutes appear

I feel this trial which took place   5
in a pictorial vista tended
to have some value when I ended
and looked upon your face

yes this vain breath limited as
it was even in its final state   10
by my poor crippled fingers has
no power to imitate

your crystalline utterly care-
less childlike laugh that charms the air.

Remembering Belgian Friends

At certain times, when no breath stirs it, all
the almost incense-hued antiquity
as I feel widowed stone let her veils fall
fold on fold furtively and visibly

Flotte ou semble par soi n'apporter une preuve
Sinon d'épandre pour baume antique le temps
Nous immémoriaux quelques-uns si contents
Sur la soudaineté de notre amitié neuve

O très chers rencontrés en le jamais banal
Bruges multipliant l'aube au défunt canal
Avec la promenade éparse de maint cygne

Quand solennellement cette cité m'apprit
Lesquels entre ses fils un autre vol désigne
A prompte irradier ainsi qu'aile l'esprit.

Chansons bas

I

(Le Savetier)

Hors de la poix rien à faire,
Le lys naît blanc, comme odeur
Simplement je le préfère
A ce bon raccommodeur.

Il va de cuir à ma paire
Adjoindre plus que je n'eus
Jamais, cela désespère
Un besoin de talons nus.

Son marteau qui ne dévie
Fixe de clous gouailleurs
Sur la semelle l'envie
Toujours conduisant ailleurs.

Il recréerait des souliers,
O pieds, si vous le vouliez!

floats or seems not to bring its proof unless   5
by pouring time out as an ancient balm
over our newborn friendship's suddenness
we immemorial few who feel so calm

O dear companions met in never trite
Bruges multiplying dawn in canals now dead   10
where various swans are voyaging outspread

when solemnly the city showed to me
those of its sons who trace another flight
to light the mind like a wing instantly.

Cheap Songs

I

(The Cobbler)

Lacking wax nothing to do,
lilies are born white, as smell
frankly I prefer them to
this man who repairs so well.

He will supplement my pair   5
with more leather than I had
ever, driving to despair
my demand for heels unclad.

His sure hammering impales
the urge to be passing through   10
constantly with cheeky nails
on the sole of this my shoe.

He'd create your shoes anew,
dear feet—if it suited you!

II

(La Marchande d'herbes aromatiques)

Ta paille azur de lavandes,
Ne crois pas avec ce cil
Osé que tu me la vendes
Comme à l'hypocrite s'il

En tapisse la muraille
De lieux les absolus lieux
Pour le ventre qui se raille
Renaître aux sentiments bleus.

Mieux entre une envahissante
Chevelure ici mets-la
Que le brin salubre y sente,
Zéphirine, Paméla

Ou conduise vers l'époux
Les prémices de tes poux.

Billet

Pas les rafales à propos
De rien comme occuper la rue
Sujette au noir vol de chapeaux;
Mais une danseuse apparue

Tourbillon de mousseline ou
Fureur éparses en écumes
Que soulève par son genou
Celle même dont nous vécûmes

Pour tout, hormis lui, rebattu
Spirituelle, ivre, immobile
Foudroyer avec le tutu,
Sans se faire autrement de bile

II

(The Seller of Scented Herbs)

Your strawy lavender so blue,
never believe that with those bold
eyelashes it may be sold
to me as to a hypocrite who

would use it as a tapestry   5
in places most convenient
so that the mocking bowels may be
reborn to true blue sentiment.

Better to set it among these
masses of overwhelming hair   10
and let the clean wisp perfume there
Paméla like a little breeze

or bring your spouse as sacrifice
the virgin firstfruits of your lice.

Note

Not the irrelevant gusts that might
seem to possess the broad highway
subjected to black hats in flight;
rather a dancer on display

a swirl of muslin in a whirl   5
or fury scattered in the sprays
which with her knee the very girl
for whom we lived our lives might raise

(enraptured, witty, yet inert)
to blast every well-trodden thing   10
beyond it with her ballet skirt
without otherwise blustering

Sinon rieur que puisse l'air
De sa jupe éventer Whistler.

Petit Air

I

Quelconque une solitude
Sans le cygne ni le quai
Mire sa désuétude
Au regard que j'abdiquai

Ici de la gloriole
Haute à ne la pas toucher
Dont maint ciel se bariole
Avec les ors de coucher

Mais langoureusement longe
Comme de blanc linge ôté
Tel fugace oiseau si plonge
Exultatrice à côté

Dans l'onde toi devenue
Ta jubilation nue

Petit Air

II

Indomptablement a dû
Comme mon espoir s'y lance
Éclater là-haut perdu
Avec furie et silence,

Voix étrangère au bosquet
Ou par nul écho suivie,
L'oiseau qu'on n'ouït jamais
Une autre fois en la vie.

unless perhaps in gay dismissal a
breeze from her tutu may fan Whistler.

Little Ditty

I

Some kind of solitude
with no swan and no pier
reflects its desuetude
in my gaze withdrawn here

from the vain pomp too high   5
for anyone to hold
mottling many a sky
with sunset's varied gold

but languorously skirt
like cast-off drapery   10
of white some fleeting bird
if nearby joyously

your naked bliss should plumb
the wave that you become.

Little Ditty

II

Utterly invincibly
as my hopes seek it in flight
must have burst lost on the height
with silence and savagery

alien to the thicket or   5
with no echo left, the bird
whose voice in this life is heard
one time only and no more.

Le hagard musicien,
Cela dans le doute expire
Si de mon sein pas du sien
A jailli le sanglot pire

Déchiré va-t-il entier
Rester sur quelque sentier!

Plusieurs Sonnets

Quand l'ombre menaça de la fatale loi
Tel vieux Rêve, désir et mal de mes vertèbres,
Affligé de périr sous les plafonds funèbres
Il a ployé son aile indubitable en moi.

Luxe, ô salle d'ébène où, pour séduire un roi
Se tordent dans leur mort des guirlandes célèbres,
Vous n'êtes qu'un orgueil menti par les ténèbres
Aux yeux du solitaire ébloui de sa foi.

Oui, je sais qu'au lointain de cette nuit, la Terre
Jette d'un grand éclat l'insolite mystère,
Sous les siècles hideux qui l'obscurcissent moins.

L'espace à soi pareil qu'il s'accroisse ou se nie
Roule dans cet ennui des feux vils pour témoins
Que s'est d'un astre en fête allumé le génie.

Le vierge, le vivace et le bel aujourd'hui
Va-t-il nous déchirer avec un coup d'aile ivre
Ce lac dur oublié que hante sous le givre
Le transparent glacier des vols qui n'ont pas fui!

Un cygne d'autrefois se souvient que c'est lui
Magnifique mais qui sans espoir se délivre
Pour n'avoir pas chanté la région où vivre
Quand du stérile hiver a resplendi l'ennui.

Singer of this haggard tone,
it must perish in a doubt 10
whether worse distress poured out
not from its breast but my own

torn apart O may it stay
whole upon some traveller's way!

A Few Sonnets

When the shade threatened with the fatal decree
that old Dream, my bones' craving and their blight,
pained to die under the funereal height
it bowed its doubt-less plumage deep in me.

Splendour—ebony hall where, to allure 5
a king, illustrious wreaths writhe in their doom—
you are merely a pride lied by the gloom
to the faith-dazzled solitary viewer.

Yes, Earth has cast into this night afar
the startling mystery of sheer dazzlingness 10
beneath dread aeons darkening it less.

Space, its own peer, whether it fail or grow
rolls in this tedium trivial fires to show
the genius kindled by a festive star.

This virginal long-living lovely day
will it tear from us with a wing's wild blow
the lost hard lake haunted beneath the snow
by clear ice-flights that never flew away!

A swan of old remembers it is he 5
superb but strives to break free woebegone
for having left unsung the territory
to live when sterile winter's tedium shone.

Tout son col secouera cette blanche agonie
Par l'espace infligée à l'oiseau qui le nie,
Mais non l'horreur du sol où le plumage est pris.

Fantôme qu'à ce lieu son pur éclat assigne,
Il s'immobilise au songe froid de mépris
Que vêt parmi l'exil inutile le Cygne.

Victorieusement fui le suicide beau
Tison de gloire, sang par écume, or, tempête!
O rire si là-bas une pourpre s'apprête
A ne tendre royal que mon absent tombeau.

Quoi! de tout cet éclat pas même le lambeau
S'attarde, il est minuit, à l'ombre qui nous fête
Excepté qu'un trésor présomptueux de tête
Verse son caressé nonchaloir sans flambeau,

La tienne si toujours le délice! la tienne
Oui seule qui du ciel évanoui retienne
Un peu de puéril triomphe en t'en coiffant

Avec clarté quand sur les coussins tu la poses
Comme un casque guerrier d'impératrice enfant
Dont pour te figurer il tomberait des roses.

Ses purs ongles très haut dédiant leur onyx,
L'Angoisse ce minuit, soutient, lampadophore
Maint rêve vespéral brûlé par le Phénix
Que ne recueille pas de cinéraire amphore

Sur les crédences, au salon vide: nul ptyx,
Aboli bibelot d'inanité sonore,
(Car le Maître est allé puiser des pleurs au Styx
Avec ce seul objet dont le Néant s'honore).

His neck will shake off this white throe that space
has forced the bird denying it to face,   10
but not the horror of earth that traps his wings.

Phantom imposed this place by his sheer gleam,
he lies immobile in scorn's frigid dream
worn by the Swan dismissed to futile things.

The fine suicide fled victoriously
blaze of fame, blood in foam, gold, storm and stress!
If, below, regal purple is to dress
only my absent tomb, what mockery!

What! out of all that brilliance not one shred   5
stays, in the dark that fêtes us (it's dead night)
except the arrogant treasure of a head
sheds its caressed nonchalance with no light,

yours yes a constant pleasure! yours alone
retaining from the heavens that have gone   10
a trace of childish triumph for your crown

of light when on the pillows you lay it prone
like some child-empress's war-morion
that in your likeness showers roses down.

With her pure nails offering their onyx high,
lampbearer Agony tonight sustains
many a vesperal fantasy burned by
the Phoenix, which no funerary urn contains

on the empty room's credences: no ptyx,   5
abolished bauble, sonorous inanity
(Master has gone to draw tears from the Styx
with that one thing, the Void's sole source of vanity).

Mais proche la croisée au nord vacante, un or
Agonise selon peut-être le décor
Des licornes ruant du feu contre une nixe,

Elle, défunte nue en le miroir, encor
Que, dans l'oubli fermé par le cadre, se fixe
De scintillations sitôt le septuor.

Le Tombeau d'Edgar Poe

Tel qu'en Lui-même enfin l'éternité le change,
Le Poëte suscite avec un glaive nu
Son siècle épouvanté de n'avoir pas connu
Que la mort triomphait dans cette voix étrange!

Eux, comme un vil sursaut d'hydre oyant jadis l'ange
Donner un sens plus pur aux mots de la tribu
Proclamèrent très haut le sortilège bu
Dans le flot sans honneur de quelque noir mélange.

Du sol et de la nue hostiles, ô grief!
Si notre idée avec ne sculpte un bas-relief
Dont la tombe de Poe éblouissante s'orne

Calme bloc ici-bas chu d'un désastre obscur
Que ce granit du moins montre à jamais sa borne
Aux noirs vols du Blasphème épars dans le futur.

Le Tombeau de Charles Baudelaire

Le temple enseveli divulgue par la bouche
Sépulcrale d'égout bavant boue et rubis
Abominablement quelque idole Anubis
Tout le museau flambé comme un aboi farouche

Yet near the vacant northward casement dies
a gold possibly from the decorations 10
of unicorns lashing a nymph with flame;

dead, naked in the looking-glass she lies
though the oblivion bounded by that frame
now spans a fixed septet of scintillations.

The Tomb of Edgar Allan Poe

Changed to Himself at last by eternity,
with a bare sword the Poet has bestirred
his age terrified that it failed to see
how death was glorying in that strange word.

The spell was drunk, so they proclaimed aloud 5
(as vile freaks writhe when seraphim bestow
purer sense on the phrases of the crowd),
in some black brew's dishonourable flow.

If our idea can carve no bas-relief
from hostile clod and cloud, O struggling grief, 10
for the adornment of Poe's dazzling tomb,

at least this block dropped by an occult doom,
this calm granite, may limit all the glum
Blasphemy-flights dispersed in days to come.

The Tomb of Charles Baudelaire

The buried shrine disgorges through its foul
sepulchral sewer-mouth slobbering sod
and ruby vilely some Anubis-god
its muzzle blazing like a savage howl

Ou que le gaz récent torde la mèche louche
Essuyeuse on le sait des opprobres subis
Il allume hagard un immortel pubis
Dont le vol selon le réverbère découche

Quel feuillage séché dans les cités sans soir
Votif pourra bénir comme elle se rasseoir
Contre le marbre vainement de Baudelaire

Au voile qui la ceint absente avec frissons
Celle son Ombre même un poison tutélaire
Toujours à respirer si nous en périssons

Hommage

Le silence déjà funèbre d'une moire
Dispose plus qu'un pli seul sur le mobilier
Que doit un tassement du principal pilier
Précipiter avec le manque de mémoire.

Notre si vieil ébat triomphal du grimoire,
Hiéroglyphes dont s'exalte le millier
A propager de l'aile un frisson familier!
Enfouissez-le moi plutôt dans une armoire.

Du souriant fracas originel haï
Entre elles de clartés maîtresses a jailli
Jusque vers un parvis né pour leur simulacre,

Trompettes tout haut d'or pâmé sur les vélins,
Le dieu Richard Wagner irradiant un sacre
Mal tu par l'encre même en sanglots sibyllins.

I

Tout Orgueil fume-t-il du soir,
Torche dans un branle étouffée
Sans que l'immortelle bouffée
Ne puisse à l'abandon surseoir!

or when new gas wrings the wicks that erase 5
shiftily insults suffered (as we know)
it lights eternal loins with a wild glow
whose flight beds out according to its rays

What foliage dried in any nightless town
could consecrate as she can do and sit 10
against the marble of Baudelaire in vain,

departed from the veils that form her gown
with shimmers—she, his Shade, a guardian bane
to breathe forever though we die of it

Homage

Already mourning, the silence of a pall
casts more than one fold on the furnishing
which the central pillar's collapse must bring
suddenly down with no memorial.

The old gay triumphs of our magic scrawl, 5
hieroglyphs by the thousand scurrying
to spread familiar flutters with their wing!
bury them in a cupboard after all.

From the original smiling noisy crowd
hated among the master lights has gushed 10
to a shrine born for their representation,

gold trumpets on the vellum swooning loud,
Wagner the god lighting a consecration
which the ink's Sibylline tears have scarcely hushed.

I

Does every Pride in the evening smoke,
a torch quenched by some sudden stroke
without the divine pre-eminent
cloud halting its abandonment!

La chambre ancienne de l'hoir
De maint riche mais chu trophée
Ne serait pas même chauffée
S'il survenait par le couloir.

Affres du passé nécessaires
Agrippant comme avec des serres
Le sépulcre de désaveu,

Sous un marbre lourd qu'elle isole
Ne s'allume pas d'autre feu
Que la fulgurante console.

II

Surgi de la croupe et du bond
D'une verrerie éphémère
Sans fleurir la veillée amère
Le col ignoré s'interrompt.

Je crois bien que deux bouches n'ont
Bu, ni son amant ni ma mère,
Jamais à la même Chimère,
Moi, sylphe de ce froid plafond!

Le pur vase d'aucun breuvage
Que l'inexhaustible veuvage
Agonise mais ne consent,

Naïf baiser des plus funèbres!
A rien expirer annonçant
Une rose dans les ténèbres.

The ancient chamber of the heir   5
to precious but outmoded ware
would surely not be warmed at all
if he should enter through the hall.

Destined agonies of the past
holding denial's tombstone fast   10
as if in eagles' claws, below

a heavy marble slab that it
isolates, not one fire is lit
except the console's lightning glow.

II

Arisen from the rump and bound
of fleeting glassware, the distraught
vigil is never flower-crowned,
the unknown neck merely stops short.

I feel sure two mouths never fed,   5
neither her lover nor my mother,
on the same Fantasy as each other,
I, sylph with cold eaves overhead!

The vase pure of any drink save
widowhood inexhaustibly   10
suffers death but does not agree,

a kiss naive and O how grave!
to breathe out any final mark
that heralds some rose in the dark.

III

Une dentelle s'abolit
Dans le doute du Jeu suprême
A n'entr'ouvrir comme un blasphème
Qu'absence éternelle de lit.

Cet unanime blanc conflit
D'une guirlande avec la même,
Enfui contre la vitre blême
Flotte plus qu'il n'ensevelit.

Mais, chez qui du rêve se dore
Tristement dort une mandore
Au creux néant musicien

Telle que vers quelque fenêtre
Selon nul ventre que le sien,
Filial on aurait pu naître.

[« Quelle soie aux baumes de temps . . . »]

Quelle soie aux baumes de temps
Où la Chimère s'exténue
Vaut la torse et native nue
Que, hors de ton miroir, tu tends!

Les trous de drapeaux méditants
S'exaltent dans notre avenue:
Moi, j'ai ta chevelure nue
Pour enfouir des yeux contents.

Non! La bouche ne sera sûre
De rien goûter à sa morsure,
S'il ne fait, ton princier amant,

III

A lace vanishes utterly
in doubt of the last Game, to spread
out only like a blasphemy
eternal absence of a bed.

This unanimous white affray 5
fought by the garland with the same,
fled to the pallid window-frame,
rather floats than buries away.

But in one gilded by his dreams
there sleeps a mandolin forlorn 10
musician of the void unknown

so that toward some pane it seems
one might filial have been born
due to no belly but its own.

['What silk with balm from advancing days . . .']

What silk with balm from advancing days
in which Chimeras writhe and pass
can match the tangled native haze
you bring beyond your looking-glass!

The holes of thoughtful banners rise 5
triumphant in our avenue:
I have your naked tresses through
which to plunge my contented eyes.

No! the mouth will not surely sense
anything in its bite unless 10
your princely lover makes the cry

Dans la considérable touffe
Expirer, comme un diamant,
Le cri des Gloires qu'il étouffe.

[« M'introduire dans ton histoire . . . »]

M'introduire dans ton histoire
C'est en héros effarouché
S'il a du talon nu touché
Quelque gazon de territoire

A des glaciers attentatoire
Je ne sais le naïf péché
Que tu n'auras pas empêché
De rire très haut sa victoire

Dis si je ne suis pas joyeux
Tonnerre et rubis aux moyeux
De voir en l'air que ce feu troue

Avec des royaumes épars
Comme mourir pourpre la roue
Du seul vespéral de mes chars

[« A la nue accablante tu . . . »]

A la nue accablante tu
Basse de basalte et de laves
A même les échos esclaves
Par une trompe sans vertu

Quel sépulcral naufrage (tu
Le sais, écume, mais y baves)
Suprême une entre les épaves
Abolit le mât dévêtu

of the Glories he stifles die
like a diamond in that dense
and fleecy ampleness.

['To introduce myself into your tale . . .']

To introduce myself into your tale
is as a mighty man afraid
if his bare footprint has been laid
on some expanse of grassy dale

I do not know what innocent   5
sin that assaults the glaciers may
laugh in loud victory today
which you did nothing to prevent

say if I am not glad to see
in the air that the fire has shot   10
full of holes where dispersed realms lie

as if in purple it must die
the wheel of my sole vesperal chariot
rubies and thunder at its axletree

['Stilled beneath the oppressive cloud . . .']

Stilled beneath the oppressive cloud
that basalt and lava base
likewise the echoes that have bowed
before a trumpet lacking grace

O what sepulchral wreck (the spray   5
knows, but it simply drivels there)
ultimate jetsam cast away
abolishes the mast stripped bare

Ou cela que furibond faute
De quelque perdition haute
Tout l'abîme vain éployé

Dans le si blanc cheveu qui traîne
Avarement aura noyé
Le flanc enfant d'une sirène

[« Mes bouquins refermés . . . »]

Mes bouquins refermés sur le nom de Paphos,
Il m'amuse d'élire avec le seul génie
Une ruine, par mille écumes bénie
Sous l'hyacinthe, au loin, de ses jours triomphaux.

Coure le froid avec ses silences de faulx,
Je n'y hululerai pas de vide nénie
Si ce très blanc ébat au ras du sol dénie
A tout site l'honneur du paysage faux.

Ma faim qui d'aucuns fruits ici ne se régale
Trouve en leur docte manque une saveur égale:
Qu'un éclate de chair humain et parfumant!

Le pied sur quelque guivre où notre amour tisonne,
Je pense plus longtemps peut-être éperdument
A l'autre, au sein brûlé d'une antique amazone.

or else concealed that, furious
failing some great catastrophe   10
all the vain chasm gaping wide

in the so white and trailing tress
would have drowned avariciously
a siren's childlike side

['My old tomes closed upon the name Paphos . . .']

My old tomes closed upon the name Paphos,
I take delight in summoning by pure genius
a ruin blessed with myriad ocean sprays
beneath the distant hyacinth of its triumphal days.

Let the cold with its scythe-like silence run,   5
I shall not howl out any void lament, not one
if this so white frolic on earth's bare face
denies the honour of some feigned vista to any place.

Satisfied by no fruits here, my starvation
finds equal savour in their learned deprivation: 10
let one burst forth in fragrant human flesh!

My foot on some wyvern where our love flames afresh,
I ponder longer, perhaps desperate, on
the other, the seared breast of an ancient Amazon.

Anecdotes ou Poèmes

Le Phénomène futur

Un ciel pâle, sur le monde qui finit de décrépitude, va peut-être partir avec les nuages: les lambeaux de la pourpre usée des couchants déteignent dans une rivière dormant à l'horizon submergé de rayons et d'eau. Les arbres s'ennuient et, sous leur feuillage blanchi (de la poussière du temps plutôt que celle des chemins), monte la maison en toile du Montreur de choses Passées: maint réverbère attend le crépuscule et ravive les visages d'une malheureuse foule, vaincue par la maladie immortelle et le péché des siècles, d'hommes près de leurs chétives complices enceintes des fruits misérables avec lesquels périra la terre. Dans le silence inquiet de tous les yeux suppliant là-bas le soleil qui, sous l'eau, s'enfonce avec le désespoir d'un cri, voici le simple boniment: « Nulle enseigne ne vous régale du spectacle intérieur, car il n'est pas maintenant un peintre capable d'en donner une ombre triste. J'apporte, vivante (et préservée à travers les ans par la science souveraine) une Femme d'autrefois. Quelque folie, originelle et naïve, une extase d'or, je ne sais quoi! par elle nommé sa chevelure, se ploie avec la grâce des étoffes autour d'un visage qu'éclaire la nudité sanglante de ses lèvres. A la place du vêtement vain, elle a un corps; et les yeux, semblables aux pierres rares, ne valent pas ce regard qui sort de sa chair heureuse: des seins levés comme s'ils étaient pleins d'un lait éternel, la pointe vers le ciel, aux jambes lisses qui gardent le sel de la mer première. » Se rappelant leurs pauves épouses, chauves, morbides et pleines d'horreur, les maris se pressent: elles aussi par curiosité, mélancoliques, veulent voir.

Quand tous auront contemplé la noble créature, vestige de quelque époque déjà maudite, les uns indifférents, car ils n'auront pas eu la force de comprendre, mais d'autres navrés et la paupière humide de larmes résignées se regarderont; tandis que les poëtes de ces temps, sentant se rallumer leurs yeux éteints, s'achemineront vers leur lampe, le cerveau ivre un instant d'une gloire confuse, hantés du Rythme et dans l'oubli d'exister à une époque qui survit à la beauté.

Anecdotes or Poems

The Future Phenomenon

A pallid sky, above the world which is dying of its own decrepitude, may possibly be departing with the clouds: shreds of wornout purple sunsets are fading within a river that sleeps on a horizon steeped in water and light-rays. The trees are bored and ill at ease, and the tent of the Showman of Past Things rises beneath their whitened leaves (whitened not with road- but with time-dust): many a streetlamp is waiting for the twilight and reviving the faces of a wretched crowd, crushed by immortal sickness and immemorial sin—men alongside their sickly accomplices, who are pregnant with the miserable fruits that will destroy the earth. In the troubled silence of all the eyes entreating the faraway sun, which plunges beneath the water with a despairing cry, here is his basic sales-pitch: 'No sign treats you to the show within, because no present-day painter could supply even a sorry shadow of it. I am bringing you, alive (and preserved throughout the ages by the supreme power of science), a Woman of ancient times. Some primordial innocent madness, some ecstasy of gold, I don't know what it is! which she calls her hair, curves down with silken grace around a face lit up by the bloodstained nakedness of her lips. Instead of vain apparel, she has a body; and though her eyes are like precious gems, they cannot match the gaze that comes from her blissful flesh: from breasts upraised as if they were full of an everlasting milk, their nipples toward the sky, to glistening legs still salty from the primeval sea.' The husbands, recalling their poor wives, bald, morbid, and filled with horror, surge forward: the latter too, melancholy wretches, are curious and want to see.

When all of them have surveyed this noble creature—this vestige of whatever already-accursed age—some of them impassively (because they didn't have the strength to understand), but others woebegone and with tears of resignation brimming from their eyes, will look at one another; while the poets of those days, feeling their lifeless eyes reillumined, will make their way back toward their lamps, their brains fleetingly rapt with a hint of glory, haunted by Rhythm and oblivious that they exist in an age that has outlived beauty.

Plainte d'automne

Depuis que Maria m'a quitté pour aller dans une autre étoile—laquelle, Orion, Altaïr, et toi, verte Vénus?—j'ai toujours chéri la solitude. Que de longues journées j'ai passées seul avec mon chat. Par *seul*, j'entends sans un être matériel et mon chat est un compagnon mystique, un esprit. Je puis donc dire que j'ai passé de longues journées seul avec mon chat et, seul, avec un des derniers auteurs de la décadence latine; car depuis que la blanche créature n'est plus, étrangement et singulièrement j'ai aimé tout ce qui se résumait en ce mot: chute. Ainsi, dans l'année, ma saison favorite, ce sont les derniers jours alanguis de l'été, qui précèdent immédiatement l'automne et, dans la journée, l'heure où je me promène est quand le soleil se repose avant de s'évanouir, avec des rayons de cuivre jaune sur les murs gris et de cuivre rouge sur les carreaux. De même la littérature à laquelle mon esprit demande une volupté sera la poésie agonisante des derniers moments de Rome, tant, cependant, qu'elle ne respire aucunement l'approche rajeunissante des Barbares et ne bégaie point le latin enfantin des premières proses chrétiennes.

Je lisais donc un de ces chers poèmes (dont les plaques de fard ont plus de charme sur moi que l'incarnat de la jeunesse) et plongeais une main dans la fourrure du pur animal, quand un orgue de Barbarie chanta languissamment et mélancoliquement sous ma fenêtre. Il jouait dans la grande allée des peupliers dont les feuilles me paraissent mornes même au printemps, depuis que Maria a passé là avec des cierges, une dernière fois. L'instrument des tristes, oui, vraiment: le piano scintille, le violon donne aux fibres déchirées la lumière, mais l'orgue de Barbarie, dans le crépuscule du souvenir, m'a fait désespérément rêver. Maintenant qu'il murmurait un air joyeusement vulgaire et qui mit la gaîté au cœur des faubourgs, un air suranné, banal: d'où vient que sa ritournelle m'allait à l'âme et me faisait pleurer comme une ballade romantique? Je la savourai lentement et je ne lançai pas un sou par la fenêtre de peur de me déranger et de m'apercevoir que l'instrument ne chantait pas seul.

Autumn Lament

Ever since Maria left me to go to another star—which one? Orion, Altair, or possibly you, green Venus?—I have always loved solitude. How many long days I have spent alone with my cat! By 'alone' I mean without a material creature: my cat is a mystic companion, a spirit. So I can say that I have spent long days alone with my cat, and alone with one of the last authors of the Latin decadence; because, singularly and strangely, ever since the fair creature passed away I have loved everything that can be summed up in the word 'fall'. Thus my favourite time of year is the final languid phase of summer that comes immediately before autumn; and the time of day when I go for a walk is the time when the sun is resting just before it vanishes, when copper-yellow shafts are on the greyish walls and copper-red shafts on the windowpanes. And likewise, the literature to which my spirit turns for pleasure is the poetry of Rome in its final death-throes—as long, that is, as it doesn't bear any whiff of the Barbarians' rejuvenating advance or babble the puerile Latin of the early Christian hymns.

So I was reading one of those beloved poems (their dabs of artificial colour are a greater delight to me than the rosy hue of youth) and I was delving a hand into the pure animal's fur, when a barbarous barrel-organ began to play mournfully and languidly below my window. It was singing in the broad avenue of poplars, whose leaves seem dismal to me even in springtime, now that Maria has passed that way with candles for the last time. Truly an instrument for mourners: pianos glitter, and violins illuminate torn fibres, but that barrel-organ, in the twilight of memory, made me dream in despair. Now, when it was murmuring a cheap and cheerful tune, a tune that would gladden the heart of the suburbs, a banal old-fashioned thing,—why did its refrain penetrate my very soul and make me weep as romantic ballads do? Slowly I savoured it, without throwing even the smallest coin out the window—for fear I would unsettle myself and see that the instrument wasn't singing alone.

Frisson d'hiver

Cette pendule de Saxe, qui retarde et sonne treize heures parmi ses fleurs et ses dieux, à qui a-t-elle été? Pense qu'elle est venue de Saxe par les longues diligences autrefois.

(De singulières ombres pendent aux vitres usées.)

Et ta glace de Venise, profonde comme une froide fontaine, en un rivage de guivres dédorées, qui s'y est miré? Ah! je suis sûr que plus d'une femme a baigné dans cette eau le péché de sa beauté; et peut-être verrais-je un fantôme nu si je regardais longtemps.

—Vilain, tu dis souvent de méchantes choses.

(Je vois des toiles d'araignées au haut des grandes croisées.)

Notre bahut encore est très vieux: contemple comme ce feu rougit son triste bois; les rideaux amortis ont son âge, et la tapisserie des fauteuils dénués de fard, et les anciennes gravures des murs, et toutes nos vieilleries? Est-ce qu'il ne te semble pas, même, que les bengalis et l'oiseau bleu ont déteint avec le temps.

(Ne songe pas aux toiles d'araignées qui tremblent au haut des grandes croisées.)

Tu aimes tout cela et voilà pourquoi je puis vivre auprès de toi. N'as-tu pas désiré, ma sœur au regard de jadis, qu'en un de mes poèmes apparussent ces mots « la grâce des choses fanées »? Les objets neufs te déplaisent; à toi aussi, ils font peur avec leur hardiesse criarde, et tu te sentirais le besoin de les user, ce qui est bien difficile à faire pour ceux qui ne goûtent pas l'action.

Viens, ferme ton vieil almanach allemand, que tu lis avec attention, bien qu'il ait paru il y a plus de cent ans et que les rois qu'il annonce

Winter Shivers

That Dresden china clock, which is running slow and strikes thirteen amid its flowers and gods—to whom did it belong? Just think how it came from Saxony by the slow stagecoaches of olden days.

(Curious shadows are hanging from the wornout windowpanes.)

And your Venetian mirror, deep as a cold spring of water, with once-gilt wyverns on its shore—who has gazed at herself in it? Ah! I am sure that more than one woman has bathed the sin of her beauty in those waters; and perhaps, if I looked for a long time, I might see a naked wraith.

'You often say such naughty things, you rascal.'

(I can see spiderwebs atop the tall casements.)

Our travelling chest is also very old: see how that fire is reddening its melancholy wood; the faded curtains are equally old, and the discoloured armchair upholstery, and the antique engravings on the walls, and all our old things? Don't you feel that even the Bengal birds and the bluebird have faded with time?

(Don't indulge in any dreams about those spiderwebs quivering atop the tall casements.)

You love all such things, which is why I can live in your company. Dear sister with the look of bygone times, didn't you wish that, in one of my poems, these words should appear: 'the grace of faded things'? New things displease you; their brazen shrillness frightens you, just as it does me; you feel obliged to wear them out—which is far from easy if you don't enjoy activity.

Come now, close the old German almanac that you are reading so attentively, even though it appeared more than a hundred years ago

soient tous morts, et, sur l'antique tapis couché, la tête appuyée
parmi tes genoux charitables dans ta robe pâlie, ô calme enfant, je te
parlerai pendant des heures; il n'y a plus de champs et les rues sont
vides, je te parlerai de nos meubles . . . Tu es distraite?

(Ces toiles d'araignées grelottent au haut des grandes croisées.)

Le Démon de l'analogie

Des paroles inconnues chantèrent-elles sur vos lèvres, lambeaux
maudits d'une phrase absurde?

Je sortis de mon appartement avec la sensation propre d'une
aile glissant sur les cordes d'un instrument, traînant et légère, que
remplaça une voix prononçant les mots sur un ton descendant:
« La Pénultième est morte », de façon que

La Pénultième

finit le vers et

Est morte

se détacha
de la suspension fatidique plus inutilement en le vide de significa-
tion. Je fis des pas dans la rue et reconnus en le son *nul* la corde
tendue de l'instrument de musique, qui était oublié et que le glorieux
Souvenir certainement venait de visiter de son aile ou d'une palme
et, le doigt sur l'artifice du mystère, je souris et implorai de vœux
intellectuels une spéculation différente. La phrase revint, virtuelle,
dégagée d'une chute antérieure de plume ou de rameau, dorénavant
à travers la voix entendue, jusqu'à ce qu'enfin elle s'articula seule,
vivant de sa personnalité. J'allais (ne me contentant plus d'une
perception) la lisant en fin de vers, et, une fois, comme un essai,
l'adaptant à mon parler; bientôt la prononçant avec un silence après
« Pénultième » dans lequel je trouvais une pénible jouissance: « La
Pénultième » puis la corde de l'instrument, si tendue en l'oubli sur le

and the kings mentioned in it are all dead; and, lying on the old carpet with my head resting on your kindly knees, I shall talk to you for hours, O placid child, in your dress that has lost its colour; there are no longer any fields, and the streets are empty, I shall speak to you of our own possessions . . . Is your mind wandering?

(Those spiderwebs are shivering atop the tall casements.)

The Demon of Analogy

Have unknown words ever sung on your lips—accursed tatters of some meaningless phrase?

I left my apartment with exactly the sensation of a wing sliding over the strings of a musical instrument, lightly and lingeringly; this was replaced by a voice that uttered the following words in descending tones: 'The Penultimate is dead'—in such a way that

> *The Penultimate*

ended a line and

> *Is dead*

detached itself from the fateful pause in a still more futile manner, into the void of meaning. I took a few steps in the street and recognized in the sound *nul* the taut string of the musical instrument—which had been forgotten, but which glorious Memory had certainly touched just now with its wing or with a palm branch; and, with my finger on the mystery's artifice, I smiled and offered up intellectual prayers to a speculation of a different kind. Back came the phrase—virtual, released from some previous fall of a feather or branch—henceforth heard through the voice, until at last it articulated itself alone, alive with its own personality. Along I went (no longer satisfied with a mere perception) reading it as a line-ending, and once experimentally adapting it to my voice; soon pronouncing it with a pause after 'Penultimate', in which I found a painful pleasure: 'The

son *nul*, cassait sans doute et j'ajoutais en matière d'oraison: « Est morte. » Je ne discontinuai pas de tenter un retour à des pensées de prédilection, alléguant, pour me calmer, que, certes, pénultième est le terme du lexique qui signifie l'avant-dernière syllabe des vocables, et son apparition, le reste mal abjuré d'un labeur de linguistique par lequel quotidiennement sanglote de s'interrompre ma noble faculté poétique: la sonorité même et l'air de mensonge assumé par la hâte de la facile affirmation étaient une cause de tourment. Harcelé, je résolus de laisser les mots de triste nature errer eux-mêmes sur ma bouche, et j'allai murmurant avec l'intonation susceptible de condoléance: « La Pénultième est morte, elle est morte, bien morte, la désespérée Pénultième », croyant par là satisfaire l'inquiétude, et non sans le secret espoir de l'ensevelir en l'amplification de la psalmodie quand, effroi!—d'une magie aisément déductible et nerveuse—je sentis que j'avais, ma main réfléchie par un vitrage de boutique y faisant le geste d'une caresse qui descend sur quelque chose, la voix même (la première, qui indubitablement avait été l'unique).

Mais où s'installe l'irrécusable intervention du surnaturel, et le commencement de l'angoisse sous laquelle agonise mon esprit naguère seigneur c'est quand je vis, levant les yeux, dans la rue des antiquaires instinctivement suivie, que j'étais devant la boutique d'un luthier vendeur de vieux instruments pendus au mur, et, à terre, des palmes jaunes et les ailes enfouies en l'ombre, d'oiseaux anciens. Je m'enfuis, bizarre, personne condamnée à porter proba-blement le deuil de l'inexplicable Pénultième.

Pauvre Enfant pâle

Pauvre enfant pâle, pourquoi crier à tue-tête dans la rue ta chanson aiguë et insolente, qui se perd parmi les chats, seigneurs des toits? car elle ne traversera pas les volets des premiers étages, derrière lesquels tu ignores de lourds rideaux de soie incarnadine.

Penultimate'—then the string of the instrument, which had been stretched so tightly in oblivion over the sound *nul*, evidently broke and I added as a sort of prayer: 'Is dead.' Constantly I kept trying to return to thoughts congruent with my tastes, arguing, to appease myself, that, after all, penultimate is the lexical term signifying the second-last syllable of a word, and its apparition was the imperfectly abandoned remnant of a linguistic task on account of which my noble poetic faculty daily grieves at being broken off: the very sonority and air of falsehood assumed by the haste of that facile affirmation were a cause of torment. Harried, I resolved to let the inherently melancholy words wander across my lips of their own accord, and I went along murmuring in consolatory tones 'The Penultimate is dead, she is dead, well and truly dead, beyond all hope, the Penultimate', thinking that this would ease my anxiety—and also harbouring some secret hope that I could bury it in the amplified chant when, alas!—by an easily explicable form of nervous magic—I felt that, as my hand, reflected in a shop window, made a gesture like a caress coming down on something, I possessed the very voice (the first one, which had certainly been the only one).

But the moment when the supernatural irrefutably intervened, and the anguish that racked my formerly magisterial spirit began, came when I raised my eyes and saw, in the antique dealers' street where I had instinctively gone, that I was in front of a lute-maker's shop, its wall being hung with the old instruments that he was selling, and, on the ground, some yellow palm branches and old birds' wings shrouded in shadow. I fled—an oddity, someone probably doomed to wear mourning for the inexplicable Penultimate.

Poor Pale Child

You poor pale child, why are you bawling your shrill and impertinent song at the top of your voice in the street, where it vanishes among the cats, those lords of the rooftops? after all, it will never pass through the first-floor shutters, behind which are heavy curtains of rose-coloured silk beyond your power to imagine.

Cependent tu chantes fatalement, avec l'assurance tenace d'un petit homme qui s'en va seul par la vie et, ne comptant sur personne, travaille pour soi. As-tu jamais eu un père? Tu n'as pas même une vieille qui te fasse oublier la faim en te battant, quand tu rentres sans un sou.

Mais tu travailles pour toi: debout dans les rues, couvert de vêtements déteints faits comme ceux d'un homme, une maigreur prématurée et trop grand à ton âge, tu chantes pour manger, avec acharnement, sans abaisser tes yeux méchants vers les autres enfants jouant sur le pavé.

Et ta complainte est si haute, si haute, que ta tête nue qui se lève en l'air à mesure que ta voix monte, semble vouloir partir de tes petites épaules.

Petit homme, qui sait si elle ne s'en ira pas un jour, quand, après avoir crié longtemps dans les villes, tu auras fait un crime? un crime n'est pas bien difficile à faire, va, il suffit d'avoir du courage après le désir, et tels qui . . . Ta petit figure est énergique.

Pas un sou ne descend dans le panier d'osier que tient ta longue main pendue sans espoir sur ton pantalon: on te rendra mauvais et un jour tu commettras un crime.

Ta tête se dresse toujours et veut te quitter, comme si d'avance elle savait, pendant que tu chantes d'un air qui devient menaçant.

Elle te dira adieu quand tu paieras pour moi, pour ceux qui valent moins que moi. Tu vins probablement au monde vers cela et tu jeûnes dès maintenant, nous te verrons dans les journaux.

Oh! pauvre petite tête!

Yet, inexorably, fatally, you keep singing, with the tenacious confidence of a little man who is making his way through life alone, relying on no one, and working only for himself. Did you ever have a father? You don't even have an old woman to make you forget your hunger by beating you when you return without a penny.

No, you are working only for yourself: standing in the streets, covered with faded clothes like those of a grown man, prematurely thin and too tall for your age, you sing for your supper with grim determination, never lowering your rapscallion eyes toward the other children playing on the pavement.

And your plaintive song is so high, so high, that your bare head, rising in the air as your voice rises, seems on the point of taking off from your little shoulders.

And who knows if it won't come off altogether some day, little man, when, after howling so long in the towns, you commit a crime? crimes aren't very hard to commit, why, all you need to do is to follow up desire with courage, and some people who . . . Your little face is full of energy.

Not a single penny falls into the wicker basket held by your scrawny hand as it dangles hopelessly over your trousers: people will make you wicked and one day you will commit a crime.

Your head is still uplifted and wanting to leave you, as if it knew in advance, while you keep singing in a way that is starting to seem ominous.

It will bid you farewell when you pay for me—and for those who are worth less than I am. Probably you came into the world for that very reason, and from this moment on you will fast, we shall see you in the papers.

O poor little head!

La Pipe

Hier, j'ai trouvé ma pipe en rêvant une longue soirée de travail, de beau travail d'hiver. Jetées les cigarettes avec toutes les joies enfantines de l'été dans le passé qu'illuminent les feuilles bleues de soleil, les mousselines et reprise ma grave pipe par un homme sérieux qui veut fumer longtemps sans se déranger, afin de mieux travailler: mais je ne m'attendais pas à la surprise que préparait cette délaissée, à peine eus-je tiré la première bouffée, j'oubliai mes grands livres à faire, émerveillé, attendri, je respirai l'hiver dernier qui revenait. Je n'avais pas touché à la fidèle amie depuis ma rentrée en France, et tout Londres, Londres tel que je le vécus en entier à moi seul, il y a un an, est apparu; d'abord les chers brouillards qui emmitouflent nos cervelles et ont, là-bas, une odeur à eux, quand ils pénètrent sous la croisée. Mon tabac sentait une chambre sombre aux meubles de cuir saupoudrés par la poussière du charbon sur lesquels se roulait le maigre chat noir; les grands feux! et la bonne aux bras rouges versant les charbons, et le bruit de ces charbons tombant du seau de tôle dans la corbeille de fer, le matin—alors que le facteur frappait le double coup solennel, qui me faisait vivre! J'ai revu par les fenêtres ces arbres malades du square désert—j'ai vu le large, si souvent traversé cet hiver-là, grelottant sur le pont du steamer mouillé de bruine et noirci de fumée—avec ma pauvre bien-aimée errante, en habits de voyageuse, une longue robe terne couleur de la poussière des routes, un manteau qui collait humide à ses épaules froides, un de ces chapeaux de paille sans plume et presque sans rubans, que les riches dames jettent en arrivant, tant ils sont déchiquetés par l'air de la mer et que les pauvres bien-aimées regarnissent pour bien des saisons encore. Autour de son cou s'enroulait le terrible mouchoir qu'on agite en se disant adieu pour toujours.

Un spectacle interrompu

Que la civilisation est loin de procurer les jouissances attribuables à cet état! on doit par exemple s'étonner qu'une

The Pipe

Yesterday, while thinking about a long evening of work (fine winter work), I found my pipe. Away went my cigarettes with all the childish joys of summer, into the past illumined by foliage blue with sunlight, muslins; and back came my solemn pipe, into the hand of a serious man who wants a good long smoke in peace and quiet so that he can work better: but I wasn't prepared for the surprise that this forsaken creature had in store for me. Hardly had I drawn the first puff when I forgot the great books I wanted to write; amazed and deeply moved, I was inhaling the return of last year's winter. I hadn't laid a hand on this faithful friend since my return to France, and now the whole of London, London as I had lived it a year ago just for myself, became visible: first the dear old fogs that muffle your brains and have, in that country, a distinctive smell of their own, when they seep in under the casements. My tobacco used to smell of a dark room on whose leather furniture, sprinkled with coal dust, the scrawny black cat would curl itself up; the big fires! and the red-armed maid pouring out the coals, and the sound of those coals falling from the sheet-metal bucket into the iron scuttle after sunrise—when the postman used to give his solemn double knock, which brought me to life! Through the windows I could see once more those sickly trees in the deserted square—I could see the open sea, crossed so often that winter, as I shivered on the drizzle-wet smoke-blackened steamer's deck—with my poor wandering beloved garbed in travelling clothes, a long drab dress the colour of road dust, a coat that stuck damply to her cold shoulders, a featherless and almost ribbonless straw hat of the kind thrown away by well-to-do ladies when they reach their destination, as being so mangled by the sea air, but which the various poor beloveds refurbish for many a season more. Around her neck was wound the terrible handkerchief that you wave when saying goodbye to each other for evermore.

An Interrupted Performance

How far civilization is from supplying the delights attributable to such a state! for instance, it's astonishing that the dreamers who live

association entre les rêveurs, y séjournant, n'existe pas, dans toute grande ville, pour subvenir à un journal qui remarque les événements sous le jour propre au rêve. Artifice que la *réalité*, bon à fixer l'intellect moyen entre les mirages d'un fait; mais elle repose par cela même sur quelque universelle entente: voyons donc s'il n'est pas, dans l'idéal, un aspect nécessaire, évident, simple, qui serve de type. Je veux, en vue de moi seul, écrire comme elle frappa mon regard de poëte, telle Anecdote, avant que la divulguent des *reporters* par la foule dressés à assigner à chaque chose son caractère commun.

Le petit théâtre des Prodigalités adjoint l'exhibition d'un vivant cousin d'Atta Troll ou de Martin à sa féerie classique *la Bête et le Génie*; j'avais, pour reconnaître l'invitation du billet double hier égaré chez moi, posé mon chapeau dans la stalle vacante à mes côtés, une absence d'ami y témoignait du goût général à esquiver ce naïf spectacle. Que se passait-il devant moi? rien, sauf que: de pâleurs évasives de mousseline se réfugiant sur vingt piédestaux en architecture de Bagdad, sortaient un sourire et des bras ouverts à la lourdeur triste de l'ours: tandis que le héros, de ces sylphides évocateur et leur gardien, un clown, dans sa haute nudité d'argent, raillait l'animal par notre supériorité. Jouir comme la foule du mythe inclus dans toute banalité, quel repos et, sans voisins où verser des réflexions, voir l'ordinaire et splendide veille trouvée à la rampe par ma recherche assoupie d'imaginations ou de symboles. Étranger à mainte réminiscence de pareilles soirées, l'accident le plus neuf! suscita mon attention: une des nombreuses salves d'applaudissements décernés selon l'enthousiasme à l'illustration sur la scène du privilège authentique de l'Homme, venait, brisée par quoi? de cesser net, avec un fixe fracas de gloire à l'apogée, inhabile à se répandre. Tout oreilles, il fallut être tout yeux. Au geste du pantin, une paume crispée dans l'air ouvrant les cinq doigts, je compris, qu'il avait, l'ingénieux! capté les sympathies par la mine d'attraper au vol quelque chose, figure (et c'est tout) de la facilité dont est par chacun prise une idée: et qu'ému au léger vent, l'ours rythmiquement et doucement levé interrogeait cet exploit, une griffe posée sur les rubans de l'épaule humaine. Personne qui ne haletât, tant

in every major city never form an association to support a journal that reports events in the light peculiar to dreams. *Reality* is a mere artifice, good for providing the average intellect with stability amid the mirages of a fact; but for that very reason, it does rest on some universal understanding: let's see, then, whether there is, in the realm of the ideal, some necessary, obvious, simple quality that can serve as a type. I want to write, purely for my own benefit, a certain Anecdote, just as it struck my gaze (a poet's gaze), before it can be divulged by the 'reporters' whom the crowd appoints to assign a common character to each individual thing.

The little theatre of the PRODIGALITIES is exhibiting a live cousin of Atta Troll or Martin in addition to its classic fairy-tale *The Beast and the Genius*; to acknowledge an invitation in the form of a double ticket, which had drifted my way yesterday, I put my hat on the empty seat beside me—a friend's absence from which bore witness to the usual dislike for naive shows of this kind. What was happening in front of me? Nothing, except this: from the evasive paleness of muslins taking refuge on twenty Baghdad-style pedestals, smiles and open arms went out to the lugubrious heaviness of the bear: while the hero who had conjured up those sylphs and was protecting them, a clown, in his exalted silvery nakedness, was taunting the animal with our own superiority. How relaxing it would be to revel, like the crowd, in a myth enclosed within every banality and, without any neighbours to receive one's outpoured reflections, to behold the commonplace splendid vigil discovered at the footlights by my search which is soothed with imaginings or symbols. An accident of the most novel kind! alien to many a recollection of similar evenings, attracted my attention: one of the numerous volleys of applause enthusiastically bestowed on this stage illustration of Man's incontestable privilege had just—broken off by what?—stopped dead, with a rigid din of acclamation at the very height, unable to expand. All ears, one really needed to be all eyes. From the puppet's gesture, a clenched fist opening its five fingers in the air, I understood that he, clever fellow! had captured the spectators' sympathies by apparently catching something in flight, an image (and nothing more than that) of the ease with which everyone grasps an idea: and that, roused by the light breeze, the bear had risen gently and rhythmically, and was questioning this exploit, with one claw on the

cette situation portait de conséquences graves pour l'honneur de la race: qu'allait-il arriver? L'autre patte s'abattit, souple, contre un bras longeant le maillot; et l'on vit, couple uni dans un secret rapprochement, comme un homme inférieur, trapu, bon, debout sur l'écartement de deux jambes de poil, étreindre pour y apprendre les pratiques du génie, et son crâne au noir museau ne l'atteignant qu'à la moitié, le buste de son frère brillant et surnaturel: mais qui, lui! exhaussait, la bouche folle de vague, un chef affreux remuant par un fil visible dans l'horreur les dénégations véritables d'une mouche de papier et d'or. Spectacle clair, plus que les tréteaux vaste, avec ce don, propre à l'art, de durer longtemps: pour le parfaire je laissai, sans que m'offusquât l'attitude probablement fatale prise par le mime dépositaire de notre orgueil, jaillir tacitement le discours interdit au rejeton des sites arctiques: « Sois bon (c'était le sens), et plutôt que de manquer à la charité, explique-moi la vertu de cette atmosphère de splendeur, de poussière et de voix, où tu m'appris à me mouvoir. Ma requête, pressante, est juste, que tu ne sembles pas, en une angoisse qui n'est que feinte, répondre ne savoir, élancé aux régions de la sagesse, aîné subtil! à moi, pour te faire libre, vêtu encore du séjour informe des cavernes où je replongeai, dans la nuit d'époques humbles ma force latente. Authentiquons, par cette embrassade étroite, devant la multitude siégeant à cette fin, le pacte de notre réconciliation. » L'absence d'aucun souffle unie à l'espace, dans quel lieu absolu vivais-je, un des drames de l'histoire astrale élisant, pour s'y produire, ce modeste théâtre! La foule s'effaçait, toute, en l'emblème de sa situation spirituelle magnifiant la scène: dispensateur moderne de l'extase, seul, avec l'impartialité d'une chose élémentaire, le gaz, dans les hauteurs de la salle, continuait un bruit lumineux d'attente.

Le charme se rompit: c'est quand un morceau de chair, nu, brutal, traversa ma vision dirigé de l'intervalle des décors, en avance de quelques instants sur la récompense, mystérieuse d'ordinaire après ces représentations. Loque substituée saignant auprès de l'ours qui, ses instincts retrouvés antérieurement à

ribbons of the human shoulder. No one's breath failed to quicken, so grave were the consequences borne by this situation for the honour of our race: what was going to happen? The other paw dropped slackly onto an arm that hung down against the tights; and you could see—a couple who had secretly been drawn closer together—something like a man, a lowly, stocky, kindly man, standing on two wide-apart furry legs, embrace the bust of his radiant supernatural brother in order to learn the practices of genius there, and his skull with the black muzzle only half reaching it: but as for him! he, his mouth frantic with vagueness, was uplifting a frightful head that shook by a thread visible in the horror the true denials of a paper-and-gold fly. A lucid spectacle, vaster than the stage, with art's appropriate gift of lasting a long time: to complete it, I, without being shocked by the probably fatal attitude adopted by the mime, that depository of our pride, allowed this speech forbidden to the descendant of arctic sites to burst forth tacitly: 'Be kind (that was the meaning) and, rather than be wanting in charity, explain to me the virtue of this atmosphere of splendour, dust, and voices, in which you have taught me to move. My request is urgent and just, as, in an anguish that is merely feigned, launched into the realms of wisdom, subtle elder! you don't seem not to know how to answer me, in order to set you free, still clad in the shapeless habitation of the caves where, in the night of humble ages, I have plunged my latent strength once more. Let us seal the pact of our reconciliation with this close embrace, in the presence of the multitude who have assembled for that very purpose.' The lack of any breath united with space, in what absolute place was I living, one of the dramas of astral history, which chose this modest theatre for its production! The crowd was vanishing altogether, magnifying the stage as the emblem of its own spiritual condition: only the gas, that modern dispenser of ecstasy, was maintaining a luminous noise of anticipation in the heights of the hall, with the impartiality of an elemental thing.

The spell was broken: that happened when a naked, brutal piece of flesh, guided from the space between the stage sets, crossed my line of sight, a few moments before the mysterious reward that usually occurs after such performances. A bleeding tatter was substituted next to the bear who, having rediscovered the instincts that he had

une curiosité plus haute dont le dotait le rayonnement théâtral, retomba à quatre pattes et, comme emportant parmi soi le Silence, alla de la marche étouffée de l'espèce, flairer, pour y appliquer les dents, cette proie. Un soupir, exempt presque de déception, soulagea incompréhensiblement l'assemblée: dont les lorgnettes, par rangs, cherchèrent, allumant la netteté de leurs verres, le jeu du splendide imbécile évaporé dans sa peur; mais virent un repas abject préféré peut-être par l'animal à la même chose qu'il lui eût fallu d'abord faire de *notre image*, pour y goûter. La toile, hésitant jusque-là à accroître le danger ou l'émotion, abattit subitement son journal de tarifs et de lieux communs. Je me levai comme tout le monde, pour aller respirer au dehors, étonné de n'avoir pas senti, cette fois encore, le même genre d'impression que mes semblables, mais serein: car ma façon de voir, après tout, avait été supérieure, et même la vraie.

Réminiscence

Orphelin, j'errais en noir et l'œil vacant de famille: au quin-conce se déplièrent des tentes de fête, éprouvai-je le futur et que je serais ainsi, j'aimais le parfum des vagabonds, vers eux à oublier mes camarades. Aucun cri de chœurs par la déchirure, ni tirade loin, le drame requérant l'heure sainte des quinquets, je souhaitais de parler avec un môme trop vacillant pour figurer parmi sa race, au bonnet de nuit taillé comme le chaperon de Dante; qui rentrait en soi, sous l'aspect d'une tartine de fromage mou, déjà la neige des cimes, le lys ou autre blancheur constitutive d'ailes au dedans: je l'eusse prié de m'admettre à son repas supérieur, partagé vite avec quelque aîné fameux jailli contre une proche toile en train des tours de force et banalités alliables au jour. Nu, de pirouetter dans sa prestesse de maillot à mon avis surprenante, lui, qui d'ailleurs commença: « Tes parents?—Je n'en ai pas.—Allons, si tu savais comme c'est farce, un père . . . même l'autre semaine que bouda la soupe, il faisait des grimaces aussi belles, quand le maître lançait les claques et les coups de pied. Mon cher! » et de triompher en élevant à moi la jambe avec aisance

possessed before he was endowed with higher curiosity by this theatrical radiance, fell back on all fours and, as if bearing the Silence away with him, trotted off with the muted tread of his species to sniff this prey so that he could sink his teeth into it. A sigh, virtually free of disappointment, incomprehensibly relieved the assembly: whose serried opera-glasses, lighting up the clarity of their lenses, sought out the acting of the splendid imbecile who had evaporated in his fear; but saw an ignoble meal preferred perhaps by the animal to the same thing that he would first have needed to make of 'our image' in order to enjoy it. The curtain, having hesitated until then to increase the danger or the emotion, suddenly lowered its announcements of prices and trifles. Like everyone else, I got up to go outside and take a breath of air, astonished that I hadn't felt, once again, the same kind of impression as my fellows, but serene: for, after all, my way of seeing had been superior, and even the true one.

Reminiscence

I, an orphan, was roaming in black and with an eye devoid of any family: at the quincunx, the tents of a fair were unfolded; did I perhaps experience the future and that I would be like this, I loved the smell of the vagabonds and was drawn toward them, oblivious of my own companions. No choral outcry through the tear in the fabric, nor any distant tirade, since the drama required the holy hour of the footlights, I wanted to speak to an urchin too unsteady on his feet to appear among his people, in a nightcap with the cut of Dante's hood; one who was bringing inside himself, in the guise of a slice of bread with cheese, the snow of mountain peaks, the lily, or some other whiteness that constituted inward wings: I would have asked him to admit me to his superior meal, which he quickly shared with some illustrious older boy who had sprung up against a nearby tent and was engaged in feats of strength and banalities consistent with the day. Naked, he pirouetted in the (to my mind surprising) nimbleness of his tights; in addition, he began: 'Your parents?' 'I don't have any.' 'Come now, if you knew what a funny thing that is, a father . . . even the other week when he was off his food, he still kept making faces just as glorious as ever, while the boss was hitting and kicking him. My dear chap!' and triumphantly, raising a leg toward

glorieuse, « il nous épate, papa, » puis de mordre au régal chaste
du très jeune: « Ta maman, tu n'en as pas, peut-être, que tu es
seul? la mienne mange de la filasse et le monde bat des mains.
Tu ne sais rien, des parents sont des gens drôles, qui font rire. »
La parade s'exaltait, il partit: moi, je soupirai, déçu tout à coup
de n'avoir pas de parents.

La Déclaration foraine

Le Silence! il est certain qu'à mon côté, ainsi que songes,
étendue dans un bercement de promenade sous les roues
assoupissant l'interjection de fleurs, toute femme, et j'en sais
une qui voit clair ici, m'exempte de l'effort à proférer un
vocable: la complimenter haut de quelque interrogatrice toi-
lette, offre de soi presque à l'homme en faveur de qui s'achève
l'après-midi, ne pouvant à l'encontre de tout ce rapproche-
ment fortuit, que suggérer la distance sur ses traits aboutie à
une fossette de spirituel sourire. Ainsi ne consent la réalité; car
ce fut impitoyablement, hors du rayon qu'on sentait avec luxe
expirer aux vernis du landau, comme une vocifération, parmi
trop de tacite félicité pour une tombée de jour sur la banlieue,
avec orage, dans tous sens à la fois et sans motif, du rire
strident ordinaire des choses et de leur cuivrerie triomphale:
au fait, la cacophonie à l'ouïe de quiconque, un instant écarté,
plutôt qu'il ne s'y fond, auprès de son idée, reste à vif devant la
hantise de l'existence.

« La fête de . . . » et je ne sais quel rendez-vous suburbain!
nomma l'enfant voiturée dans mes distractions, la voix claire
d'aucun ennui; j'obéis et fis arrêter.

Sans compensation à cette secousse qu'un besoin d'explica-
tion figurative plausible pour mes esprits, comme symétrique-
ment s'ordonnent des verres d'illumination peu à peu éclairés
en guirlandes et attributs, je décidai, la solitude manquée, de

me with glorious ease, 'he amazes us, Papa does'; then, biting into the youngster's chaste meal: 'Your Mama, maybe you don't have one, you're alone? Mine eats bits of string and everyone claps. You can't imagine how funny parents are, how much they make you laugh.' The parade was building up, he went away: as for me, I gave a sigh, suddenly disappointed that I had no parents.

The Announcement at the Fair

Silence! certainly any woman outspread beside me, as if in a dream, amid the swaying motion of the ride that muffled the inter-jected flowers beneath the wheels—and I know one woman who sees this clearly—would excuse me from the effort of uttering a single word: to compliment her aloud on some question-mark of a costume, virtually offering herself to the man in whose favour the afternoon is drawing to its close, evoking (contrary to all this fortuitous conjunc-tion of circumstances) only the distance that ends on her features in the dimple of an intelligent smile. Reality doesn't allow it to be so; for, mercilessly, beyond the sunbeam that you could sense expiring luxuriously on the landau's varnished surface, amid too much silent bliss for a nightfall on the outskirts of town, there was a kind of stormy outcry, everywhere all at once and without any cause, of the ordinary shrill laughter of things and their triumphal brassy reson-ance: in fact, a cacophony to the ears of anyone who, having with-drawn to spend a moment in the company of his own thought (rather than to melt into it), remains painfully sensitive to the obsessiveness of existence.

'The festival of . . .' plus I don't know what suburban meeting-place! declared the little girl who had been transported into my absentmindedness, her voice clear of any frustration; I obeyed and called a halt.

Without any compensation for this shock except the need for some figurative explanation plausible to my mind, like a series of gradually illuminated lamps symmetrically arranged in garlands and symbols,

m'enfoncer même avec bravoure en ce déchaînement exprès et haïssable de tout ce que j'avais naguères fui dans une gracieuse compagnie: prête et ne témoignant de surprise à la modification dans notre programme, du bras ingénu elle s'en repose sur moi, tandis que nous allons parcourir, les yeux sur l'enfilade, l'allée d'ahurissement qui divise en écho du même tapage les foires et permet à la foule d'y renfermer pour un temps l'univers. Subséquemment aux assauts d'un médiocre dévergondage en vue de quoi que ce soit qui détourne notre stagnation amusée par le crépuscule, au fond, bizarre et pourpre, nous retint à l'égal de la nue incendiaire un humain spectacle, poignant: reniée du châssis peinturluré ou de l'inscription en capitales une baraque, apparemment vide.

A qui ce matelas décousu pour improviser ici, comme les voiles dans tous les temps et les temples, l'arcane! appartînt, sa fréquentation durant le jeûne n'avait pas chez son possesseur excité avant qu'il le déroulât comme le gonfalon d'espoirs en liesse, l'hallucination d'une merveille à montrer (que l'inanité de son famélique cauchemar); et pourtant, mû par le caractère frérial d'exception à la misère quotidienne qu'un pré, quand l'institue le mot mystérieux de fête, tient des souliers nombreux y piétinant (en raison de cela poind aux profondeurs des vêtements quelque unique velléité du dur sou à sortir à seule fin de se dépenser), lui aussi! n'importe qui de tout dénué sauf de la notion qu'il y avait lieu pour être un des élus, sinon de vendre, de fair voir, mais quoi, avait cédé à la convocation du bienfaisant rendez-vous. Ou, très prosaïquement, peut-être le rat éduqué à moins que, lui-même, ce mendiant sur l'athlétique vigueur de ses muscles comptât, pour décider l'engouement populaire, faisait défaut, à l'instant précis, comme cela résulte souvent de la mise en demeure de l'homme par les circonstances générales.

« Battez la caisse! » proposa en altesse Madame . . . seule tu sais Qui, marquant un suranné tambour duquel se levait, les bras

I decided, having lost my solitude, to plunge (even boldly) into this explicit and detestable unleashing of everything I had lately shunned in such gracious company: ready, and showing no surprise at the change in our plans, she leans an ingenuous arm on me as, with our eyes on the serried rows, we make our way down the lane of chaos that divides a fairground into an echo of the same noise and allows the crowd for a while to encompass the universe there. After the onslaughts of a mediocre licentiousness aimed at diverting (in any way whatever) our stagnation entertained by the sunset, a touching human spectacle detained us no less than the fiery cloud in the background, strange and purple: a booth, apparently empty, repudiated by its gaudily painted frame and inscription in capital letters.

Whoever may have owned this mattress, which had been ripped apart in order to improvise here, like the veils in all times and temples, Mystery itself! association with it during his fast had not roused in its possessor—before he unrolled it as the banner of his joyous hopes—the hallucination of some wonder to be put on show (except for the inanity of his famished nightmare); and yet, stirred by the fraternal character of exception to daily misery which a meadow, when the mysterious word 'fair' initiates it, derives from the many shoes that trample upon it (because of which, there dawns in the depths of clothes some singular whim of a hard penny to come out for the sole purpose of being spent), he too! anyone at all, stripped of everything except the notion that he ought to be one of the elect, if not to sell, then at least to show something (but what?), had yielded to the summons of the beneficent meeting-place. Or, rather more prosaically, perhaps the trained rat—unless the beggar himself was counting on the athletic vigour of his muscles to establish himself as a popular craze—was missing at that particular moment, as so often results when man is given an ultimatum by general circumstances.

'Beat the drum!' Madame you-alone-know-Who proposed haughtily, pointing out an antiquated drum from which arose, with his arms

décroisés afin de signifier inutile l'approche de son théâtre sans prestige, un vieillard que cette camaraderie avec un instrument de rumeur et d'appel, peut-être, séduisit à son vacant dessein; puis comme si, de ce que tout de suite on pût, ici, envisager de plus beau, l'énigme, par un bijou fermant la mondaine, en tant qu'à sa gorge le manque de réponse, scintillait! la voici engouffrée, à ma surprise de pitre coi devant une halte du public qu'empaume l'éveil des ra et des fla assourdissant mon invariable et obscur pour moi-même d'abord « Entrez, tout le monde, ce n'est qu'un sou, on le rend à qui n'est pas satisfait de la représentation. » Le nimbe en paillasson dans le remerciement joignant deux paumes séniles vidé, j'en agitai les couleurs, en signal, de loin, et me coiffai, prêt à fendre la masse debout en le secret de ce qu'avait su faire avec ce lieu sans rêve l'initiative d'une contemporaine de nos soirs.

A hauteur du genou, elle émergeait, sur une table, des cent têtes.

Net ainsi qu'un jet égaré d'autre part la dardait électriquement, éclate pour moi ce calcul qu'à défaut de tout, elle, selon que la mode, une fantaisie ou l'humeur du ciel circonstanciaient sa beauté, sans supplément de danse ou de chant, pour la cohue amplement payait l'aumône exigée en faveur d'un quelconque; et du même trait je comprends mon devoir en le péril de la subtile exhibition, ou qu'il n'y avait au monde pour conjurer la défection dans les curiosités que de recourir à quelque puissance absolue, comme d'une Métaphore. Vite, dégoiser jusqu'à éclaircissement, sur maintes physionomies, de leur sécurité qui, ne saisissant tout du coup, se rend à l'évidence, même ardue, impliquée en la parole et consent à échanger son billon contre des présomptions exactes et supérieures, bref, la certitude pour chacun de n'être pas refait.

uncrossed as evidence that it was useless to approach his marvel-less theatre, an old man whom this companionship with an instrument of noise and invitation may have seduced to her unspecified scheme; then, as if, because of what could instantly be imagined here as most beautiful, the enigma glittered! clasping this woman of the world with a jewel like the lack of any answer at her breast, lo and behold she was swallowed up, to the surprise of the nonplussed clown whom I was, before the public halted, caught by the summons of the rum-tum-tum that muffled my unwavering and at first obscure even to myself: 'Step up, everyone, it's only a penny, anyone who isn't satis-fied with the show will get a refund.' The straw halo was emptied into the gratitude that pressed two senile palms together; I wave its colours as a signal from afar and cover my head, ready to cut through the crowd standing in the secret of what the initiative of a con-temporary of our evenings had known to make of this unimaginative place.

Knee high, on a table, she was emerging from a hundred heads.

Clear as a stray light-beam from somewhere else that was flashing her forth electrically, there burst on me the deduction that, minus everything, she, according as fashion, fantasy, or heaven's caprice might particularize her beauty, was amply paying the crowd, without the addition of dance or song, for the charitable handout that had been exacted to provide aid for someone or other; and at the same moment I understood my duty in the peril of that subtle exhibition, or that the sole earthly method of averting her defection to mere curiosity was by relying on some absolute power, such as Metaphor. Quickly, chatter away until the elucidation, on many faces, of an impercipience which, failing to grasp everything at once, surrenders, with whatever difficulty, to the evidence implied in the word and agrees to exchange its cheap coin for precise and superior presumptions, in short, the certainty that each person hasn't been cheated.

Un coup d'œil, le dernier, à une chevelure où fume puis éclaire de fastes de jardins le pâlissement du chapeau en crêpe de même ton que la statuaire robe se relevant, avance au spectateur, sur un pied comme le reste hortensia.

Alors:

> *La chevelure vol d'une flamme à l'extrême*
> *Occident de désirs pour la tout déployer*
> *Se pose (je dirais mourir un diadème)*
> *Vers le front couronné son ancien foyer*

> *Mais sans or soupirer que cette vive nue*
> *L'ignition du feu toujours intérieur*
> *Originellement la seule continue*
> *Dans le joyau de l'œil véridique ou rieur*

> *Une nudité de héros tendre diffame*
> *Celle qui ne mouvant astre ni feux au doigt*
> *Rien qu'à simplifier avec gloire la femme*
> *Accomplit par son chef fulgurante l'exploit*

> *De semer de rubis le doute qu'elle écorche*
> *Ainsi qu'une joyeuse et tutélaire torche*

Mon aide à la taille de la vivante allégorie qui déjà résignait sa faction, peut-être faute chez moi de faconde ultérieure, afin d'en assoupir l'élan gentiment à terre: « Je vous ferai observer, ajoutai-je, maintenant de plain-pied avec l'entendement des visiteurs, coupant court à leur ébahissement devant ce congé par une affectation de retour à l'authenticité du spectacle, Messieurs et Dames, que la personne qui a eu l'honneur de se soumettre à votre jugement, ne

A glance, the last one, at a lock of hair, on which there smoulders—
and then lights up with the gardens' opulent riches—the paleness of
a crepe hat exactly the same shade as the statuesque dress which rises
over a foot as hydrangea-coloured as the rest, advancing toward the
spectators.

Then:

> *The hair flight of a flame to the extreme*
> *west of desire if it should all unlace*
> *settles (a diadem dying it would seem)*
> *near the crowned brow its former fireplace*

> *but without sighing for more gold than this*
> *live cloud kindling the fire ever within*
> *at first the only one continues in*
> *the jewel of the eye true or remiss*

> *a tender naked hero would degrade*
> *her who stirring no star or fire would*
> *just condensing with glory womanhood*
> *flashing with her head wreak the escapade*

> *of strewing rubies on the doubt she would scorch*
> *like a joyous and tutelary torch.*

As I supported the waist of the living allegory (who was already
resigning her post, perhaps because of a failure on my part to emit
any further stream of words) and gracefully cushioned her arrival on
the ground: 'I would have you note, Ladies and Gentlemen,' I added,
now on a level with the visitors' understanding, cutting short their
astonishment at this dismissal by a pretence that I was returning
to the authenticity of the show, 'that the person who has had the
honour of submitting herself to your judgement needs no costume

requiert pour vous communiquer le sens de son charme, un costume ou aucun accessoire usuel de théâtre. Ce naturel s'accommode de l'allusion parfaite que fournit la toilette toujours à l'un des motifs primordiaux de la femme, et suffit, ainsi que votre sympathique approbation m'en convainc. » Un suspens de marque appréciative sauf quelques confondants « Bien sûr! » ou « C'est cela! » et « Oui » par les gosiers comme plusieurs bravos prêtés par des paires de mains généreuses, conduisit jusqu'à la sortie sur une vacance d'arbres et de nuit la foule où nous allions nous mêler, n'était l'attente en gants blancs encore d'un enfantin tourlourou qui les rêvait dégourdir à l'estimation d'une jarretière hautaine.

—Merci, consentit la chère, une bouffée droit à elle d'une constellation ou des feuilles bue comme pour y trouver sinon le rassérènement, elle n'avait douté d'un succès, du moins l'habitude frigide de sa voix: j'ai dans l'esprit le souvenir de choses qui ne s'oublient.

—Oh! rien que lieu commun d'une esthétique . . .

—Que vous n'auriez peut-être pas introduit, qui sait? mon ami, le prétexte de formuler ainsi devant moi au conjoint isolement par exemple de notre voiture—où est-elle—regagnons-la:—mais ceci jaillit, forcé, sous le coup de poing brutal à l'estomac, que cause une impatience de gens auxquels coûte que coûte et soudain il faut proclamer quelque chose fût-ce la rêverie . . .

—Qui s'ignore et se lance nue de peur, en travers du public; c'est vrai. Comme vous, Madame, ne l'auriez entendu si irréfutablement, malgré sa réduplication sur une rime du trait final, mon boniment d'après un mode primitif du sonnet ([1]), je le gage, si chaque terme ne s'en était répercuté jusqu'à vous par de variés tympans, pour charmer un esprit ouvert à la compréhension multiple.

—Peut-être! accepta notre pensée dans un enjouement de souffle nocturne la même.

---

[1] Usité à la Renaissance anglaise.

or any of the other standard theatrical accessories to impress you with her charm. This naturalness is thoroughly at home with the perfect allusion which dress always provides to one of woman's primordial motives, and is quite enough, as your kind approval persuades me.' An appreciative silence, apart from some mingling cries of 'Sure!' or 'That's right!' and 'Yes' from various throats, as well as several bravos supplied by generous pairs of hands, led the crowd with which we were going to merge to an exit that opened onto a void of trees and night, were it not for a soldier boy still waiting in white gloves and dreaming that he was taking the stiffness out of them by the appraisal of a haughty garter.

'Thank you', consented the dear woman, having drunk a gust blown straight at her from a constellation or some leaves, as if to find there, if not renewed equanimity (for she had never doubted that she would be a success), at least the habitual coolness of her voice: 'I am holding memories of unforgettable things in my mind.'

'Oh, nothing but the commonplace of an aesthetic . . .'

'Which you yourself might not necessarily have introduced, who knows? my friend, the pretext of formulating before me in such a way in the joint isolation, for instance, of my carriage—where is it—let's get back to it:—but this simply gushed out under the impact of a brutal blow to the stomach, which was caused by the impatience of people to whom, instantly and at whatever cost, one must announce something, even if it is a daydream . . .'

'Which has no knowledge of itself and merely rushes, naked with fear, through the public; that's true. As you, Madame, would not have grasped so decisively, in spite of its duplicated rhyme on the final stroke, my little spiel based on a primitive form of the sonnet[1], if each term had not echoed to you from various drums, to charm a mind open to multiplicities of meaning.'

'Perhaps!' agreed our thought in a playfulness of nocturnal breeze, identically.

----

[1] In use during the English Renaissance [*Mallarmé's note*].

Le Nénuphar blanc

J'avais beaucoup ramé, d'un grand geste net assoupi, les yeux au dedans fixés sur l'entier oubli d'aller, comme le rire de l'heure coulait alentour. Tant d'immobilité paressait que frôlé d'un bruit inerte où fila jusqu'à moitié la yole, je ne vérifiai l'arrêt qu'à l'étincellement stable d'initiales sur les avirons mis à nu, ce qui me rappela à mon identité mondaine.

Qu'arrivait-il, où étais-je?

Il fallut, pour voir clair en l'aventure, me remémorer mon départ tôt, ce juillet de flamme, sur l'intervalle vif entre ses végétations dormantes d'un toujours étroit et distrait ruisseau, en quête des floraisons d'eau et avec un dessein de reconnaître l'emplacement occupé par la propriété de l'amie d'une amie, à qui je devais improviser un bonjour. Sans que le ruban d'aucune herbe me retînt devant un paysage plus que l'autre chassé avec son reflet en l'onde par le même impartial coup de rame, je venais échouer dans quelque touffe de roseaux, terme mystérieux de ma course, au milieu de la rivière: où tout de suite élargie en fluvial bosquet, elle étale un nonchaloir d'étang plissé des hésitations à partir qu'a une source.

L'inspection détaillée m'apprit que cet obstacle de verdure en pointe sur le courant, masquait l'arche unique d'un pont prolongé, à terre, d'ici et de là, par une haie clôturant des pelouses. Je me rendis compte. Simplement le parc de Madame . . ., l'inconnue à saluer.

Un joli voisinage, pendant la saison, la nature d'une personne qui s'est choisi retraite aussi humidement impénétrable ne pouvant être que conforme à mon goût. Sûr, elle avait fait de ce cristal son miroir intérieur à l'abri de l'indiscrétion éclatante des après-midi; elle y venait et la buée d'argent glaçant des saules ne fut bientôt que la limpidité de son regard habitué à chaque feuille.

The White Water Lily

I had been rowing for a long time, with a strong, clean, soporific motion, my eyes turned inward and utterly oblivious of my journey, as the laughter of the hour was flowing all around. So much motionlessness was idling away the time that, brushed by a dull sound into which my skiff half slid, I was able to confirm that it had come to a stop only by the steady glittering of initials on the bared oars, which reminded me of my worldly identity.

What was happening, where was I?

To understand the episode properly, I had to remember my early departure, on this flaming July day, through the lively gap between the drowsing vegetation of a persistently narrow and wayward stream, in search of water flowers and with the intention of exploring a property that belonged to the friend of a friend, to whom I should say hello on the spur of the moment. Without having been detained by any strip of grass before one vista more than another, as all alike were borne away with their reflections in the water by the same impartial oar-strokes, I had just run aground and mysteriously ended my little voyage on some clump of reeds in the middle of the stream: where, suddenly widening into a fluvial grove, it displays all the indifference of a pool rippled with a well-spring's reluctance to depart.

Detailed inspection showed me that this obstacle of tapering greenery in the current masked the single arch of a bridge that was extended on land, in both directions, by a hedge enclosing a series of lawns. I understood. Merely the gardens of Madame ——, the unknown lady whom I was to greet.

A pretty enough neighbourhood during the season; the character of a person who had chosen so watery and impenetrable a retreat for herself could only be in harmony with my own tastes. Surely she had formed this crystal into an internal mirror to shelter her from the brilliant tactlessness of the afternoons; she would come there, and the silvery mist icing the willows would soon be only the limpidity of her gaze familiar with every leaf.

Toute je l'évoquais lustrale.

Courbé dans la sportive attitude où me maintenait de la
curiosité, comme sous le silence spacieux de ce que s'annonçait
l'étrangère, je souris au commencement d'esclavage dégagé
par une possibilité féminine: que ne signifiaient pas mal
les courroies attachant le soulier du rameur au bois de
l'embarcation, comme on ne fait qu'un avec l'instrument de
ses sortilèges.

«—Aussi bien une quelconque . . . » allais-je terminer.

Quand un imperceptible bruit me fit douter si l'habitante du
bord hantait mon loisir, ou inespérément le bassin.

Le pas cessa, pourquoi?

Subtil secret des pieds qui vont, viennent, conduisent
l'esprit où le veut la chère ombre enfouie en de la batiste et les
dentelles d'une jupe affluant sur le sol comme pour circonvenir
du talon à l'orteil, dans une flottaison, cette initiative par quoi
la marche s'ouvre, tout au bas et les plis rejetés en traîne, une
échappée, de sa double flèche savante.

Connaît-elle un motif à sa station, elle-même la promeneuse:
et n'est-ce, moi, tendre trop haut la tête, pour ces joncs à ne
dépasser et toute la mentale somnolence où se voile ma
lucidité, que d'interroger jusque-là le mystère.

«—A quel type s'ajustent vos traits, je sens leur précision,
Madame, interrompre chose installée ici par le bruissement
d'une venue, oui! ce charme instinctif d'en dessous que ne
défend pas contre l'explorateur la plus authentiquement

I conjured her up, utterly lustral.

Bent forward in the sporting posture in which curiosity held me, as if beneath the spacious silence through which the stranger would announce herself, I smiled at this dawn of a slavery released by a feminine possibility: which was symbolized pretty well by the straps tying the rower's shoes to the wooden hull of the boat, for we are always one with the instrument of our enchantments.

'Just like any woman at all . . .' I was going to conclude.

When an imperceptible noise made me wonder whether the inhabitant of the shore was haunting my leisure time or, unexpectedly, the pond.

The footsteps stopped, why?

Subtle secret of feet that come and go, leading the mind wherever she may choose, dear shadow buried in cambric and the lace of a skirt flowing down over the ground as if to surround from heel to toe, floatingly, this initiative by walking opens up a transient space with its knowing double arrow, very low and with the folds thrown back in a train.

Has she some conscious reason for standing still, this walker: and would I myself be holding my head too high if, to penetrate the mystery, I raised it above these reeds and all the mental somnolence in which my lucidity is shrouded.

'Whatever may be the pattern of your features, Madame, I can feel their precision interrupt something established here by the rustlings of an arrival, yes! this instinctive charm of something underneath, which is not defended against the explorer by even the most authen-

nouée, avec une boucle en diamant, des ceintures. Si vague concept se suffit: et ne transgressera le délice empreint de généralité qui permet et ordonne d'exclure tous visages, au point que la révélation d'un (n'allez point le pencher, avéré, sur le furtif seuil où je règne) chasserait mon trouble, avec lequel il n'a que faire. »

Ma présentation, en cette tenue de maraudeur aquatique, je la peux tenter, avec l'excuse du hasard.

Séparés, on est ensemble: je m'immisce à de sa confuse intimité, dans ce suspens sur l'eau où mon songe attarde l'indécise, mieux que visite, suivie d'autres, l'autorisera. Que de discours oiseux en comparaison de celui que je tins pour n'être pas entendu, faudra-t-il, avant de retrouver aussi intuitif accord que maintenant, l'ouïe au ras de l'acajou vers le sable entier qui s'est tu!

La pause se mesure au temps de ma détermination.

Conseille, ô mon rêve, que faire?

Résumer d'un regard la vierge absence éparse en cette solitude et, comme on cueille, en mémoire d'un site, l'un des ces magiques nénuphars clos qui y surgissent tout à coup, enveloppant de leur creuse blancheur un rien, fait de songes intacts, du bonheur qui n'aura pas lieu et de mon souffle ici retenu dans la peur d'une apparition, partir avec: tacitement, en déramant peu à peu sans du heurt briser l'illusion ni que le clapotis de la bulle visible d'écume enroulée à ma fuite ne jette aux pieds survenus de personne la ressemblance transparante du rapt de mon idéale fleur.

Si, attirée par un sentiment d'insolite, elle a paru, la Méditative ou la Hautaine, la Farouche, la Gaie, tant pis pour cette indicible mine que j'ignore à jamais! car j'accomplis selon les règles la manœuvre: me dégageai, virai et je contournais

tically fastened sash with a diamond buckle. So vague an idea is enough: and will not transgress the delight tinged with a generality that allows and demands the exclusion of all faces, to the point where any revelation of one (please do not bend it confirmingly on the secret threshold where I reign) would banish my passion, which has nothing to do with it.'

I can try to present myself in this pirate costume with the excuse that it happened by chance.

Apart, we are together: I merge into her obscure intimacy, in this moment suspended on the water where my dream is delaying the indecisive creature, better than any visit (followed by others) could do. How many trivial conversations there would have to be, in comparison with this one which I have made in order not to be heard, before we could regain an understanding as intuitive as our present one, my ear flat against the mahogany and facing all the now-silent sand!

The pause is measured by the time it takes me to decide.

Tell me, my dream, what shall I do?

Sum up in a glance the virgin absence dispersed in this solitude and depart with it, as, to remember a certain place, you pluck one of the magical closed water lilies that suddenly rise up, enveloping nothing in their hollow whiteness, made of untouched dreams, from a happiness that will never be realized, and from the breath that I am now holding for fear of some apparition: silently, rowing away little by little, without breaking the illusion by any sudden shock, and without allowing the rippling visible bubble of foam unfurled by my flight to throw at anyone's arriving feet a transparent likeness of my abducted ideal blossom.

If, drawn by some unusual feeling, that Pensive or Haughty, Cruel or Happy creature appeared, so much the worse for the indescribable face that I shall never know! for I performed the manoeuvre according to the rules: pushed off, turned about, and was already tracing a

déjà une ondulation du ruisseau, emportant comme un noble
œuf de cygne, tel que n'en jaillira le vol, mon imaginaire tro-
phée, qui ne se gonfle d'autre chose sinon de la vacance
exquise de soi qu'aime, l'été, à poursuivre, dans les allées de
son parc, toute dame, arrêtée parfois et longtemps, comme au
bord d'une source à franchir ou de quelque pièce d'eau.

L'Ecclésiastique

Les printemps poussent l'organisme à des actes qui, dans
une autre saison, lui sont inconnus et maint traité d'histoire
naturelle abonde en descriptions de ce phénomène, chez les
animaux. Qu'il serait d'un intérêt plus plausible de recueillir
certaines des altérations qu'apporte l'instant climatérique dans
les allures d'individus faits pour la spiritualité! Mal quitté par
l'ironie de l'hiver, j'en retiens, quant à moi, un état équivoque
tant que ne s'y substitue pas un naturalisme absolu ou naïf,
capable de poursuivre une jouissance dans la différentiation de
plusieurs brins d'herbes. Rien dans le cas actuel n'apportant
de profit à la foule, j'échappe, pour le méditer, sous quelques
ombrages environnant d'hier la ville: or c'est de leur mystère
presque banal que j'exhiberai un exemple saisissable et
frappant des inspirations printanières.

Vive fut tout à l'heure, dans un endroit peu fréquenté du bois
de Boulogne, ma surprise quand, sombre agitation basse, je vis,
par les mille interstices d'arbustes bons à ne rien cacher, total
et des battements supérieurs du tricorne s'animant jusqu'à des
souliers affermis par des boucles en argent, un ecclésiastique,
qui à l'écart de témoins, répondait aux sollicitations du gazon.
A moi ne plût (et rien de pareil ne sert les desseins provi-
dentiels) que, coupable à l'égal d'un faux scandalisé se saisis-
sant d'un caillou du chemin, j'amenasse par mon sourire même
d'intelligence, une rougeur sur le visage à deux mains voilé de
ce pauvre homme, autre que celle sans doute trouvée dans son
solitaire exercice! Le pied vif, il me fallut, pour ne produire par
ma présence de distraction, user d'adresse; et fort contre la

ripple in the stream, carrying away, like a noble swan's egg of a kind that will never burst into flight, my imaginary trophy, swollen with nothing except the exquisite emptiness of self that every lady loves to pursue in summer through the avenues of her gardens, while she pauses occasionally and for some considerable time, as if at the edge of a spring to be crossed or some other body of water.

The Ecclesiastic

Springtime incites an organism to actions which, in any other season, are alien to it, and many a natural history treatise teems with descriptions of this phenomenon among animals. How much more plausibly interesting it would be to list some of the changes caused by this climactic moment in the behaviour of individuals who have been created for spirituality! In my own instance, when the irony of winter has barely left me, I still cling to some of its ambivalent condition, until it is replaced by a naive or absolute naturalism capable of seeking pleasure in the differentiation of various blades of grass. Nothing in the present case could bring profit to the crowd, so I escape, in order to meditate on it, I escape beneath some shade trees lately surrounding the town: now, it is from their almost banal mystery that I shall exhibit a tangible and striking example of springtime impulses.

Keen was my surprise just now when, in a seldom-frequented corner of the Bois de Boulogne, I saw a lowly sombre commotion through the chinks within the myriad bushes that are no good for hiding anything: an ecclesiastic, in a complete state and arousing himself from the lofty tremors of his three-cornered hat all the way down to his silver-buckled shoes, who was responding to the lawn's solicitations far away from all witnesses. Far be it from me (and nothing of the kind would serve the designs of providence), like a scandalized hypocrite seizing a single pebble from the road, to bring by a smile—even of understanding—a blush to this poor man's face hidden by his two hands, other than the blush doubtless elicited by his solitary exercise! I had to use some skill, with fleetness of foot, to avoid creating a distraction by my presence; and, steeled against the

tentation d'un regard porté en arrière, me figurer en esprit
l'apparition quasi-diabolique qui continuait à froisser le
renouveau de ses côtes, à droite, à gauche et du ventre, en
obtenant une chaste frénésie. Tout, se frictionner ou jeter les
membres, se rouler, glisser, aboutissait à une satisfaction: et
s'arrêter, interdit du chatouillement de quelque haute tige de
fleur à de noirs mollets, parmi cette robe spéciale portée avec
l'apparence qu'on est pour soi tout même sa femme. Solitude,
froid silence épars dans la verdure, perçus par des sens moins
subtils qu'inquiets, vous connûtes les claquements furibonds
d'une étoffe; comme si la nuit absconse en ses plis en sortait
enfin secouée! et les heurts sourds contre la terre du squelette
rajeuni; mais l'énergumène n'avait point à vous contempler.
Hilare, c'était assez de chercher en soi la cause d'un plaisir ou
d'un devoir, qu'expliquait mal un retour, devant une pelouse,
aux gambades du séminaire. L'influence du souffle vernal
doucement dilatant les immuables textes inscrits en sa chair,
lui aussi, enhardi de ce trouble agréable à sa stérile pensée, était
venu reconnaître par un contact avec la Nature, immédiat, net,
violent, positif, dénué de toute curiosité intellectuelle, le bien-
être général; et candidement, loin des obédiences et de la con-
trainte de son occupation, des canons, des interdits, des cen-
sures, il se roulait, dans la béatitude de sa simplicité native,
plus heureux qu'un âne. Que le but de sa promenade atteint se
soit, droit et d'un jet, relevé non sans secouer les pistils et
essuyer les sucs attachés à sa personne, le héros de ma vision,
pour rentrer, inaperçu, dans la foule et les habitudes de son
ministère, je ne songe à rien nier; mais j'ai le droit de ne point
considérer cela. Ma discrétion vis-à-vis d'ébats d'abord
apparus n'a-t-elle pas pour récompense d'en fixer à jamais
comme une rêverie de passant se plut à la compléter, l'image
marquée d'un sceau mystérieux de modernité, à la fois baroque
et belle?

La Gloire

La Gloire! je ne la sus qu'hier, irréfragable, et rien ne
m'intéressera d'appelé par quelqu'un ainsi.

temptation of a backward glance, to merely imagine the quasi-diabolical apparition who continued to rumple the new season right and left with his sides and stomach, thus achieving a chaste frenzy. Everything, rubbing himself or twitching his limbs, rolling, slithering, resulted in satisfaction: pausing too, unsettled by some tall flower stem that was tickling his black calves through that special gown worn with the appearance that one is everything to oneself, even one's own wife. The frantic flappings of a cloth have been familiar to you, O solitude, cold silence strewn through the greenery, perceived by senses less subtle than troubled; as if the darkness hidden in its folds was finally shaken out of it! and the rejuvenated skeleton's dull thuds against the earth; but the demon-possessed man did not need to contemplate you at all. He had only to look cheerily within himself for the cause of a pleasure or duty which, in the presence of a lawn, could hardly be explained by a return to the gambols of the seminary. As the influence of the vernal breeze softly enlarged the immutable texts inscribed on his flesh, he too, emboldened by this disturbance that pleased his sterile thinking, had come to acknowledge the general well-being by an immediate, clean, violent, positive contact with Nature, stripped of all intellectual curiosity; and far from the obediences and constraints of his occupation, from canons and prohibitions and censures, he was rolling in the bliss of his innate simplicity, happier than a donkey. When the object of his outing had been attained, I should not dream of denying that the hero of my vision stood up straight in a single bound, not without shaking off the pistils and wiping off the sap that clung to his person, so that he could return unperceived into the crowd and the habits of his ministry; but I have the right to avoid considering such matters. Surely my discretion in regard to those incipiently glimpsed frolics has been rewarded by being fixed forever as the daydream of a passer-by who was pleased to complete it, an image stamped with a mysterious seal of modernity, at once baroque and beautiful.

Glory

Glory! until yesterday I had no knowledge of it, an indisputable thing; and from now on, nothing else that is so called by anyone can interest me.

Cent affiches s'assimilant l'or incompris des jours, trahison de la lettre, ont fui, comme à tous confins de la ville, mes yeux au ras de l'horizon par un départ sur le rail traînés avant de se recueillir dans l'abstruse fierté que donne une approche de forêt en son temps d'apothéose.

Si discord parmi l'exaltation de l'heure, un cri faussa ce nom connu pour déployer la continuité de cimes tard évanouies, Fontainebleau, que je pensai, la glace du compartiment violentée, du poing aussi étreindre à la gorge l'interrupteur: Tais-toi! Ne divulgue pas du fait d'un aboi indifférent l'ombre ici insinuée dans mon esprit, aux portières de wagons battant sous un vent inspiré et égalitaire, les touristes omniprésents vomis. Une quiétude menteuse de riches bois suspend alentour quelque extraordinaire état d'illusion, que me réponds-tu? qu'ils ont, ces voyageurs, pour ta gare aujourd'hui quitté la capitale, bon employé vociférateur par devoir et dont je n'attends, loin d'accaparer une ivresse à tous départie par les libéralités conjointes de la nature et de l'État, rien qu'un silence prolongé le temps de m'isoler de la délégation urbaine vers l'extatique torpeur de ces feuillages là-bas trop immobilisés pour qu'une crise ne les éparpille bientôt dans l'air; voici, sans attenter à son intégrité, tiens, une monnaie.

Un uniforme inattentif m'invitant vers quelque barrière, je remets sans dire mot, au lieu du suborneur métal, mon billet.

Obéi pourtant, oui, à ne voir que l'asphalte s'étaler net de pas, car je ne peux encore imaginer qu'en ce pompeux octobre exceptionnel du million d'existences étageant leur vacuité en tant qu'une monotonie énorme de capitale dont va s'effacer ici la hantise avec le coup de sifflet sous la brume, aucun furtivement évadé que moi

A hundred posters absorbing the days' misunderstood gold—a betrayal of letters—fled past, as if to every corner of the town, my eyes being drawn to the level of the horizon by a departure on the rails before being drawn into the abstruse pride bestowed by a forest at its time of apotheosis.

Amid the exaltation of that hour, so discordantly did a cry distort the name 'Fontainebleau', known for its unfolding of a continuous succession of lately vanished treetops, that I thought of outraging the glass of the compartment with my fist and then throttling the interrupter: Be quiet! Don't, with any commonplace howl, reveal the shadow that has now been instilled in my mind to the carriage doors banging beneath an inspired and egalitarian wind, when the ever-present tourists have been spewed out. All around, a deceptive tranquillity of opulent woodlands is holding some extraordinary state of illusion poised, what answer can you give me? that those travellers left the capital today for your station, O worthy employee vociferating out of duty and from whom I expect, far from a greedy hoarding of the rapture lavished on all and sundry by the joint liberalities of nature and the State, merely a silence long enough for me to isolate myself from the urban delegation and seek the ecstatic torpor of those leaves over there, which are so motionless that some flurry must soon scatter them into the air; here, without trying to corrupt your integrity, have a coin.

An unresponsive uniform invites me to a certain barrier, and without a word I hand over my ticket instead of the metallic bribe.

Having been obeyed nonetheless, yes, at least by the look of the asphalt stretching out untrodden before me, for among the million existences piling up their vacuity as an immense monotony of the capital—whose spell is going to be wiped out here when the whistle blows through the mist—I still can't imagine that I am the only one

n'ait senti qu'il est, cet an, d'amers et lumineux sanglots, mainte indécise flottaison d'idée désertant les hasards comme des branches, tel frisson et ce qui fait penser à un automne sous les cieux.

Personne et, les bras de doute envolés comme qui porte aussi un lot d'une splendeur secrète, trop inappréciable trophée pour paraître! mais sans du coup m'élancer dans cette diurne veillée d'immortels troncs au déversement sur un d'orgueils surhumains (or ne faut-il pas qu'on en constate l'authenticité?) ni passer le seuil où des torches consument, dans une haute garde, tous rêves antérieurs à leur éclat répercutant en pourpre dans la nue l'universel sacre de l'intrus royal qui n'aura eu qu'à venir: j'attendis, pour l'être, que lent et repris du mouvement ordinaire, se réduisit à ses proportions d'une chimère puérile emportant du monde quelque part, le train qui m'avait là déposé seul.

Conflit

Longtemps, voici du temps—je croyais—que s'exempta mon idée d'aucun accident même vrai; préférant aux hasards, puiser, dans son principe, jaillissement.

Un goût pour une maison abandonnée, lequel paraîtrait favorable à cette disposition, amène à me dédire: tant le contentement pareil, chaque année verdissant l'escalier de pierres extérieur, sauf celle-ci, à pousser contre les murailles un volet hivernal puis raccorder comme si pas d'interruption, l'œillade d'à présent au spectacle immobilisé autrefois. Gage de retours fidèles, mais voilà que ce battement, vermoulu, scande un vacarme, refrains, altercations, en-dessous: je me rappelle comment la légende de la malheureuse demeure dont je hante le coin intact, envahie par une bande de travailleurs en train d'offenser le pays parce que tout de solitude, avec une voie ferrée, survint, m'angoissa au départ, irais-je ou pas, me fit presque hésiter—à revoir, tant pis!

who has stolen away stealthily, feeling that there are bitter and luminous sobbings this year, many a wavering indefinite idea shunning haphazard things like branches, a certain quivering that makes you think of some autumn beneath the skies.

Nobody and, since the arms of doubt have flown away like someone who carries off a prize in secret splendour, a trophy too insignificant to be visible! but without dashing straight away into that diurnal vigil of immortal tree-trunks pouring down superhuman prides over one individual (surely its authenticity needs to be experienced) or crossing the threshold where torch-flames aloft on watch are devouring all dreams that antedate their brilliance, echoing through the clouds in purple the universal consecration of the royal intruder who will merely have had to arrive: I waited, in order to be that very person, until the train that had set me down there alone, once more under the influence of its habitual motion, slowly shrank in scale to the proportions of childish monster carrying various people somewhere.

Conflict

For a long time, for some time now—so I believed—my thought abstained from any accidents, even true ones; preferring to draw from the fountain of its own essence, instead of chance.

A fondness for an abandoned house, which might seem to favour such a state of mind, now leads me to issue a retraction: the contentment is so much the same, except this, as each year turns the outdoor stone stairs green, pushing wintry shutters back against the walls then coupling today's glance with the formerly immobilized scene, as though there had been no interruption. A reward for faithful returns; but now the banging of those (worm-eaten) shutters is rhythmically beating a raucous din, refrains, altercations, from below: I recall how the legend of the unfortunate abode whose intact corner I inhabit, when it was invaded by a band of workers in the process of offending the country (because it had been totally secluded) with a railway, arrived, distressed me when I was on the

ce sera à défendre, comme mien, arbitrairement s'il faut, le local et j'y suis. Une tendresse, exclusive dorénavant, que ç'ait été lui qui, dans la suppression concernant des sites précieux, reçût la pire injure; hôte, je le deviens, de sa déchéance: invraisemblablement, le séjour chéri pour la désuétude et de l'exception, tourné par les progrès en cantine d'ouvriers de chemin de fer.

Terrassiers, puisatiers, par qui un velours hâve aux jambes, semble que le remblai bouge, ils dressent, au repos, dans une tranchée, la rayure bleu et blanc transversale des maillots comme la nappe d'eau peu à peu (vêtement oh! que l'homme est la source qu'il cherche): ce les sont, mes co-locataires jadis ceux, en esprit, quand je les rencontrai sur les routes, choyés comme les ouvriers quelconques par excellence: la rumeur les dit chemineaux. Las et forts, grouillement partout où la terre a souci d'être modifiée, eux trouvent, en l'absence d'usine, sous les intempéries, indépendance.

Les maîtres si quelque part, dénués de gêne, verbe haut.—Je suis le malade des bruits et m'étonne que presque tout le monde répugne aux odeurs mauvaises, moins au cri. Cette cohue entre, part, avec le manche, à l'épaule, de la pioche et de la pelle: or, elle invite, en sa faveur, les émotions de derrière la tête et force à procéder, directement, d'idées dont on se dit *c'est de la littérature!* Tout à l'heure, dévot ennemi, pénétrant dans une crypte ou cellier en commun, devant la rangée de l'outil double, cette pelle et cette pioche, sexuels—dont le métal, résumant la force pure du travailleur, féconde les terrains sans culture, je fus pris de religion, outre que de mécontentement, émue à m'agenouiller. Aucun homme de loi ne se targue de déloger l'intrus—baux tacites, usages locaux—établi par surprise et ayant même payé aux propriétaires: je dois jouer le rôle ou restreindre, à mes droits, l'empiètement. Quelque langage, la chance que je le tienne, comporte du dédain, bien sûr, puisque la promiscuité, couramment, me déplaît: ou, serai-je, d'une note juste, conduit à discourir ainsi?—Camarades—par exemple—vous ne supposez pas l'état

point of departure, would I go or not, made me almost hesitate—to
see it again, so much the worse! the place will have to be defended as
my own property, by arbitrary means if necessary, and there I am. A
henceforth exclusive feeling of tenderness that, in the process of
suppressing lovely places, this was the one that suffered the greatest
insult; I am becoming the host of its decline: unbelievably, the
resting-place prized for its disuse and exceptional status has been
transformed by progress into a canteen for railway workers.

Earth-diggers, well-diggers, with worn-out corduroy on their
legs—evidence that the embankment must be making progress; relax-
ing in a trench, they gradually arrange the blue and white transverse
stripes of their jerseys like a sheet of water (clothing oh! how man is
the source that he himself is seeking): they are the people in question,
formerly my co-tenants, in my mind, when I met them on the roads,
cherished like nondescript working men par excellence: rumour
says they are itinerant workers. Weary and strong, a teeming mass
wherever the earth is in need of alteration, they find their independ-
ence in the absence of a factory, throughout inclement weather.

The masters, if anywhere, are unconstrained, loud of speech.—
Noise has made me ill, and I am astonished that almost everyone is
repelled by bad smells, less so by shouting. These hordes come and
go, their pick- and shovel-handles on their shoulders: they invite
favourable emotions in the back of your mind and force you to move
on, directly, from ideas that you privately call 'literature'! Just now,
while I was plunging as a devout enemy into some crypt or common
storeroom, faced by the row of double tools, those sexual shovels and
picks—whose metal sums up the worker's unalloyed strength and
fertilizes the uncultivated soil, I was seized by a religious impulse,
not to mention a feeling of discontent, and was so deeply moved that
I knelt down. No man of law prides himself on ousting an intruder—
silent leases, local customs—established by surprise and even after
paying the owners: I must play the role or else restrict the trespass
as far as I have the right to do. If I happened to utter any language,
it would sound scornful, of course, because promiscuous things
generally displease me: or will I be driven to make a speech in the
proper tone, along these lines? 'Comrades,' for instance, 'you cannot
imagine the state of someone who is scattered across a landscape like

de quelqu'un épars dans un paysage celui-ci, où toute foule s'arrête, en tant qu'épaisseur de forêt à l'isolement que j'ai voulu tutélaire de l'eau; or mon cas, tel et, quand on jure, hoquète, se bat et s'estropie, la discordance produit, comme dans ce suspens lumineux de l'air, la plus intolérable si sachez, invisible des déchirures.—Pas que je redoute l'inanité, quant à des simples, de cet aveu, qui les frapperait, sûrement, plus qu'autres au monde et ne commanderait le même rire immédiat qu'à onze messieurs, pour voisins: avec le sens, pochards, du merveilleux et, soumis à une rude corvée, de délicatesses quelque part supérieures, peut-être ne verraient-ils, dans mon douloureux privilège, aucune démarcation strictement sociale pour leur causer ombrage, mais personnelle—s'observeraient-ils un temps, bref, l'habitude plausiblement reprend le dessus; à moins qu'un ne répondît, tout de suite, avec égalité.—Nous, le travail cessé pour un peu, éprouvons le besoin de se confondre, entre soi: qui a hurlé, moi, lui? son coup de voix m'a grandi, et tiré de la fatigue, aussi est-ce, déjà, boire, gratuitement, d'entendre crier un autre.—Leur chœur, incohérent, est en effect nécessaire. Comme vite je me relâche de ma défense, avec la même sensibilité qui l'aiguisa; et j'introduis, par la main, l'assaillant. Ah! à l'exprès et propre usage du rêveur se clôture, au noir d'arbres, en spacieux retirement, la Propriété, comme veut le vulgaire: il faut que je l'aie manquée, avec obstination, durant mes jours—omettant le moyen d'acquisition—pour satisfaire quelque singulier instinct de ne rien posséder et de seulement passer, au risque d'une résidence comme maintenant ouverte à l'aventure qui n'est pas, tout à fait, le hasard, puisqu'il me rapproche, selon que je me fis, de prolétaires.

Alternatives, je prévois la saison, de sympathie et de malaise . . .

—Ou souhaiterais, pour couper court, qu'un me cherchât querelle: en attendant et seule stratégie, s'agit de clore un jardinet, sablé, fleuri par mon art, en terrasse sur l'onde, la pièce d'habitation à la campagne . . . Qu'étranger ne passe

this, where the forest is so dense that no crowds ever reach the isolation which, I used to hope, would guard the water; in fact, that is my position and, when there is swearing, hiccuping, fighting, and mutual mangling, the discord produces the most unbearable, let me inform you, and invisible of destructions, just as it does in this luminous uncertainty of air.' Not that I fear the futility of admitting that to these unsophisticated people; surely it would touch them more than many other people in the world, and would not elicit the same immediate laughter that it would from eleven gentlemen, considered as neighbours: being drunkards, they have a sense of the marvellous and, being subject to arduous drudgery, of the somewhat greater difficulties involved; in my melancholy privilege they might not see any strictly social distinction that might offend them, but a merely personal one—should they be quiet for a while, presumably habit would quickly get the upper hand again; unless one of them immediately answered on equal terms. 'When we've stopped work for a short time, people like us need to get together; who was bawling, me, him? his shout enlarged me, and drew me out of my tiredness; also, when you hear someone else shouting, it's like having a free drink.' Their chorus—an incoherent one—is indeed necessary. So I withdraw my defence just as quickly, with the same sensitivity that had heightened it; and I introduce the beseiger with my own hand. Ah! the Property, as the vulgar herd would call it, is enclosed in the trees' shade, in spacious retirement, for the express and proper use of the dreamer: I must let the opportunity go by, stubbornly, in my own lifetime—not to mention the means of acquisition—in order to satisfy some strange instinct to own no possessions and merely to pass, at the risk of a residence like this one now open to an adventure which isn't entirely a matter of chance, since it brings me nearer to these proletarians, as I mature.

Alternatives, I can foresee this time, one of sympathy and uneasiness. —

Or, to put an end to this, I would like someone to pick a quarrel with me: in the meantime and purely as a matter of strategy, it is a question of enclosing a little garden, adorned with flowers by my art and gravelled, a rural living room on a terrace above the water . . .

le seuil, comme vers un cabaret, les travailleurs iront à leur chantier par un chemin loué et fauché dans les moissons.

« Fumier! » accompagné de pieds dans la grille, se profère violemment: je comprends qui l'aménité nomme, eh! bien même d'un soûlaud, grand gars le visage aux barreaux, elle me vexe malgré moi; est-ce caste, du tout, je ne mesure, individu à individu, de différence, en ce moment, et ne parviens à ne pas considérer le forcené, titubant et vociférant, comme un homme ou à nier le ressentiment à son endroit. Très raide, il me scrute avec animosité. Impossible de l'annuler, mentalement: de parfaire l'œuvre de la boisson, le coucher, d'avance, en la poussière et qu'il ne soit pas ce colosse tout à coup grossier et méchant. Sans que je cède même par un pugilat qui illustrerait, sur le gazon, la lutte des classes, à ses nouvelles provocations débordantes. Le mal qui le ruine, l'ivrognerie, y pourvoira, à ma place, au point que le sachant, je souffre de mon mutisme, gardé indifférent, qui me fait complice.

Un énervement d'états contradictoires, oiseux, faussés et la contagion jusqu'à moi, par du trouble, de quelque imbécile ébriété.

Même le calme, obligatoire dans une région d'échos, comme on y trempe, je l'ai, particulièrement les soirs de dimanche, jusqu'au silence. Appréhension quant à cette heure, qui prend la transparence de la journée, avant les ombres puis l'écoule lucide vers quelque profondeur. J'aime assister, en paix, à la crise et qu'elle se réclame de quelqu'un. Les compagnons apprécient l'instant, à leur façon, se concertent, entre souper et coucher, sur les salaires ou interminablement disputent, en le décor vautrés. M'abstraire ni quitter, exclus, la fenêtre, regard, moi-là, de l'ancienne bâtisse sur l'endroit qu'elle sait; pour faire au groupe des avances, sans effet. Toujours le cas:

May no stranger cross its threshold as if to a tavern, the workers will
go to their workplace by a rented road mown through the fields.

'Filthy scum!' is hurled violently, accompanied by a few kicks at
the gate: I understand at whom the compliment is aimed, well! even
from a drunkard, a big lad with his face against the railings, it annoys
me in spite of myself; is this class prejudice, not at all, at this
moment I am not measuring any individual differences and cannot
help regarding the staggering, jabbering lunatic as a man or harbour-
ing resentment against him. He studies me with hostility, looking
very stiff. Impossible to blot him out mentally: to finish what drink
has begun, to bring him down, for a start, into the dust and prevent
him from being this suddenly coarse and malevolent giant. Nor can I
even succumb to his copious new provocations by a fist-fight that
would illustrate the class struggle on the lawn. The evil that is ruin-
ing him, drunkenness, will do that job for me, so completely that I,
knowing it, am suffering from my own silence; my continuing
impassivity has made me an accomplice.

I have even been affected by a nervous weakness due to indolent,
warped, contradictory states of mind and the contagiousness, caused
by agitation, of a certain imbecile intoxication.

All the same, when you steep yourself in a realm of echoes, tran-
quillity is required; and I have so much of it that I am silent,
especially on Sunday evenings. Some misgivings about the hour,
which, before the shadows fall, becomes as transparent as the day,
and then sheds it lucidly into some deep place. I like to be present
calmly during this crisis, so that it may have a witness of some kind.
My companions appreciate the moment in their own way; between
supper and bedtime they hold a consultation about their wages or
else argue interminably, as they sprawl in the scenery. Although
shut out, I neither depart nor leave the window of the old house built
on its familiar site; in order to make advances to the group, but

pas lieu de se trouver ensemble; un contact peut, je le crains, n'intervenir entre des hommes.—« Je dis » une voix « que nous trimons, chacun ici, au profit d'autres. »—« Mieux, » interrompais-je bas, « vous le faites, afin qu'on vous paie et d'être légalement, quant à vous seuls. »—« Oui, les bourgeois, » j'entends, peu concerné « veulent un chemin de fer ».—« Pas moi, du moins » pour sourire « je ne vous ai pas appelés dans cette contrée de luxe et sonore, bouleversée autant que je suis gêné ». Ce colloque, fréquent, en muettes restrictions de mon côté, manque, par enchantement; quelle pierrerie, le ciel fluide! Toutes les bouches ordinaires tues au ras du sol comme y dégorgeant leur vanité de parole. J'allais conclure: « Peut-être moi, aussi, je travaille . . . — A quoi? n'eût objecté aucun, admettant, à cause de comptables, l'occupation transférée des bras à la tête. A quoi—tait, dans la conscience seule, un écho— du moins, qui puisse servir, parmi l'échange général. Tristesse que ma production reste, à ceux-ci, par essence, comme les nuages au crépuscule ou des étoiles, vaine.

Véritablement, aujourd'hui, qu'y a-t-il?

L'escouade du labeur gît au rendez-vous mais vaincue. Ils ont trouvé, l'un après l'autre qui la forment, ici affalée en l'herbe, l'élan à peine, chancelant tous comme sous un projectile, d'arriver et tomber à cet étroit champ de bataille: quel sommeil de corps contre la motte sourde.

Ainsi vais-je librement admirer et songer.

Non, ma vue ne peut, de l'ouverture où je m'accoude, s'échapper dans la direction de l'horizon, sans que quelque chose de moi n'enjambe, indûment, avec manque d'égard et de convenance à mon tour, cette jonchée d'un fléau; dont, en ma qualité, je dois comprendre le mystère et juger le devoir: car, contrairement à la majorité et beaucoup de plus fortunés, le

ineffectually. Always the same story: no means of coming together; men, I fear, cannot always make contact. A voice: 'I think we're all doing drudgery here for other people's benefit.' 'What's more,' I interpolate *sotto voce*, 'you are doing it to be paid and have a legitimate existence, from your own point of view.' 'Yes, the middle classes want a railway', I hear without too much concern. 'Not me, at least,' having to smile, 'I never summoned you to this land of luxury and sonority, which is being turned upside down to such an extent that it inconveniences me.' This frequent dialogue, my side being composed of unspoken reservations, falls magically silent: what a piece of jewellery the fluid sky is! Quieted, all commonplace mouths are flush with the ground, as though they were disgorging their vain speeches there. I was going to conclude: 'Perhaps I am working too.' 'At what?' nobody would have uttered such an objection; in view of paymasters, they admit that work can be transposed from the arm to the head. At what—an echo, in the mind alone, falls silent—at least, something that might be useful in general trading. How sad that my products should remain, for these men, in a state of essence, as vain as the evening clouds or stars!

In reality, today, what is the matter?

The work gang lies at its meeting-place, but vanquished. Its individual members, slumped in the grass, and staggering as if shot down, have hardly found the strength to arrive and drop on this tiny battlefield: how they sleep, these bodies, on the dull sod!

So I am going to marvel and muse freely.

No, my gaze cannot escape toward the horizon from the window where I am leaning, without some part of me inappropriately overstepping those scattered plague victims, which would show a lack of courtesy and propriety in my turn; from my own standpoint, I must appreciate their mysteriousness and assess their task: for bread was

pain ne lui a pas suffi—ils ont peiné une partie notable de la semaine, pour l'obtenir, d'abord; et, maintenant, la voici, demain, ils ne savent pas, rampent par le vague et piochent sans mouvement—qui fait en son sort, un trou égal à celui creusé, jusqu'ici, tous les jours, dans la réalité des terrains (fondation, certes, de temple). Ils réservent, honorablement, sans témoigner de ce que c'est ni que s'éclaire cette fête, la part du sacré dans l'existence, par un arrêt, l'attente et le momentané suicide. La connaissance qui resplendirait—d'un orgueil inclus à l'ouvrage journalier, résister, simplement et se montrer debout—alentour magnifiée par une colonnade de futaie; quelque instinct la chercha dans un nombre considérable, pour les déjeter ainsi, de petits verres et ils en sont, avec l'absolu d'un accomplissement rituel, moins officiants que victimes, à figurer, au soir, l'hébétement de tâches si l'observance relève de la fatalité plus que d'un vouloir.

Les constellations s'initient à briller: comme je voudrais que parmi l'obscurité qui court sur l'aveugle troupeau, aussi des points de clarté, telle pensée tout à l'heure, se fixassent, malgré ces yeux scellés ne les distinguant pas—pour le fait, pour l'exactitude, pour qu'il soit dit. Je penserai, donc, uniquement, à eux, les importuns, qui me ferment, par leur abandon, le lointain vespéral; plus que, naguères, par leur tumulte. Ces artisans de tâches élémentaires, il m'est loisible, les veillant, à côté d'un fleuve limpide continu, d'y regarder le peuple—une intelligence robuste de la condition humaine leur courbe l'échine journellement pour tirer, sans l'intermédiaire du blé, le miracle de vie qui assure la présence: d'autres ont fait les défrichements passés et des aqueducs ou livreront un terre-plein à telle machine, les mêmes, Louis-Pierre, Martin, Poitou et le Normand, quand ils ne dorment pas, ainsi s'invoquent-ils selon les mères ou la province; mais plutôt des naissances sombrèrent en l'anonymat et l'immense sommeil l'ouïe à la génératrice, les prostrant, cette fois, subit un accablement et un élargissement de tous les siècles et, autant cela possible— réduite aux proportions sociales, d'éternité.

not enough for them (unlike the majority and more fortunate ones)—first they worked for a substantial part of the week to gain it; and now here they are, with no knowledge of tomorrow, crawling through the haze and digging motionlessly—making as big a hole in their destiny as the one they have dug daily till now in the reality of the ground (a foundation for a temple, assuredly). By stopping, waiting, and momentarily committing suicide, they honourably retain the sacred part of existence, without witnessing what it is or what lightning-bolts this festal occasion is shedding. The knowledge that would become resplendent—of a certain pride in their daily work, simply to resist and stand tall—is magnified on all sides by a colonnade of trees; some instinct sought that knowledge in a large number of drinks, to contort them in this way, and at dusk, victims rather than officers, with the absoluteness of a ritual consummation, they have reached the point of representing the stupefaction of tasks when they are imposed by necessity instead of some desire.

The constellations are starting to shine: how I would wish that points of light, a certain recent thought, should also be fixed in the darkness that falls over the blind herd, in spite of the fact that their sealed eyes cannot discern them—for the sake of fact and exactness, so that it may be said. Thus I shall think only of them, the intruders, who are shutting out the distant twilight from me, more effectively by their current surrender than by their previous hubbub. As I watch over them alongside a limpid unwavering river, I may see these artisans of elementary tasks as the people—a healthy understanding of the human condition is daily bending their backs in order to draw forth, without the intermediary of wheat, the miracle of life that assures presence: others have cleared the land completely and erected aqueducts, or will subject a strip of soil to a certain machine, the same people, Louis-Pierre, Martin, Poitou, and the Norman, as they call each other when awake according to their mother or their homeland; instead, however, births have sunk into anonymity, and at the moment, with their ear to mother earth, they sleep an immense sleep that exhausts them, undergoing a prostration and an extension of all the ages and also, as far as such a thing is possible—when reduced to social proportions, of eternity.

Poème

Un coup de dés jamais
n'abolira le hasard

[French text on pages 139–159]

Poem

A Dice Throw At Any Time
Never Will Abolish Chance

[English text on pages 161–181]

UN COUP DE DÉS

JAMAIS

QUAND BIEN MÊME LANCÉ DANS DES CIRCONSTANCES

ÉTERNELLES

DU FOND D'UN NAUFRAGE

SOIT
    que

          l'Abîme

     blanchi
         étale
           furieux

               sous une inclinaison
                  plane désespérément

                        d'aile

                    la sienne

                          par

avance retombée d'un mal à dresser le vol
              et couvrant les jaillissements
                          coupant au ras les bonds

          très à l'intérieur résume

l'ombre enfouie dans la profondeur par cette voile alternative

                jusqu'adapter
                        à l'envergure

          sa béante profondeur en tant que la coque

                d'un bâtiment

            penché de l'un ou l'autre bord

LE MAÎTRE

surgi
    inférant

        de cette conflagration

        que se

        comme on menace

      l'unique Nombre qui ne peut pas

          hésite
       cadavre par le bras

   plutôt
      que de jouer
        en maniaque chenu
         la partie
        au nom des flots

            un

        naufrage cela

hors d'anciens calculs
où la manœuvre avec l'âge oubliée

jadis il empoignait la barre

à ses pieds
de l'horizon unanime

prépare
s'agite et mêle
au poing qui l'étreindrait
un destin et les vents

être un autre

Esprit
pour le jeter
dans la tempête
en reployer la division et passer fier

écarté du secret qu'il détient

envahit le chef
coule en barbe soumise

direct de l'homme

sans nef
n'importe
où vaine

ancestralement à n'ouvrir pas la main

               crispée

          par delà l'inutile tête

  legs en la disparition

            à quelqu'un

                  ambigu

        l'ultérieur démon immémorial

ayant

     de contrées nulles

          induit

le vieillard vers cette conjonction suprême avec la probabilité

             celui

                  son ombre puérile

caressé et polie et rendue et lavée

         assoupie par la vague et soustraite

     aux durs os perdus entre les ais

             né

              d'un ébat

la mer par l'aïeul tentant ou l'aïeul contre la mer

     une chance oiseuse

                              Fiançailles

dont

     le voile d'illusion rejailli leur hantise

     ainsi que le fantôme d'un geste

            chancellera

            s'affalera

               folie

N'ABOLIRA

COMME SI

Une insinuation

au silence

dans quelque proche

voltige

simple

enroulée avec ironie
                    ou
                        le mystère
                                précipité
                                        hurlé

tourbillon d'hilarité et d'horreur

autour du gouffre
                sans le joncher
                            ni fuir

                et en berce le vierge indice

COMME SI

plume solitaire éperdue

sauf

que la rencontre ou l'effleure une toque de minuit
et immobilise
au velours chiffonné par un esclaffement sombre

cette blancheur rigide

dérisoire

en opposition au ciel
trop
pour ne pas marquer
exigüment
quiconque

prince amer de l'écueil

s'en coiffe comme de l'héroïque
irrésistible mais contenu
par sa petite raison virile

en foudre

soucieux

      expiatoire et pubère

                        muet

La lucide et seigneuriale aigrette
          au front invisible
    scintille
        puis ombrage
une stature mignonne ténébreuse
     en sa torsion de sirène

par d'impatientes squames ultimes

rire

     que

        SI

de vertige

debout

   le temps
      de souffleter
bifurquées

    un roc

  faux manoir
      tout de suite
        évaporé en brumes

      qui imposa
        une borne à l'infini

C'ÉTAIT
issu stellaire

CE SERAIT

pire

       non

             davantage ni moins

                     indifféremment mais autant

LE NOMBRE

EXISTÂT-IL

autrement qu'hallucination éparse d'agonie

COMMENÇÂT-IL ET CESSÂT-IL

sourdant que nié et clos quand apparu

enfin

par quelque profusion répandue en rareté

SE CHIFFRÂT-IL

évidence de la somme pour peu qu'une

ILLUMINÂT-IL

LE HASARD

Choit
       la plume
             rythmique suspens du sinistre
                                 s'ensevelir
                     aux écumes originelles
        naguères d'où sursauta son délire jusqu'à une cime
                      flétrie
            par la neutralité identique du gouffre

RIEN

de la mémorable crise
ou se fût
l'évènement

accompli en vue de tout résultat nul
                        humain

                N'AURA EU LIEU
            une élévation ordinaire verse l'absence

                                QUE LE LIEU
inférieur clapotis quelconque comme pour disperser l'acte vide
                abruptement qui sinon
                par son mensonge
                        eût fondé
                        la perdition

dans ces parages
                du vague
                        en quoi toute réalité se dissout

EXCEPTÉ
à l'altitude
PEUT-ÊTRE
aussi loin qu'un endroit

fusionne avec au–delà

        hors l'intérêt
      quant à lui signalé
            en général
selon telle obliquité par telle déclivité
            de feux

  vers
    ce doit être
      le Septentrion aussi Nord

           UNE CONSTELLATION

    froide d'oubli et de désuétude
          pas tant
        qu'elle n'énumère
     sur quelque surface vacante et supérieure
        le heurt successif
            sidéralement
     d'un compte total en formation

veillant
    doutant
      roulant
        brillant et méditant

           avant de s'arrêter
        à quelque point dernier qui le sacre

        Toute Pensée émet un Coup de Dés

A DICE THROW

AT ANY TIME

EVEN WHEN CAST IN

EVERLASTING CIRCUMSTANCES

FROM THE DEPTH OF A SHIPWRECK

WHETHER
            the

                    Chasm

                whitish
                        fulltide
                            frenzied
                                down a declivity
                                    desperately glides

                                        on a wing

                                            its own

                                                    in

advance fallen back from a failure to guide its flight
and covering all the outspurts
cutting off all the surges

far far within recalls

the shadow buried in the deep veiled by this variant sail

to the point of matching
the span

with its gaping trough like the shell

of a ship

listing to this side or that

THE MASTER

risen
inferring

from this conflagration

that there

as you threaten

the one and only Number that cannot

hesitates
a corpse cut off

rather
than play
the game
like a hoary maniac
in the name of the waves
one

direct shipwreck

      gone beyond the old reckonings
      helmsmanship now forgotten with age

             he used to grip the helm

at his feet
          of the united horizon

is in preparation
          tossed and blended
              in the fist that seeks to grasp it
some destiny and also the winds

be any other

          Spirit
              in order to cast it
                    into the blast
                closing the division and passing proudly on

by its arm from the secret it withholds

surges over his head
spills down as a submissive beard

of man this

        with no vessel
       no matter
             where vain

ancestrally not to open his hand
                    which is clenched
            far beyond his useless head

    a bequest on his disappearance

                        to someone
                            ambiguous

        the ulterior immemorial demon

having
        from non-lands
                led
the old man toward this ultimate conjunction with probability

                    he
                        his puerile shadow
caressed and polished and restored and washed
                softened by the waves and set free
        from the hard bones lost amid the timbers

                    born
                            from a frolic
the sea attempting via the old man or the latter versus the sea
                an idle chance
                                        Nuptials
whose
        veil of illusion being splashed back their obsession
        along with the wraith of a gesture

                will falter
                and fall

                    sheer folly

NEVER WILL ABOLISH

AS IF

A simple

in the silence

in some imminent

hovers

insinuation

inrolled ironically
                    or
                        the mystery
                                    hurled down
                                                howled out

swirl of hilarity and horror

on the brink of the abyss
                        without sprinkling it
                                        or escaping

                    and draws from it the soothing virgin sign

                                                    AS IF

an utterly lost and lonely quill

except

that a cap of midnight abuts it or grazes it
                    and fixes
        on the velvet crumpled by a dark burst of laughter

                    this rigid whiteness

ridiculous

                            opposed to the sky
            too vividly
                    not to mark
                        in miniature detail
                                whoever

        a bitter prince of the reef

                caps himself with it heroically
                irresistible but restrained
                by his limited reason manly

                                    in a flash of lightning

anxious

  expiatory and pubescent

                                        mute

                          The lucid and lordly plume
                              on the invisible brow
              shimmers
                      then overshadows
                          a dim and dainty form
                      in her siren sinuosity

              with forked and impatient terminal

laughter

      that

             IF

of vertigo

erect

   long enough
      to slap
scales

     some rock

    a false mansion
         suddenly
            dispelled in mists

        which laid
          a limit on the infinite

IT WAS
a product of the stars

IT WOULD BE

no

worse

neither more nor less

but as much indifferently as

THE NUMBER

MIGHT HAVE EXISTED

except as the fragmentary hallucination of some death throe

MIGHT HAVE BEGUN AND ENDED

seeping out though denied and enclosed when manifest

eventually

outspread with a certain profusion in a rare state

MIGHT HAVE BEEN RECKONED

evidence of the total sum however scant

MIGHT HAVE ENLIGHTENED

CHANCE

Down falls

the quill

a rhythmic suspension of disaster

to bury itself

in the primordial spray

whose frenzy formerly leapt from there to a peak

that is blasted

in the constant neutrality of the abyss

NOTHING

of the unforgettable crisis
or else
the deed

might have been achieved keeping in view every result that is non

human

WILL HAVE TAKEN PLACE
a commonplace upsurge is shedding absence

OTHER THAN THE PLACE
a lowly splashing of some kind as if to scatter the vacuous action
at once which otherwise
by its deceit
would have established
the loss

in these indefinite regions
of the swell
where all reality is dissolved

EXCEPT

       on high

              PERHAPS

                      as far away as a place

merges with the beyond

outside any interest
assigned to it
in a general way
by a certain obliquity in a certain declivity
of flames

toward
what must be
Septentrion as well as North

A CONSTELLATION

cold with neglect and disuse
not so much
that it fails to number
on some vacant and higher surface
the successive impact
starrily
of a full reckoning in the making

keeping watch
wondering
rolling on
shining and pondering

before finally halting
at some last point that sanctifies it

Every Thought emits a Dice Throw

Poems Uncollected by Mallarmé

Soleil d'hiver

A Monsieur Éliacim Jourdain

Phébus à la perruque rousse
De qui les lames de vermeil,
O faunes ivres dans la mousse,
Provoquaient votre lourd sommeil.

Le bretteur aux fières tournures
Dont le brocart était d'ors fins,
Et qui par ses égratignures
Saignait la pourpre des raisins.

Ce n'est plus qu'un Guritan chauve
Qui, dans son ciel froid verrouillé,
Le long de sa culotte mauve
Laisse battre un rayon rouillé:

Son aiguillette, sans bouffette,
Triste, pend aux sapins givrés,
Et la neige qui tombe est faite
De tous ses cartels déchirés!

L'Enfant prodigue

I

Chez celles dont l'amour est une orange sèche
Qui garde un vieux parfum sans le nectar vermeil,
J'ai cherché l'Infini qui fait que l'homme pèche,
Et n'ai trouvé qu'un Gouffre ennemi du sommeil.

Poems Uncollected by Mallarmé

Winter Sun

For Monsieur Éliacim Jourdain

Red-wigged Apollo
whose scarlet swordblades
used to prod the deep slumbers
of fauns drunk in the moss.

The brigand in bold garb   5
brocaded with fine gold
who slashed the grapes
till they bled purple.

Now merely a bald old Guritan
in his cold and bolted sky,   10
letting a rusty sunbeam
slap against his mauve breeches.

His aglet with no rosette
dangles sadly in the frosted firs,
and the falling snow is composed   15
of all his shredded challenges!

The Prodigal Son

I

Among the girls whose love is oranges' dried skin
with no nectar despite the old scents they still keep,
I sought the Boundless that impels mankind to sin
and found only a Chasm inimical to sleep. —

—L'Infini, rêve fier qui berce dans sa houle
Les astres et les cœurs ainsi qu'un sable fin!
—Un Gouffre, hérissé d'âpres ronces, où roule
Un fétide torrent de fard mêlé de vin!

II

O la mystique, ô la sanglante, ô l'amoureuse
Folle d'odeurs de cierge et d'encens, qui ne sus
Quel Démon te tordait le soir où, douloureuse,
Tu léchas un tableau du saint-cœur de Jésus,

Tes genoux qu'ont durcis les oraisons rêveuses,
Je les baise, et tes pieds qui calmeraient la mer;
Je veux plonger ma tête en tes cuisses nerveuses
Et pleurer mon erreur sous ton cilice amer;

Là, ma sainte, enivré de parfums extatiques,
Dans l'oubli du noir Gouffre et de l'Infini cher,
Après avoir chanté tout bas de longs cantiques
J'endormirai mon mal sur votre fraîche chair.

. . . Mysticis umbraculis

(Prose des Fous)

Elle dormait: son doigt tremblait, sans améthyste
Et nu, sous sa chemise: après un soupir triste,
Il s'arrêta, levant au nombril la batiste.

Et son ventre sembla de la neige où serait,
Cependant qu'un rayon redore la forêt,
Tombé le nid moussu d'un gai chardonneret.

The Boundless, that proud dream lulling all stars and souls   5
like tiny grains of sand within its surging brine!—
A Chasm bristling with sharp thistles, through which rolls
a foetid torrent of commingled rouge and wine!

II

O woman, lacerated, mystic, amorous too,
with the madness that censer and candlestick impart,   10
not knowing what Demon wrung you in the dark when you
dolefully licked a picture of Christ's sacred heart,

I kiss your knees that self-communing prayers chastize,
I kiss your feet that would appease the open sea;
I wish to plunge my head between your vital thighs   15
and in your hair-shirt weep for my iniquity;

there, my dear saint, in that oblivion of the dim
Chasm and the Boundless, rapt with scents vibrant and fresh,
when I have finished softly chanting my long hymn,
I shall assuage my torment on your wholesome flesh.   20

. . . In the Mystical Shadows

(Liturgy for the Feast of Fools)

She was asleep; her bare and jewelless finger, placed
beneath her nightgown, quivered; after a deep sigh
it grew still, hitching up the cambric to her waist.

And her belly seemed like a snowdrift where,
while a gold sunbeam lit its forest lair,   5
the mossy nest of some bright finch might lie.

Sonnet

A Emmanuel des Essarts

Souvent la vision du Poète me frappe:
Ange à cuirasse fauve, il a pour volupté
L'éclair du glaive, ou, blanc songeur, il a la chape,
La mitre byzantine et le bâton sculpté.

Dante, au laurier amer, dans un linceul se drape,
Un linceul fait de nuit et de sérénité:
Anacréon, tout nu, rit et baise une grappe
Sans songer que la vigne a des feuilles, l'été.

Pailletés d'astres, fous d'azur, les grands bohèmes,
Dans les éclairs vermeils de leur gai tambourin,
Passent, fantastiquement coiffés de romarin.

Mais j'aime peu voir, Muse, ô reine des poèmes
Dont la toison nimbée a l'air d'un ostensoir,
Un poète qui polke avec un habit noir.

Haine du pauvre

Ta guenille nocturne étalant par ses trous
Les rousseurs de tes poils et de ta peau, je l'aime
Vieux spectre, et c'est pourquoi je te jette vingt sous.

Ton front servile et bas n'a pas la fierté blême:
Tu comprends que le pauvre est le frère du chien
Et ne vas pas drapant ta lésine en poème.

Comme un chacal sortant de sa pierre, ô chrétien
Tu rampes à plat ventre après qui te bafoue.
Vieux, combien par grimace? et par larme, combien?

Mets à nu ta vieillesse et que la gueuse joue,
Lèche, et de mes vingt sous chatouille la vertu.
A bas! . . . —les deux genoux! . . . —la barbe dans la boue!

Sonnet

For Emmanuel des Essarts

Often the Poet catches my gaze:
an angel in a fulvid breastplate, who delights
in the sword's flashing rays; or else, bright dreamer, displays
the mitre, ornamental staff, and cope of Byzantine rites.

Dante wears bitter laurels and funereal drapes   5
where night and serenity entwine;
Anacreon laughs, stark naked, and kisses a cluster of grapes,
heedless of summer's leaves on the vine.

Amid the scarlet flashes of their gay tambourine
all the great Bohemians, fantastically decked in rosemary,   10
pass by, spangled with stars, maddened with the Absolute.

But I scarcely care to behold, O Muse, poetry's queen
with radiant hair like an ostensory,
a poet who polkas in a black suit.

Hatred of the Poor

Those midnight rags of yours, with holes exposing
    your freckles and red bristles—I love them all:
so I am tossing you twenty sous, old phantom.

    Your brow is servile, base, with no wan pride;
you, knowing paupers are dogs' brothers, never   5
    dress up your stinginess in poetry.

Like a jackal leaving its lair, dear Christian,
    you grovel after those who mock at you.
What price a tear, old man? what price a grimace?

    Bare your senility; let it swindle, coax,   10
wheedle the virtue that my twenty sous have.
    Down!—on your knees!—with your beard in the mire!

Que veut cette médaille idiote, ris-tu?
L'argent brille, le cuivre un jour se vert-de-grise,
Et je suis peu dévot et je suis fort têtu,

Choisis.—Jetée? alors, voici ma pièce prise.
Serre-la dans tes doigts et pense que tu l'as
Parce que j'en tiens trop, ou par simple méprise.

—C'est le prix, si tu n'as pas peur, d'un coutelas.

[« Parce que de la viande . . . »]

Parce que de la viande était à point rôtie,
Parce que le journal détaillait un viol,
Parce que sur sa gorge ignoble et mal bâtie
La servante oublia de boutonner son col,

Parce que d'un lit, grand comme une sacristie,
Il voit, sur la pendule, un couple antique et fol,
Ou qu'il n'a pas sommeil, et que, sans modestie,
Sa jambe sous les draps frôle une jambe au vol,

Un niais met sous lui sa femme froide et sèche,
Contre ce bonnet blanc frotte son casque-à-mèche
Et travaille en soufflant inexorablement:

Et de ce qu'une nuit, sans rage et sans tempête,
Ces deux êtres se sont accouplés en dormant,
O Shakspeare et toi, Dante, il peut naître un poëte!

Le Château de l'espérance

Ta pâle chevelure ondoie
Parmi les parfums de ta peau
Comme folâtre un blanc drapeau
Dont la soie au soleil blondoie.

Why that silly old coin, you scoff? The money
  is glittering, some day it must verdigris,
I am scarcely devout and very stubborn,   15

  make your choice.—Flung? my cash is captured, then!
Clutch it tight, tell yourself you have it only
  out of scorn—or because I own too much.

It will—if you're not afraid—buy you a cutlass.

['Because a bit of roast was done to a turn . . .']

Because a bit of roast was done to a turn,
because the paper reported a rape,
because the maid had forgotten to button her blouse
over her tawdry and ill-shaped breasts,

because on the clock he could see a naughty old couple   5
from a bed as big as a vestry,
or because he lay awake with his leg
shamelessly brushing another leg beneath the sheets,

some simpleton plants his cold dry wife underneath him,
rubs his tasselled crown against her white cap   10
and toils inexorably, puffing and panting:

and because those two creatures coupled in their sleep
one night with no storm and no bluster,
O Shakespeare, and ah Dante, a poet may be born!

The Castle of Hope

Your fair hair is fluttering
across the scents of your skin
like a white flag frolicking
as its silk glints yellow in the sunlight.

Las de battre dans les sanglots
L'air d'un tambour que l'eau défonce,
Mon cœur à son passé renonce
Et, déroulant ta tresse en flots,

Marche à l'assaut, monte,—ou roule ivre
Par des marais de sang, afin
De planter ce drapeau d'or fin
Sur un sombre château de cuivre

—Où, larmoyant de nonchaloir,
L'Espérance rebrousse et lisse
Sans qu'un astre pâle jaillisse
La Nuit noire comme un chat noir.

[« Une négresse par le démon secouée . . . »]

Une négresse par le démon secouée
Veut goûter une enfant triste de fruits nouveaux
Et criminels aussi sous leur robe trouée,
Cette goinfre s'apprête à de rusés travaux:

A son ventre compare heureuses deux tétines
Et, si haut que la main ne le saura saisir,
Elle darde le choc obscur de ses bottines
Ainsi que quelque langue inhabile au plaisir.

Contre la nudité peureuse de gazelle
Qui tremble, sur le dos tel un fol éléphant
Renversée elle attend et s'admire avec zèle,
En riant de ses dents naïves à l'enfant;

Et, dans ses jambes où la victime se couche,
Levant une peau noire ouverte sous le crin,
Avance le palais de cette étrange bouche
Pâle et rose comme un coquillage marin.

My heart wearies of beating a ditty   5
in tears on a drum that has burst with such fluid,
renounces its past
and, unfurling your tresses in waves,

marches off and mounts an attack, scales the heights—
or else rolls drunkenly over marshes of blood,   10
to plant that banner of finest gold
on a dark-hued copper castle—

where Hope, listlessly weeping,
rubs up and smooths down
Night black as a black cat   15
without one pallid star gleaming.

['A negress aroused by the devil . . .']

A negress aroused by the devil is longing
to taste a young girl saddened by strange
forbidden fruits under their tattered dress,
and is toiling, the glutton, at cunning little schemes:

on her belly she compares a pair of sprightly nipples   5
and thrusts the dark shock from between her booted legs,
like some tongue inexpert at pleasure,
so high up that no hand could reach it.

Against the quivering gazelle's timid nudity
as she lies upturned on her back like a frenzied elephant   10
she waits and admires herself eagerly,
smiling with innocent teeth at the girl;

and between her legs where the victim is bedded,
arching her black skin parted beneath its fleece,
she pushes out the palate of that alien mouth   15
as rosy and pale as a seashell.

Hérodiade

Ouverture

LA NOURRICE
(INCANTATION)

Abolie, et son aile affreuse dans les larmes
Du bassin, aboli, qui mire les alarmes,
De l'or nu fustigeant l'espace cramoisi,
Une Aurore a, plumage héraldique, choisi
Notre tour cinéraire et sacrificatrice,
Lourde tombe qu'a fuie un bel oiseau, caprice
Solitaire d'aurore au vain plumage noir . . .
Ah! des pays déchus et tristes le manoir!
Pas de clapotement! L'eau morne se résigne,
Que ne visite plus la plume ni le cygne
Inoubliable: l'eau reflète l'abandon
De l'automne éteignant en elle son brandon:
Du cygne quand parmi le pâle mausolée
Ou la plume plongea la tête, désolée
Par le diamant pur de quelque étoile, mais
Antérieure, qui ne scintilla jamais.

Crime! bûcher! aurore ancienne! supplice!
Pourpre d'un ciel! Étang de la pourpre complice!
Et sur les incarnats, grand ouvert, ce vitrail.

La chambre, singulière en un cadre, attirail
De siècles belliqueux, orfèvrerie éteinte,
A le neigeux jadis pour ancienne teinte,
Et la tapisserie, au lustre nacré, plis
Inutiles avec les yeux ensevelis
De sibylles, offrant leur ongle vieil aux Mages.
Une d'elles, avec un passé de ramages
Sur sa robe blanchie en l'ivoire fermé
Au ciel d'oiseaux parmi l'argent noir parsemé,
Semble, de vols partis costumée et fantôme,
Un arôme qui porte, ô roses! un arôme,

Herodias

Overture

THE NURSE
UTTERS AN INCANTATION:

Abolished, and her dread wing in the tears
of the abolished pool reflecting fears,
lashing the crimson space of naked gold,
a Dawn has, with heraldic plumage, chosen
our cinerary sacrificial tower,   5
a leaden tomb shunned by a lovely bird—
dawn's lone caprice in dark vain plumage . . . O
this mansion of degenerate dismal country!
No lapping waves! The drab water, no longer
visited by a feather or unforgettable swan,   10
is calm: the water mirrors the dejection
of autumn leaves quenching their flames in it,
of the swan when it plunged its head into
its pallid tomb or feathers, devastated
by the pure diamond of some star, although   15
it was an earlier one, and never glittered.

Crime! funeral pyre! ancient sunrise! torment!
Purple sky! Pool, accomplice of that purple!
Wide open, over the rose hues, this stained-glass window.

The curious room within a frame—the pomp of   20
a warlike era, all the goldwork tarnished—
used to be tinged with snowy yesteryear;
its lustrous pearly tapestries are useless
folds with the buried eyes of Sibyls offering
their aged fingernails toward the Magi.   25
One of them, with a woven past of flowers
on her gown bleached in a locked ivory chest
and with a bird-strewn sky on the black silver,
ghostly and garbed in risen flights, seems an
aroma carrying, O roses! an aroma,   30

Loin du lit vide qu'un cierge soufflé cachait,
Un arôme d'os froids rôdant sur le sachet,
Une touffe de fleurs parjures à la lune,
(A la cire expirée, encor! s'effeuille l'une,)
De qui le long regret et les tiges de qui
Trempent en un seul verre à l'éclat alangui . . .
Une Aurore traînait ses ailes dans les larmes!

Ombre magicienne aux symboliques charmes!
Une voix, du passé longue évocation,
Est-ce la mienne prête à l'incantation?
Encore dans les plis jaunes de la pensée
Traînant, antique, ainsi qu'une toile encensée
Sur un confus amas d'ostensoirs refroidis,
Par les trous anciens et par les plis roidis
Percés selon le rythme et les dentelles pures
Du suaire laissant par ses belles guipures
Désespéré monter le vieil éclat voilé
S'élève, (ô quel lointain en ces appels celé!)
Le vieil éclat voilé du vermeil insolite,
De la voix languissant, nulle, sans acolyte,
Jettera-t-il son or par dernières splendeurs,
Elle, encore, l'antienne aux versets demandeurs,
A l'heure d'agonie et de luttes funèbres!
Et, force du silence et des noires ténèbres,
Tout rentre également en l'ancien passé,
Fatidique, vaincu, monotone, lassé,
Comme l'eau des bassins anciens se résigne.

Elle a chanté, parfois incohérente, signe
Lamentable!
         le lit aux pages de vélin,
Tel, inutile et si claustral, n'est pas le lin!
Qui des rêves par plis n'a plus le cher grimoire,
Ni le dais sépulcral à la déserte moire,
Le parfum des cheveux endormis. L'avait-il?
Froide enfant, de garder en son plaisir subtil
Au matin grelottant de fleurs, ses promenades,
Et quand le soir méchant a coupé les grenades!

far from the void bed veiled by a spent candle, an
aroma of cold bones roaming over the sachet,
a bunch of flowers faithless to the moon
(one is still shedding petals on the dead wax);
their stalks and their prolonged regret are steeped   35
in one solitary vase with languid brilliance.
A Dawn was dragging her wings in the pool's tears!

Sorceress shadow with symbolic charms!
A voice, a distant evocation of the past,
is it mine, is it ready to utter incantations?   40
still lingering in the yellow folds of thought,
drifting, antique, like incense-scented cloth
above a chaos of long-cold ostensories,
through all the ancient holes and stiffened folds
pierced in the rhythm and the shroud's pure lacework   45
letting old veiled gleam, desperate, ascend
through its lovely embroideries, there shall
rise: (O what distance hidden in those calls!)
the old veiled glimmer of a strange gilt-silver,
of the voice languishing, null, lacking acolytes,   50
will it—the antiphon still for petitions—
will it scatter its gold in final splendours
in the hour of death-agony and deadly struggles!
And so, by means of silence and dark shadows,
all things alike return to the long-distant past,   55
fateful, defeated, weary, and monotonous,
like water settling in some ancient pool.

She has sung, sometimes incoherently,
a lamentable sign!
                    the bed with vellum pages,
which, useless and so claustral, is not linen!   60
no longer with the crumpled scrawl of dreams
nor the sepulchral canopy in desolate watered silk,
the scent of sleeping hair. Did it ever possess that?
Cold little girl, preserving as her subtle pleasure
her walks in the dawn shivering with flowers   65
and when wicked dusk slit the pomegranates!

Le croissant, oui le seul est au cadran de fer
De l'horloge, pour poids suspendant Lucifer,
Toujours blesse, toujours une nouvelle heurée,
Par la clepsydre à la goutte obscure pleurée,
Que, délaissée, elle erre, et, sur son ombre, pas
Un ange accompagnant son indicible pas!
Il ne sait pas cela, le roi qui salarie
Depuis longtemps la gorge ancienne et tarie.
Son père ne sait pas cela, ni le glacier
Farouche reflétant de ses armes l'acier,
Quand, sur un tas gisant de cadavres sans coffre
Odorant de résine, énigmatique, il offre
Ses trompettes d'argent obscur aux vieux sapins!
Reviendra-t-il un jour des pays cisalpins!
Assez tôt? car tout est présage et mauvais rêve!
A l'ongle qui parmi le vitrage s'élève
Selon le souvenir des trompettes, le vieux
Ciel brûle, et change un doigt en un cierge envieux.
Et bientôt sa rougeur de triste crépuscule
Pénétrera du corps la cire qui recule!
De crépuscule, non, mais de rouge lever,
Lever du jour dernier qui vient tout achever,
Si triste se débat, que l'on ne sait plus l'heure
La rougeur de ce temps prophétique qui pleure
Sur l'enfant, exilée en son cœur précieux
Comme un cygne cachant en sa plume ses yeux,
Comme les mit le vieux cygne en sa plume, allée,
De la plume détresse, en l'éternelle allée
De ses espoirs, pour voir les diamants élus
D'une étoile, mourante, et qui ne brille plus!

Et . . .

The crescent moon, yes, the sole one is on the clock's
steel dial, with Lucifer slung as a weight,
constantly wounding, always some new hourful
wept by the dark drops of the water-clock   70
when she wanders abandoned, with not one angel over
her shadow to escort her inexpressible steps!
He knows nothing of that, the king whose pay
has so long hired those dried and aged breasts.
Her father does not know it, nor the wild   75
glacier mirroring his arms of steel,
when on some sprawling heap of corpses with no
resinous coffins, enigmatically he
offers his dim silvery trumpets to the old pines!
Will he return some day from the Cisalpine lands!   80
Soon enough? For all things are bad dreams and ill omens!
On the fingernail raised amid the stained-glass window
according to the memory of those trumpets,
the old sky burns, turning a finger into
an envious candle. Soon its sad dusk redness   85
will penetrate the body's waning wax!
Not dusk, no, but red dawn, dawn of the last day
that puts an end to everything, the redness of this
prophetic time struggles so sadly that
no-one can tell the hour any more; it weeps   90
over the child exiled in her own precious heart
like a swan veiling its eyes in its plumage
as the old swan plunged them there, and passed through
from the perturbed quills into the timeless avenue
leaving all hope, to see the diamond prize   95
of a star that no longer shines, but dies.

And . . .

Dans le jardin

La jeune dame qui marche sur la pelouse
Devant l'été paré de pommes et d'appas,
Quand des heures Midi comblé jette les douze,
Dans cette plénitude arrêtant ses beaux pas,

A dit un jour, tragique abandonnée—épouse—
A la Mort séduisant son Poëte: Trépas!
Tu mens. O vain climat nul! je me sais jalouse
Du faux Eden que, triste, il n'habitera pas.

Voilà pourquoi les fleurs profondes de la terre
L'aiment avec silence et savoir et mystère,
Tandis que dans leur cœur songe le pur pollen:

Et lui, lorsque la brise, ivre de ces délices,
Suspend encore un nom qui ravit les calices,
A voix faible, parfois, appelle bas: Ellen!

Sonnet

2 novembre 1877

—« Sur les bois oubliés quand passe l'hiver sombre
Tu te plains, ô captif solitaire du seuil,
Que ce sépulcre à deux qui fera notre orgueil
Hélas! du manque seul des lourds bouquets s'encombre.

Sans écouter Minuit qui jeta son vain nombre,
Une veille t'exalte à ne pas fermer l'œil
Avant que dans les bras de l'ancien fauteuil
Le suprême tison n'ait éclairé mon Ombre.

Qui veut souvent avoir la Visite ne doit
Par trop de fleurs charger la pierre que mon doigt
Soulève avec l'ennui d'une force défunte.

In the Garden

One day the young lady strolling over the lawn
before summer adorned with fruits and allurements,
when sated Noon had scattered the twelfth of the hours,
halted her fair steps amid such bounty

and, tragic abandoned bride, declared   5
to Death enticing her Poet: 'O vain and void realm,
Doom, you are telling a lie! I know I am jealous
of the false Eden where he, in his grief, will never be dwelling.'

Therefore the earth's profound flowers
adore her in silence and wisdom and mystery   10
while the pure pollen is dreaming within their hearts:

and he, when the breeze, ravished by such delights,
still holds in suspense a name that enraptures the blossoms,
at times, in frail tones, softly calls: 'Ellen!'

Sonnet

2 November 1877

'When sombre winter sweeps over the forgotten woods
you lament, O lonely prisoner of the threshold,
that this tomb for two, in which we will take pride
alas! is burdened only with the weight of absent bouquets.

'Heedless of Midnight tolling its vain number,   5
a vigil is rousing you never to close your eyes
till the final ember has illumined my Shadow
in the old armchair's embrace.

'Someone who longs to be Visited often should never
load too many flowers on the stone which my finger   10
is lifting with the weariness of a departed strength.

Ame au si clair foyer tremblante de m'asseoir,
Pour revivre il suffit qu'à tes lèvres j'emprunte
Le souffle de mon nom murmuré tout un soir. »

[« Rien, au réveil, que vous n'ayez . . . »]

Rien, au réveil, que vous n'ayez
Envisagé de quelque moue
Pire si le rire secoue
Votre aile sur les oreillers.

Indifféremment sommeillez
Sans crainte qu'une haleine avoue
Rien, au réveil, que vous n'ayez
Envisagé de quelque moue.

Tous les rêves émerveillés,
Quand cette beauté les déjoue,
Ne produisent fleur sur la joue
Dans l'œil diamants impayés
Rien, au réveil, que vous n'ayez.

Sonnet

pour elle

O si chère de loin et proche et blanche, si
Délicieusement toi, Méry, que je songe
A quelque baume rare émané par mensonge
Sur aucun bouquetier de cristal obscurci.

Le sais-tu, oui! pour moi voici des ans, voici
Toujours que ton sourire éblouissant prolonge
La même rose avec son bel été qui plonge
Dans autrefois et puis dans le futur aussi.

'To revive me, a soul trembling to sit at so bright a fireplace,
I need only borrow from your lips
the breath of my name murmured all evening.'

['Nothing on waking . . .']

Nothing on waking that you never had
contemplated with a kind of pout
worse still if a laugh should shake
your wing upon the pillows.

Sleep on impassively with no fear   5
that a breath might confess
something on waking that you never had
contemplated with a kind of pout.

All the dreams that are amazed
when they are baffled by such beauty   10
lend not one flower to the cheek
unpaid diamonds in the eye
anything on waking that you never had.

Sonnet

for her

O so dear from afar and nearby and sheer white, so
deliciously yourself, dear Méry, that I
dream of some rare balm shed by deceit
on whichever vase of darkened crystal

do you know, yes! for me it is years ago, it is   5
forever that your dazzling smile has prolonged
the same rose with its fair summertime plunging
into the past and the future as well.

Mon cœur qui dans les nuits parfois cherche à s'entendre
Ou de quel dernier mot t'appeler le plus tendre,
S'exalte en celui rien que chuchoté de Sœur—

N'était, très grand trésor et tête si petite,
Que tu m'enseignes bien toute une autre douceur
Tout bas par le baiser seul dans tes cheveux dite.

[« Dame Sans trop d'ardeur . . . »]

Dame
          Sans trop d'ardeur à la fois enflammant
La rose qui cruelle ou déchirée, et lasse
Même du blanc habit de pourpre, le délace
Pour ouïr dans sa chair pleurer le diamant

Oui, sans ces crises de rosée et gentiment
Ni brise quoique, avec, le ciel orageux passe
Jalouse d'apporter je ne sais quel espace
Au simple jour le jour très vrai du sentiment

Ne te semble-t-il pas, disons, que chaque année
Dont sur ton front renaît la grâce spontanée
Suffise selon quelque apparence et pour moi

Comme un éventail frais dans la chambre s'étonne
A raviver du peu qu'il faut ici d'émoi
Toute notre native amitié monotone.

[« Si tu veux nous nous aimerons . . . »]

          Si tu veux nous nous aimerons
          Avec tes lèvres sans le dire
          Cette rose ne l'interromps
          Qu'à verser un silence pire

My heart which sometimes at night strives to listen
or call you by whatever ultimate tenderest word   10
rejoices in none but a whisper of 'Sister'—

were it not that you, a treasure so great and a head so tiny,
are teaching me quite another endearment
uttered softly by the kiss in your hair alone.

['Lady Without too much passion . . .']

Lady
        Without too much passion at one time inflaming
the rose who, cruel or tattered and weary
of even her white robe, unlaces it with crimson
to hear the diamond weeping deep in her flesh

yes, without those crises of dew and gently   5
nor any breeze, though with it the stormy sky clears,
jealous to bring some unknown space
to the mere day, the true day of feeling

have you perhaps a sense, let us say, that each year
whose spontaneous grace is reborn on your brow   10
is enough in certain apparent respects and for me,

as a cool fan in the room is amazed
to revive with what little stir here is required
the whole of our natural monochrome friendship.

['If you wish we shall make love . . .']

            If you wish we shall make love
            with your lips wordlessly
            never break off that rose
            except to shed worse silence

Jamais de chants ne lancent prompts
Le scintillement du sourire
Si tu veux nous nous aimerons
Avec tes lèvres sans le dire

Muet muet entre les ronds
Sylphe dans la pourpre d'empire
Un baiser flambant se déchire
Jusqu'aux pointes des ailerons
Si tu veux nous nous aimerons

Types de la rue

Le Marchand d'ail et d'oignons

L'ennui d'aller en visite
Avec l'ail nous l'éloignons.
L'élégie au pleur hésite
Peu si je fends des oignons.

Le Cantonnier

Ces cailloux, tu les nivelles
Et c'est, comme troubadour,
Un cube aussi de cervelles
Qu'il me faut ouvrir par jour.

Le Crieur d'imprimés

Toujours, n'importe le titre,
Sans même s'enrhumer au
Dégel, ce gai siffle-litre
Crie un premier numéro.

La Femme du carrier

La femme, l'enfant, la soupe
En chemin pour le carrier
Le complimentent qu'il coupe
Dans l'us de se marier.

no song can ever spark 5
the sudden gleam of a smile
if you wish we shall make love
with your lips wordlessly

softly softly between the rounds
sylph in imperial purple 10
a flaming kiss is sundered
on the very tips of the pinions
if you wish we shall make love

Street Folk

The Seller of Garlic and Onions

With garlic we distance the tedium
of paying a visit;
whenever I cut an onion
weeping Elegy can hardly wait.

The Roadmender

You level those pebbles
and, being a troubadour,
I too must crack open
a cube of brains each day.

The Newsboy

Over and over, whatever the headline,
without even catching a cold when the
ice thaws, this cheery little half-pint
keeps calling out some new number.

The Quarryman's Wife

Wife and child and soup
en route to the quarryman
congratulate him for cutting into
the habit of getting married.

La Marchande d'habits

Le vif œil dont tu regardes
Jusques à leur contenu
Me sépare de mes hardes
Et comme un dieu je vais nu.

Le Vitrier

Le pur soleil qui remise
Trop d'éclat pour l'y trier
Ote ébloui sa chemise
Sur le dos du vitrier.

Éventail

de Méry Laurent

De frigides roses pour vivre
Toutes la même interrompront
Avec un blanc calice prompt
Votre souffle devenu givre

Mais que mon battement délivre
La touffe par un choc profond
Cette frigidité se fond
En du rire de fleurir ivre

A jeter le ciel en détail
Voilà comme bon éventail
Tu conviens mieux qu'une fiole

Nul n'enfermant à l'émeri
Sans qu'il y perde ou le viole
L'arôme émané de Méry.

The Old Clothes Woman

Your keen eye parts me from my togs
peering right into their contents
so that like a god I
go naked.

The Glazier

The bright sun shedding
a brilliance too great to be sorted
dazzled takes off its shirt
on the glazier's back.

Fan

Belonging to Méry Laurent

Frigid roses to exist
all alike will interrupt
your frosted breath
with a quick white calyx

but should my fluttering liberate   5
the whole bunch with a profound shock
that frigidity will melt into the laughter
of a rapturous blossoming

see how like a good fan
you are better than a phial   10
at carving the sky into fragments

no flask could be stoppered
without losing or violating
the fragrance of Méry.

Hommage

Toute Aurore même gourde
A crisper un poing obscur
Contre des clairons d'azur
Embouchés par cette sourde

A le pâtre avec la gourde
Jointe au bâton frappant dur
Le long de son pas futur
Tant que la source ample sourde

Par avance ainsi tu vis
O solitaire Puvis
De Chavannes
            jamais seul

De conduire le temps boire
A la nymphe sans linceul
Que lui découvre ta gloire

Petit Air

(*guerrier*)

Ce me va hormis l'y taire
Que je sente du foyer
Un pantalon militaire
A ma jambe rougeoyer

L'invasion je la guette
Avec le vierge courroux
Tout juste de la baguette
Au gant blanc des tourlourous

Nue ou d'écorce tenace
Pas pour battre le Teuton
Mais comme une autre menace
A la fin que me veut-on

Homage

Every Dawn however numb
when she lifts a dark fist to
grip the trumpets of the blue
which she blows though deaf and dumb

has the shepherd with the gourd   5
plus the rod struck forcibly
where his future steps will be
till the vast spring is outpoured

So you live facing the brink
O Puvis far from the crowd   10
de Chavannes
               never alone

as you lead our time to drink
at the nymph without a shroud
which your glory will make known.

Little Ditty

(*Warlike*)

When I feel my leg reddish–dyed
dressed in a pair of military
pantaloons by the fireside
it (not to keep my peace) suits me

I wait for onslaughts to begin   5
with the virgin hostility
of nothing but a drumstick in
the white gloves of the soldiery

stark bare or keeping its bark yet,
not to outgeneral Germany   10
but as a different kind of threat
to the end that is sought from me,

De trancher ras cette ortie
Folle de la sympathie

[« Toute l'âme résumée . . . »]

Toute l'âme résumée
Quand lente nous l'expirons
Dans plusieurs ronds de fumée
Abolis en autres ronds

Atteste quelque cigare
Brûlant savamment pour peu
Que la cendre se sépare
De son clair baiser de feu

Ainsi le chœur des romances
A ta lèvre vole-t-il
Exclus-en si tu commences
Le réel parce que vil

Le sens trop précis rature
Ta vague littérature

Tombeau

Anniversaire—Janvier 1897

Le noir roc courroucé que la bise le roule
Ne s'arrêtera ni sous de pieuses mains
Tâtant sa ressemblance avec les maux humains
Comme pour en bénir quelque funeste moule.

Ici presque toujours si le ramier roucoule
Cet immatériel deuil opprime de maints
Nubiles plis l'astre mûri des lendemains
Dont un scintillement argentera la foule.

to cut short all the lunacy
of the wild nettle Sympathy.

['All the soul that we evoke . . .']

All the soul that we evoke
when we shed it lingering
into various rings of smoke
each effaced by a new ring

testifies to some cigar   5
burning with much artifice
as the ash falls away far
from its lucid fiery kiss

should the choir of lyric art
fly toward your own lips thus   10
exclude from it if you start
the real which is villainous

sense too definite cancels your
indistinct literature.

Tomb

Anniversary—January 1897

The black rock, cross (how the north wind has rolled
it on!) won't stop even by pious throngs
handling its parity with human wrongs
as if that consecrates some fatal mould.

Here almost always if the dove has cooed,   5
with nubile folds its immaterial sorrow
oppresses the ripe star of that tomorrow
whose glint will silver all the multitude.

Qui cherche, parcourant le solitaire bond
Tantôt extérieur de notre vagabond—
Verlaine? Il est caché parmi l'herbe, Verlaine

A ne surprendre que naïvement d'accord
La lèvre sans y boire ou tarir son haleine
Un peu profond ruisseau calomnié la mort.

[« Au seul souci de voyager . . . »]

Au seul souci de voyager
Outre une Inde splendide et trouble
—Ce salut va, le messager
Du temps, cap que ta poupe double

Comme sur quelque vergue bas
Plongeante avec la caravelle
Écumait toujours en ébats
Un oiseau d'ivresse nouvelle

Qui criait monotonement
Sans que la barre ne varie
Un inutile gisement
Nuit, désespoir et pierrerie

Par son chant reflété jusqu'au
Sourire du pâle Vasco.

Hérodiade

Le Cantique de saint Jean

Le soleil que sa halte
Surnaturelle exalte
Aussitôt redescend
Incandescent

Who, following our vagabond's withdrawn
leap (once external) still desires to see   10
Verlaine? Verlaine is hidden in the lawn

to catch no more than in plain harmony
before the lip drank there or spent its breath
a much-maligned and shallow trickle, death.

['For the sole task of travelling . . .']

For the sole task of travelling
beyond India fraught and sublime—
goes this salute, envoy from time,
the cape your stern is compassing

as on some spar lowly in station   5
plummeting with the caravel
constantly frolicked through the swell
a bird of new intoxication

which cried in a drab monotone
though the helm never swerved aside   10
a bearing that could be no guide
night and despair and precious stone

by its song mirrored all the while
as far as pale-cheeked Vasco's smile.

Herodias

Canticle of John the Baptist

The sun that was exalted
when it miraculously halted
is once more sinking low
brightly aglow

Je sens comme aux vertèbres
S'éployer des ténèbres
Toutes dans un frisson
  A l'unisson

Et ma tête surgie
Solitaire vigie
Dans les vols triomphaux
  De cette faux

Comme rupture franche
Plutôt refoule ou tranche
Les anciens désaccords
  Avec le corps

Qu'elle de jeûnes ivre
S'opiniâtre à suivre
En quelque bond hagard
  Son pur regard

Là-haut où la froidure
Éternelle n'endure
Que vous le surpassiez
  Tous ô glaciers

Mais selon un baptême
Illuminée au même
Principe qui m'élut
  Penche un salut.

I seem to feel shadowy   5
wings unfurl in my vertebrae
which are shuddering one
    and all in unison

and my head now full-blown
a watchman on its own   10
in the victory flights made
    by the scythe's blade

as a clean severance may
suppress or cut away
the immemorial war so   15
    long fought against the torso

rather than drunk with fasting
commit itself to lasting
pursuit of its pure sight
    in some wild flight   20

on high where the perpetual
coldness cannot endure that all
of you O frozen glaciers
    are its superiors

but as an act of baptism my   25
head was illuminated by
the principle of my salvation
    and bows in salutation.

APPENDIX 2

Vers de circonstances

Les Loisirs de la poste

[Cette publication tout à l'honneur de la Poste. Aucune des adresses en vers reproduites ici n'a manqué son destinaire.

Le poëte ajoute que l'idée lui en vint à cause d'un rapport évident entre le format des enveloppes et la disposition d'un quatrain—par pur sentiment esthétique. Il les multiplia au gré de ses relations.]— THE EDITOR.

Leur rire avec la même gamme
Sonnera si tu te rendis
Chez Monsieur Whistler et Madame,
Rue Antique du Bac 110.

Rue, au 23, Ballu.
                    J'exprime
Sitôt Juin à Monsieur Degas
La satisfaction qu'il rime
Avec la fleur des syringas.

Monsieur Monet que l'hiver ni
L'été, sa vision ne leurre,
Habite, en peignant, Giverny
Sis auprès de Vernon, dans l'Eure.

Villa des Arts, près l'avenue
De Clichy, peint Monsieur Renoir
Qui devant une épaule nue
Broie autre chose que du noir.

APPENDIX 2

Occasional Verses

Postal Recreations

[A publication entirely to the glory of the Postal Service. None of the verse addresses reproduced below failed to reach its destination.

The poet adds that the idea came to him purely for aesthetic reasons, because of an obvious similarity between the format of a postal address and the layout of a quatrain. He has penned many such things to entertain his friends.]—THE EDITOR.

> Their laughter will resound
> in harmony if you should visit
> Mr and Mrs Whistler,
> 110 old Rue du Bac.

> 23 Rue Ballu.
>   Now June is here
> I express my satisfaction
> that Monsieur Degas rhymes
> with the mock-orange blossom.

> Monsieur Monet, whose vision
> goes astray neither in winter nor in summer,
> lives painting at Giverny
> located near Vernon, in the Eure.

> At the Villa des Arts, near the Avenue
> de Clichy, paints Monsieur Renoir
> who gets something other than the blues
> when faced with a bare shoulder.

Paris, chez Madame Méry
Laurent, qui vit loin des profanes
Dans sa maisonnette *very*
Select du 9 Boulevard Lannes.

Pour rire se restaurant
La rate ou le charmant foie
Madame Méry Laurent
Aux eaux d'Évian
                              Savoie.

Dans sa douillette d'astrakan
Sans qu'un vent coulis le jalouse
Monsieur François Coppée à Caen
Rue, or c'est *des Chanoines*, 12.

Monsieur Mendès aussi Catulle
A toute la Muse debout
Dispense la brise et le tulle
Rue, au 66, Taitbout.

Adieu l'orme et le châtaignier!
Malgré ce que leur cime a d'or
S'en revient Henri de Régnier
Rue, au six même, Boccador.

Notre ami Vielé Griffin
Savoure très longtemps sa gloire
Comme un plat solitaire et fin
A Nazelles dans Indre-et-Loire.

Paris, the home of Madame Méry
Laurent, who dwells far from the vulgar herd
in her *très chic* little house
at 9 Boulevard Lannes.

Amusing herself by fattening up
her spleen or charming liver
Madame Méry Laurent
at the waters of Évian
                    Savoy.

Envied by no draught
in his astrakhan overcoat
Monsieur François Coppée at 12
Rue—now it's *des Chanoines*, Caen.

Monsieur Mendès a.k.a. Catulle
attentive to the Muse
distributes breeze and tulle
at 66 Rue Taitbout.

Farewell to the elm and chestnut!
Despite the gold of their crowns
Henri de Régnier has come back
to exactly 6 Rue Boccador.

Our friend Vielé-Griffin
is savouring his fame very slowly
like a lone and exquisite dish
at Nazelles in Indre-et-Loire.

Apte à ne point te cabrer, hue!
Poste et j'ajouterai: dia!
Si tu ne fuis 11 bis rue
Balzac chez cet Hérédia.

Apporte ce livre, quand naît
Sur le Bois l'Aurore amaranthe,
Chez Madame Eugène Manet
Rue au loin Villejust 40.

Sans t'étendre dans l'herbe verte
Naïf distributeur, mets-y
Du tien, cours chez Madame Berthe
Manet, par Meulan, à Mézy.

Mademoiselle Ponsot, puisse
Notre compliment dans sa fleur
Vous saluer au Châlet-Suisse
Sis route de Trouville, Honfleur.

Rue, et 8, de la Barouillère
Sur son piano s'applique à
Jouer, fée autant qu'écolière,
Mademoiselle Wrotnowska.

Si tu veux un médecin tel
Sans perruque ni calvitie
Qu'est le cher docteur Hutinel
Treize, entends—de la Boétie.

Never inclined to buck, gee up!
Postal Service and I'll add: whoa!
if you don't shun 11b Rue Balzac,
the home of a certain Heredia.

Bear this book, when amaranthine
Dawn is born above the Woods,
to Madame Eugène Manet
at 40 faraway Rue Villejust.

Without taking a tumble in the grass
innocent distributor, do
your part, hurry to Madame Berthe
Manet, at Mézy, by Meulan.

Mademoiselle Ponsot, may our best
wishes in full bloom
greet you at Châlet-Suisse
located at Route de Trouville, Honfleur.

8 and Rue de la Barouillère
where Mademoiselle Wrotnowska,
fairy and student alike,
is working hard at her piano-playing.

If you are seeking a medico like
with neither wig nor baldness
dear Doctor Hutinel
13, see—de la Boétie.

Prends ta canne à bec de corbin
Vieille Poste (ou je fais t'en battre)
Et cours chez le docteur Robin
Rue, oui, de Saint-Pétersbourg 4.

Au fond de Saint-James, Neuilly,
Le docteur Fournier n'a d'idée,
Songeur, prudent et recueilli,
Que de courtiser l'orchidée.

Augusta Holmès accourue
En tant qu'une blanche parente
Des rois joueurs de harpe, rue
Juliette Lamber, 40.

Arrête-toi, porteur, au son
Gémi par les violoncelles,
C'est chez Monsieur Ernest Chausson,
22 Boulevard de Courcelles.

Rue, ouïs! 22 Lavoisier
Madame Degrandi qui lance
La richesse de son gosier
Aussi haut que notre silence.

Au 137, avenue
Malakoff, Madame Tola
Dorian; celle qui vola
Le feu de la céleste nue.

L'âge aidant à m'appesantir
Il faut que toi, ma pensée, ailles
Seule rue 11 de Traktir
Chez l'aimable Monsieur Séailles.

Take your walking-stick (or I'll
beat you with it) old Postal Service
and run to the home of Doctor Robin,
4 Rue, yes, de Saint-Pétersbourg.

In the depths of Saint-James, Neuilly,
Doctor Fournier, pensive, prudent, reflective,
thinks of courting
only an orchid.

Augusta Holmès sought after
as a fair relative
of the harp-playing kings, at 40
Rue Juliette Lamber.

Halt, postman, at the sound
groaned by the cellos: it's
the home of Monsieur Ernest Chausson,
22 Boulevard de Courcelles.

22 Rue, hear ye! Lavoisier
Madame Degrandi who casts
the riches of her throat
so high that they reach our silence.

At 137 Avenue
Malakoff, Madame Tola
Dorian; she who stole
the fire from the clouds of heaven.

Age is helping to weigh me down
so you, my thought, must go alone
to 11 Rue de Traktir,
the home of the charming Monsieur Séailles.

A Montigny, Monsieur Grosclaude
Vise un lapin sans dévier
Ou, vêtu de sa verte blaude
Jette dans le Loing l'épervier.

Monsieur Mirbeau, Pont de l'Arche
(Eure)
         Toi qui vois les Damps
Facteur, ralentis la marche
Et jette ceci dedans.

A moins qu'il ne hante la nue,
Ne vogue où mûrit le letchi,
Monsieur Léon Dierx, avenue
Ci proche, 13, de Clichy.

Tapi sous ton chaud mac-ferlane,
Ce billet, quand tu le recois
Lis le haut; 6, cour Saint-François
Rue, est-ce Moreau? cher Verlaine.

Éventails

Mme M. R.

Simple, tendre, aux prés se mêlant,
Ce que tout buisson a de laine
Quand a passé le troupeau blanc
Semble l'âme de Madeleine.

Jadis frôlant avec émoi
Ton dos de licorne ou de fée,
Aile ancienne, donne-moi
L'horizon dans une bouffée.

At Montigny, Monsieur Grosclaude
takes unwavering aim at a rabbit
or else, clad in his green smock,
casts a sweep-net into the Loing.

Monsieur Mirbeau, Pont de l'Arche
(Eure)
          O postman who sees Les Damps,
tarry a little
and drop this there.

Unless he is haunting the clouds
or sailing where the litchi ripens,
Monsieur Léon Dierx, 13
Avenue de Clichy, close at hand.

Ensconced in your warm Inverness cape,
when you receive this note
read it aloud; 6 Cour Saint-François,
Rue—is it Moreau? dear Verlaine.

Fans

Mme M. R.

Simple, soft, blending with the fields,
the fleece that all the shrubbery yields
when the white flocks have crossed the plain
might be the soul of Madeleine.

Formerly brushing vibrantly
across your unicorn's or fair-
y's back, O ancient wing, grant me
whole vistas in one gust of air.

Mme N. M.

Autour de marbres le lis croît—
Brise, ne commence par taire,
Fière et blanche, son regard droit,
Nelly pareille à ce parterre.

Mlle G. M.

Là-bas de quelque vaste aurore
Pour que son vol revienne vers
Ta petite main qui s'ignore
J'ai marqué cette aile d'un vers.

Mme de R.

Fermé, je suis le sceptre aux doigts
Et, contente de cet empire,
Ne m'ouvrez, aile, si je dois
Dissimuler votre sourire.

Offrandes à divers du Faune

Ce Faune, s'il vous eût assise
Dans un bosquet, n'en serait pas
A gonfler sa flûte indécise
Du trouble épars de ses vieux pas.

Faune, qui dans une éclaircie
Vas te glisser tout en dormant
Avec quatre vers remercie
Dujardin ton frère normand.

Faune, si tu prends un costume
Simple comme les liserons
Dujardin et moi non posthume
Nous te populariserons.

Mme N. M.

Amid the marbles a lily grows—
never, O breeze, seek to oppose
her frank gaze, fair high-spirited
Nelly so like this flowerbed.

Mlle G. M.

From some far-flung dawn in a far-off land
so that its flight may now reverse
toward your tiny unconscious hand
I have marked this wing with a little verse.

Mme de R.

Shut, I am the fingers' sceptre; and,
content simply to rule that land,
do not spread me out, wing, as I'll
be obliged to disguise your smile.

Presenting the *Faun* to Various People

Had he sat you down in a grove,
this Faun would not have been reduced
to swelling his hesitant flute
with the desultory pangs of his old steps.

O Faun, as you steal through a clearing
fast asleep,
thank your Norman brother Dujardin
in four lines.

Faun, if you should wear a garb
simple as bindweed
Dujardin and I will make you popular
not posthumously.

Fallait-il que tu t'assoupisses,
Faune qu'aujourd'hui l'on connaît,
Pour attendre ces temps propices
Avant d'aller chez Baronet.

Sa flûte un peu de côté
Il en joue et se recule
L'espoir de connaître ôté
A qui va cet opuscule.

Laid Faune! comme passe aux bocages un train
Qui siffle ce que bas le chalumeau soupire
Vas-tu par trop de flamme empêcher ce quatrain
Maladroit à la taire ou, s'il la disait, pire.

Satyre aux baisers inexperts
Qui pourchasses outre la brune
La fauve Nymphe, tu les perds
Il n'est d'extase qu'avec une.

Invitation à la soirée d'inauguration
de la Revue indépendante

Caressé par la réussite
Et dans les gants les plus étroits,
Édouard Dujardin sollicite
Qu'autour de neuf heures, le trois

Mars, pas même l'ombre endossée
D'un habit à crachats divers!
Vous visitez, onze, Chaussée
D'Antin, son magasin de vers:

Rightly did you have a little doze,
O Faun now so well-known,
and wait for these auspicious days
when you can go to Baronet.

With his flute a bit askance
he plays a tune and retreats
having taken away all hope of cognizance
from this little book's recipient.

Must you hoot like a passing train in the thickets
what the pipe alone sighs *sotto voce*, ugly Faun!—
must you show too much passion and obstruct this
   little quatrain,
clumsy at stifling such feelings—and even worse, if they
   were uttered.

O Satyr pursuing not only the brunette
but the shy Nymph as well,
you are wasting your clumsy kisses
there is rapture only with one.

Invitation to the Inaugural Soirée of the *Revue indépendante*

Coddled by success
and in gloves of the tightest kind,
Édouard Dujardin requests
that on the third of March, around nine,

without wearing the tiniest jot
of formal dress or badge of rank!
you visit his poetry shop
at 11 Chaussée-d'Antin:

5

La REVUE avec bruit qu'on nomme
INDÉPENDANTE, Monsieur, pend
Une crémaillère d'or comme
Le gaz en son local pimpant.

Toast

Comme un cherché de sa province
Sobre convive mais lecteur
Vous aimâtes que je revinsse
Très cher Monsieur le Directeur

Partager la joie élargie
Jusqu'à m'admettre dans leur rang
De ceux couronnant une orgie
Sans la fève ni le hareng

Aussi je tends
                    avec le rire
—Écume sur ce vin dispos—
Qui ne saurait se circonscrire
Entre la lèvre et des pipeaux

A vous dont un regard me coupe
La louange
                    haut notre Coupe

the REVIEW called INDEPENDENT by
the talk of the town, my dear Sir, is   10
warming its house with gold like
the gas in its smart premises.

Toast

As a man sought from his own province
a sober guest yet a reader
you wished me to return
dearest Headmaster

and share the happiness that extends   5
even to finding myself a place in the ranks
of those who are crowning a revel
with neither beans nor herring

So I raise
                with a smile
—a foam set on this wine—   10
which could not be confined
between lips and pipes

to you whose merest glance cuts short
my praise
                our Cup high

EXPLANATORY NOTES

In the prefatory note he reluctantly provided for the *Cosmopolis* edition of *A Dice Throw At Any Time Never Will Abolish Chance*, Mallarmé wrote: 'I would prefer this Note not to be read, or to be glanced at and then actually forgotten; it teaches the practised Reader little that is located beyond his perception: yet may cause trouble for the novice.' He himself rarely attempted to elucidate his works 'in plain prose', and on the few occasions when he did so, his explanations fell far short of the verse originals in power and significance. Notes by any later writer must be even less satisfactory; they too should either not be read at all, or else be glanced at and then forgotten. The 'meaning' of these poems is located in the poems themselves, not in anything that can be written about them.

The notes below are keyed to the line numbers in the margin of the English translations. In the case of *A Dice Throw* . . ., pages are customarily numbered from 1 to 11 (reckoning each opening—verso plus recto—as a single page). Thus '3: 8' is the eighth line down on the poem's third page (regardless of whether that line appears on the verso or the recto, or even on both).

Poetical Works

Mallarmé first collected his *Poésies* in a de-luxe edition of about forty copies, published by *La Revue indépendante* in October 1887. The poems were grouped in nine sections as follows:

I. First Poems ('Ill Fortune', 'Apparition', 'Futile Petition', 'A Punishment for the Clown').

II. The *Parnasse satirique* ('A negress . . .').

III. The first *Parnasse contemporain* series ('The Windows', 'The Flowers', 'Renewal', 'Anguish', 'Weary of bitter rest . . .', 'The Bell-Ringer', 'Summer Sadness', 'The Blue', 'Sea Breeze', 'Sigh', 'Alms').

IV. Other Poems ('Fan', 'Saint', 'Gift of the Poem').

V. 'Herodias'.

VI. 'A Faun in the Afternoon'.

VII. 'Funerary Toast'.

VIII. 'Prose'.

IX. Last Sonnets ('This virginal long-living lovely day . . .', 'When the shade threatened . . .', 'The fine suicide . . .', 'With her pure nails . . .', 'The Tomb of Edgar Allan Poe', 'Homage' ['Already mourning . . .'], 'My old tomes closed . . .', 'What silk with balm . . .', 'Sonnet-Cycle' ['Does every Pride in the evening smoke . . .', 'Arisen from the rump and bound . . .', 'A lace vanishes utterly . . .'], 'To introduce myself into your tale . . .').

For the revised edition, prepared in 1894, Mallarmé omitted the headings but kept the same main sections: the early poems; the poems from the first (1866) series of *Le Parnasse contemporain* (an anthology that brought together

the work of various younger poets reacting against the literary orthodoxy of the time); the four relatively long and ambitious poems 'Herodias', 'A Faun', 'Funerary Toast', and 'Prose'; finally the later sonnets (first the tetralogy, then the poems of homage, then the others).

The 1894 arrangement differed in prefacing the collection with a dedicatory sonnet ('Toast'), omitting 'A negress . . .', redistributing the 'Other Poems' ('Fan', plus eight other short occasional pieces, now formed a new section between 'Prose' and the late sonnets), and reshuffling somewhat the order of the 'Last Sonnets' (to which two recently composed poems were added). But these differences were relatively minor; as Mallarmé acknowledged in his bibliographical note at the end of the book, its basic structure had already been settled by 1887.

The volume prepared in 1894 was not actually published until 1899 (a year after Mallarmé's death), when his daughter Geneviève inserted three further items. However, the present edition restores the 1894 arrangement, which is the last known to have been approved by the author himself.

In a letter to Verlaine on 16 November 1885, Mallarmé characterized the collection as 'an album rather than a book'. Its design was not random, but its author did not claim for it the overall unity attempted in, for example, Baudelaire's *Les Fleurs du mal* (1857) or Hugo's *Les Contemplations* (1856) and *La Légende des siècles* (1859–83).

Poésies is a more formal word than *poèmes*, the term that Mallarmé applied to his prose poems. Our rendering 'poetical works' is an attempt to suggest something of the difference.

Toast ['Nothing, this foam, this virgin verse . . .']

Written January 1893; recited by Mallarmé at a literary banquet on 9 February, and published in *La Plume* on 15 February. The speaker addresses his colleagues, raising his glass and comparing its foam to the poem he is reciting.

6   *with myself on the poop-deck now*: the speaker presents himself as lagging behind the younger and more adventurous writers in his audience.

12   *solitude, star, or rocky coast*: the syntax is characteristically ambiguous and double-edged; the three items could be either literary goals ('things . . . deserving of our sail's white preoccupation') or dangers that might oppose the attainment of those goals.

Ill Fortune

Written early 1862, and partly published 15 March 1862 in *L'Artiste*; substantially revised in 1887. A sardonic reply to Baudelaire's poem of the same title; it suggests that the effects of 'Ill Fortune' are often less glamorous and more pedestrian than the older poet had claimed.

The illustrious writers of ll. 1–19, who see misfortune as something noble ('A mighty angel') and draw sustenance from it ('They suck Sorrow's teat'— an image used by Baudelaire in 'Le Cygne'), are contrasted with their numerous ill-starred 'brothers', who suffer wretchedly in the pursuit of art,

mocked (ll. 52–60) by those who have sold out to please the public. In 1862 Baudelaire might well have seemed to belong in the first category; he was still in excellent health and had just issued the successful revised edition of *Les Fleurs du mal*. In the second class Mallarmé was evidently thinking of Gérard de Nerval (whose body was found hanging from a streetlamp in 1855)—and also of himself. 'Remember my poem "Ill Fortune"? I, alas, am in the second class', he wrote to his friend Henri Cazalis on 4 June 1862. In both form and content, the poem is particularly indebted to Théophile Gautier's 1837 'Ténèbres'.

25   *Prometheus with no vulture*: in Classical mythology, Prometheus stole fire from heaven and brought it to humanity; as a punishment, the gods bound him to a mountain with a vulture devouring his entrails. These poets do Promethean deeds but suffer less illustrious punishments.

Apparition

Written mid-1863; published 24 November 1883 in Verlaine's essay on Mallarmé in *Lutèce*. The apparition of a dreamlike female figure, intangible and unidentifiable, transforms the evening scene: the poem starts with a sad moon, and ends with showers of 'scented stars'.

Futile Petition

Written early 1862 for Anne-Marie Gaillard (Nina de Villard, 1843–84), an active supporter of the young 'Parnassian' poets; published 25 February 1862 in *Le Papillon*, and substantially revised in 1887. In a letter of 24 May 1862 Mallarmé described it as 'a Louis XV style sonnet'—that is, an eighteenth-century pastiche of a kind fashionable during the 1850s and 1860s, which will be most familiar to present-day readers from Verlaine's *Fêtes galantes* (1869). The beloved, surrounded by stock rococo accessories (lapdog, lozenge, fan, abbé in attendance) and portrayed as both princess and shepherdess, is raising to her lips a cup of Sèvres porcelain decorated with a naked figure of Hebe (the Classical goddess of youth and cupbearer to the gods).

The earliest surviving draft (1862), entitled simply 'Placet' ('Petition'), reads as follows:

> J'ai longtemps rêvé d'être, ô duchesse, l'Hébé
> Qui rit sur votre tasse au baiser de tes lèvres,
> Mais je suis un poète, un peu moins qu'un abbé,
> Et n'ai point jusqu'ici figuré sur le Sèvres.
>
> Puisque je ne suis pas ton bichon embarbé,
> Ni tes bonbons, ni ton carmin, ni les Jeux mièvres
> Et que sur moi pourtant ton regard est tombé,
> Blonde, dont les coiffeurs divins sont des orfèvres,
>
> Nommez-nous . . .—vous de qui les souris framboisés
> Sont un troupeau poudré d'agneaux apprivoisés

Qui vont broutant les cœurs et bêlant aux délires,—
Nommez-nous . . .—et Boucher sur un rose éventail
Me peindra, flûte aux mains, endormant ce bercail,
Duchesse, nommez-nous berger de vos sourires.

[Duchess, I have long wished to be the Hebe who
is smiling on the Sèvres cup which your lips kiss,
but I am a mere poet—less than an abbé, this!—
and on that cup I never was placed hitherto.

Because I am not your bewhiskered lapdog, nor
your lipstick, your sweets, or coquettish Revelries
and since you nonetheless yielded to me, therefore,
O blonde whose hair is dressed by goldsmith deities,

appoint us—you whose many teasing brambled wiles
form a powder-wigged flock of little tame pet sheep
nibbling at every heart, bleating with no restraint,—

appoint us—and Boucher on a pink fan will paint
me, flute in my hand, as I lull the lambs to sleep,
dear Duchess, do appoint us shepherd of your smiles.]

François Boucher (1703–70) was a well-known painter of rococo pastoral scenes for the eighteenth-century aristocracy.

A Punishment for the Clown

Written by March 1864; after radical revision, published October 1887 in the *Revue indépendante* edition of Mallarmé's *Poésies*. The speaker is not only a poet writing with a pen by lamplight, but also a plume-hatted actor, a 'bad Hamlet' before the footlights. Yearning to break out of this world, he plunges into the lakes of someone's eyes (in the 1864 draft, his beloved's; but the 1887 text is less specific) and is washed pure from his greasepaint—only to find himself in a sterile, glacial realm: without the 'base' props of the stage, he no longer has his 'genius' (1864 text), his 'consecration' (1887 text). The poem was suggested by Théodore de Banville's virtuoso showpiece 'Le Saut du tremplin' (from *Odes funambulesques*, 1857), in which a leaping circus clown bursts through the tent and soars up into the stars.

The earliest surviving draft (1864) reads as follows:

Pour ses yeux,—pour nager dans ces lacs, dont les quais
Sont plantés de beaux cils qu'un matin bleu pénètre,
J'ai, Muse,—moi, ton pitre,—enjambé la fenêtre
Et fui notre baraque où fument tes quinquets,

Et d'herbes enivré, j'ai plongé comme un traître
Dans ces lacs défendus, et, quand tu m'appelais,

Baigné mes membres nus dans l'onde aux blancs galets,
Oubliant mon habit de pitre au tronc d'un hêtre.

Le soleil du matin séchait mon corps nouveau
Et je sentais fraîchir loin de ta tyrannie
La neige des glaciers dans ma chair assainie,

Ne sachant pas, hélas! quand s'en allait sur l'eau
Le suif de mes cheveux et le fard de ma peau,
Muse, que cette crasse était tout le génie!

[For her eyes—just to swim within those lakes, whose edge
is sown with fair eyelashes through which a blue dawn broke,
I—I, your clown, Muse—leapt over the window-ledge
and fled from our booth where your footlights shed their smoke,

and I, ravished with grass, dived like a traitor down
in those forbidden lakes, and, while you summoned me,
on the trunk of a beech I shunned my jester's gown,
bathing my naked limbs in the white-shingled sea.

Within the morning sunlight my new body dried
and I could feel the glaciers' snow grow cool and fresh
far from your tyranny in my now-wholesome flesh,

not knowing, alas, when the greasepaint and the grime
from my skin and my hair slipped away on the tide,
O Muse, that all the genius was that slime!]

The Windows

Written May 1863; published 12 May 1866 in *Le Parnasse contemporain*. On 3 June 1863 Mallarmé sent it to Cazalis with the prefatory remarks: 'Drink deeply of the Ideal. The happiness of the world below is base—your hands have to be very calloused to seize it. The statement "I am happy" means "I am a coward"—and very often "I am a fool," because either you can't see the heaven of the Ideal above this ceiling of happiness, or else you must be wilfully shutting your eyes to it. On this theme I've written a little poem, "The Windows", which I'm sending you.' The speaker, like a sick man in hospital, longs to escape from the drab world around him and die, passing through 'mysticism or art' into the heaven of the Ideal. But there is a danger in that process: the 'angel' that he becomes may well be a fallen one, eternally condemned.

38   *that monster*: the Inane.

The Flowers

Written March 1864; published 12 May 1866 in *Le Parnasse contemporain*. Nature, Mother and Lady, is addressed; the poem contemplates her generative power in creating both life (the opening lines echo the creation scene of Hugo's 1859 'Le Sacre de la femme' in *La Légende des siècles*) and death.

11   *Herodias*: the girl who danced before Herod the tetrarch and asked for the head of the prophet John the Baptist as her reward. For Mallarmé's choice of this name, see the notes on *Herodias*: 'Scene' (p. 242 below).

22   *blooms to sway phials*: the swaying corollas of toxic flowers are depicted as phials containing poison.

Renewal

Written May–June 1862; published 12 May 1866 in *Le Parnasse contemporain*. Sending the poem to Cazalis on 4 June 1862, Mallarmé wrote of 'a curious barrenness that springtime had imposed within me. I am rid of it at last, after three months of impotence, and my first sonnet is devoted to a description—i.e. a curse—of it. This is poetry of a new kind, in which material results (those of the blood and nerves) are examined and combined with mental results (those of the mind and soul). It could be termed "springtime depression" [*spleen printanier*].'

12   *though*: the French (*cependant*) suggests both concomitance ('while') and contrast ('though').

Anguish

Written early 1864; published 12 May 1866 in *Le Parnasse contemporain*. In 1864 the title was 'To a Whore', and in 1866 'To One who is Calm'—a Baudelairean phrase befitting the poem's Baudelairean subject and approach. As usual with Mallarmé, the poem reveals more of its author's inner life than of his external circumstances: it was composed within six or seven months of his marriage.

14   *dying*: an early (1864?) draft read *penser* ('thinking').

['Weary of bitter rest . . .']

Written 1864; published 12 May 1866 in *Le Parnasse contemporain*, with the title 'Epilogue' (it was Mallarmé's final poem in that booklet). The speaker, unable to create—he feels his brain to be merely an 'immense cemetery' (ll. 5–6 and the first draft of ll. 9–10 make clear that this is the sense intended)—seeks to turn his back on the 'ravenous Art' that his 'antiquated' world prefers. Instead, he wants to imitate Chinese art—an aspiration that has been interpreted very differently by different critics (is he lowering his sights, for instance, or is he striving for loftier goals than ever?). It may be crucial to note that the Chinese art described by the speaker is an alien, elusive thing (like the lines in which he describes it), painting what cannot be painted (not a flower, but 'the end of a flower')—in which case any attempt to reduce it to critical paraphrase may be doomed to failure.

The Bell-Ringer

Written early 1862, around the same time as 'Ill Fortune' (compare their last lines); published 15 March 1862 in *L'Artiste*.

4   *Ave*: in traditional Roman Catholic ritual, a prayer offered when the Angelus bell is rung in the morning.

5   *enlightened*: in the 1862 text the light is stated to come from 'a pale candle'; this information disappeared when Mallarmé revised the sonnet in 1866.

7   *secular*: hundred-year-old; but the context encourages the reader to think also of *séculier*, 'lacking any religious significance'.

Summer Sadness

Written 1862; after substantial revision, published 30 June 1866 in *Le Parnasse contemporain*. In 1862 the sonnet was grouped with 'Renewal' under the general heading 'Unwholesome Suns': summer, like spring, is traditionally depicted by poets in positive terms, but in these poems both seasons are blighted and blighting. 'Summer Sadness' may date from the time when Mallarmé began to court his future wife, but any temptation to see it as simple autobiography should be resisted: the pallid, insubstantial creature addressed in this poem, stereotypically gold-haired and unresponsive, is as much a fantasy construct created for the purposes of a specific poem as the prostitute of 'Anguish'.

The earliest surviving draft (1862?) reads as follows:

> Le Soleil, sur la mousse où tu t'es endormie,
> A chauffé comme un bain tes cheveux ténébreux,
> Et, dans l'air sans oiseaux et sans brise ennemie,
> Évaporé ton fard en parfums dangereux.
>
> De ce blanc flamboiement l'immuable accalmie
> Me fait haïr la vie et notre amour fiévreux,
> Et tout mon être implore un sommeil de momie
> Morne comme le sable et les palmiers poudreux!
>
> Ta chevelure, est-elle une rivière tiède
> Où noyer sans frissons mon âme qui m'obsède
> Et jouir du Néant où l'on ne pense pas?
>
> Je veux boire le fard qui fond sous tes paupières
> Si ce poison promet au cœur que tu frappas
> L'insensibilité de l'azur et des pierres!
>
> [The Sun, like a bath, has warmed your shadowy hair
> upon the moss where you lie somnolent,

evaporating your rouge, in the birdless air
without a hostile breeze, to dangerous scent.

The never-varied calm of this white gleam
makes me hate life and our hot passion, and
my very being craves a mummy's dream
bleak as the dusty palm trees and the sand!

Your hair—is it a tepid river to
drown undisturbed the soul obsessing me
and tease the Void where thought is all unknown?

Let me sup kohl drawn from your eyes, and see
if that bane gives this heart stricken by you
the impassivity of sky and stone.]

The Blue

Written by early January 1864; published 12 May 1866 in *Le Parnasse contemporain*. Shortly after the poem's composition, Mallarmé sent a detailed analysis of it to Cazalis. 'To take a broader view at the outset, and deepen the whole work, I myself don't appear in the first stanza. The blue torments the impotent in general. The second stanza raises a suspicion that I suffer from this cruel disease because of my flight before the possessive sky. In this stanza too I start to develop, with the blasphemous boast "And what wild night", the strange notion of summoning up the fogs. The prayer to "dear Tedium" confirms my impotence. In the third stanza, I am as frantic as a man who sees a desperate appeal granted. The fourth stanza [in all known drafts, it is the sixth stanza] begins with a freed schoolboy's grotesque exclamation: "The Sky has died!" And instantly, armed with that admirable assurance, I appeal to Matter. Verily, behold the joy of the Impotent! Weary of the illness that ravages me, I long to taste the common happiness of the multitude, and to await an obscure death . . . I say "I long". But the enemy is a ghost, the sky *returns from the dead*, and I hear it singing in the blue bells. It goes past, lazy and victorious, without being sullied by the mist, and it simply runs me through. At which I (being full of pride, and not seeing that it's a just punishment for my cowardice) howl that I am suffering immense "torment". I long to flee once more, but I recognize my error and acknowledge that I am "haunted" . . . For those who seek something more than word-music in poetry, there is a real drama here.'

Sea Breeze

Written May 1865; published 12 May 1866 in *Le Parnasse contemporain*. In a letter of 8 February 1866, Mallarmé summarized the subject as 'the inexplicable desire that sometimes grips us—to leave those who are dear to us, and *depart*!'

13–15 *mast . . . no mast*: the awkward syntax of these lines enacts the chaotic shipwreck in which the mast disappears.

Sigh

Written by April 1864; published 12 May 1866 in *Le Parnasse contemporain*. An 'autumn reverie' (Mallarmé's description in a letter of 8 February 1868), to be compared with the prose poem 'Autumn Lament'.

Alms

Written 1862; after substantial revision, published 12 May 1866 in *Le Parnasse contemporain*; further revised in 1887. The speaker gives alms to a beggar, sardonically urging him to lavish it on 'some immense strange sin' rather than hoarding it stingily or spending it on necessities. Mallarmé is identified by some critics with the speaker, by others with the beggar; perhaps it is better to see both speaker and beggar as imaginative creations who draw their attributes from their creator.

The earliest surviving draft (1862?), entitled 'A un mendiant' ('To a Beggar'), reads as follows:

Pauvre, voici cent sous . . . Longtemps tu cajolas
—Ce vice te manquait,—le songe d'être avare?
Ne les enterre pas pour qu'on te sonne un glas.

Évoque de l'Enfer un péché plus bizarre.
Tu peux ensanglanter tes brumeux horizons
D'un Rêve ayant l'éclair vermeil d'une fanfare:

Changeant en verts treillis les barreaux des prisons
Qu'illumine l'azur charmant d'une éclaircie,
Le tabac fait grimper de sveltes feuillaisons;

L'opium est à vendre en mainte pharmacie;
Veux-tu mordre au rabais quelque pâle catin
Et boire en sa salive un reste d'ambroisie?

T'attabler au café jusqu'à demain matin?
Les plafonds sont fardés de faunesses sans voiles,
Et l'on jette deux sous au garçon, l'œil hautain.

Puis quand tu sors, vieux dieu, grelottant sous tes toiles
D'emballage, l'aurore est un lac de vin d'or
Et tu jures avoir le gosier plein d'étoiles!

Tu peux aussi, pour bien gaspiller ton trésor,
Mettre une plume rouge à ta coiffe; à complies,
Brûler un cierge au saint à qui tu crois encor.

Ne t'imagine pas que je dis des folies:
Que le Diable ait ton corps si tu crêves de faim,
Je hais l'aumône *utile*, et veux que tu m'oublies;

Et, surtout, ne vas pas, drôle, acheter du pain!

[Here, have a coin, poor man . . . Did you pursue
your dream of greed (a vice you lacked) a long time?
Don't bury it, lest they toll a knell for you.

Conjure from Hell something more strangely sinful;
you could bloody your hazy vistas by
means of a Dream blazing red like a fanfare:

tobacco makes slim tendrils ramify,
and transforms prison bars into green lattice
lit by a pretty patch of clear blue sky;

opium is on sale at any chemist's;
would you nibble at cheap rates some forlorn
whore, taste the honeyed dregs of her saliva,

or eat in cafés till tomorrow morn?
The snobs toss waiters twopence, and the ceilings
are rouged with she-fauns whom no veils adorn.

When you leave, old god shivering in your burlap,
a lake of golden wine is break of day
and you swear that the stars must fill your gullet!

To waste your treasure better still, you may
deck yourself with a red plume, burning at compline
a candle to the saint whom you still pray.

Do not imagine that my words are folly:
Devil take your body if you die unfed!
I hate all *useful* handouts; please forget me.

Above all, rascal, don't go and buy bread!]

Gift of the Poem

Written October 1865; published in an untraced French magazine before 2
February 1867, when it was reprinted by *L'Avant-Coureur* in Louisiana. As its
position in Mallarmé's *Poésies* and its first line indicate, the poem acts as a
dedication of 'Herodias'. In a letter of 31 December 1865, its author described

it as 'a little poem composed after the nocturnal toil to which my spirit has grown accustomed . . . When the wicked dawn breaks, the poet is terrified by the funereal offspring that enraptured him during the illuminated night, and sees that it is lifeless; he feels a need to bring it to his wife, who will give life to it.'

1   *an Idumaean night*: a night spent working on the topic of Herodias, who was of Idumaean ancestry. Idumaea, in Hellenistic and Roman times, was a province south of Judaea; Mallarmé invests it with familiar Oriental attributes: gold, spices, palm trees (suggested by a well-known passage of Virgil, *Georgics*, iii. 12), Sibyls.

6   *that relic*: the poem.

9   *your little daughter*: Mallarmé's daughter Geneviève was born on 19 November 1864, during the first phase of his work on 'Herodias'.

13   *Sibylline*: arcane or esoteric.

Herodias: Scene

Written 1865; published November 1871 in *Le Parnasse contemporain*. Herodias, in Mallarmé's writings, is the girl who danced before Herod the tetrarch and asked for the head of John the Baptist as her reward. None of the Scripture narratives mentions her name; Josephus (not the most reliable of historians) calls her Salome, but as Mallarmé pointed out in a February 1865 letter to Eugène Lefébure, some later sources give her the same name as her mother—Herodias. (English readers will be familiar with this tradition from Browning, 'Fra Lippo Lippi', ll. 196–7: 'Herodias . . . who went and danced and got men's heads cut off.') In the same letter Mallarmé also declared: 'What little inspiration I've had, I owe to that name; I think that even if my heroine had been called *Salomé*, I'd have invented the word *Hérodiade*, dark and red as an open pomegranate. Anyhow, I mean to make her a creature of sheer fantasy, utterly independent of history.'

On this topic Mallarmé planned an extended cycle of poems, which was begun in October 1864 and continued to occupy him intermittently till his death; however, only one of the projected poems—the present one—was completed to his satisfaction. As presented in this 'Scene', Herodias is fiercely committed to virginity, like her 'sister' the moon (the Diana of Classical mythology); she draws back even from the Nurse's touch, and still more from the idea that her 'secrets' are being 'reserved' for some as yet unknown male ('he'); by the end of the poem she is withdrawing into a state of total separation from the world. Yet the very intensity of her commitment contains the seeds of its own destruction: as she herself is more than half aware, her lips are 'speaking a lie'.

Mallarmé is quoted as saying that the final lines of the 'Scene' anticipate 'the future violation of the mystery of her being by a glance from John, who will look at her and pay for that sacrilege by his death—because the untamed virgin can never again feel herself intact, fully restored, and whole, until she holds in her hands the severed head that still dares to preserve the memory of

the glimpsed virgin' (Robert de Montesquiou, *Diptyque de Flandre, Triptyque de France* (Paris, 1921), 235). But that explanation is concerned mainly with the poem's relation to other, uncompleted (and largely unwritten) pieces of the Herodias cycle, not with its sense in the separate state ultimately published by Mallarmé.

2   *some unknown era*: the Nurse perceives Herodias as out of touch with the present.

17–19   *I strip away . . . the pale lilies within me*: Herodias is seeking to rid herself of what is 'natural' and living.

22   *lions*: Mallarmé's feminine noun *bêtes* does not accord with the masculine *épris* in l. 17; it was therefore posthumously altered in proof (the handwriting is probably his daughter Geneviève's) to *lions*. We have preserved the original reading in the French text, but adopted the rendering 'lions' in translation.

30   *funereal*: the liquid is 'funereal' because it is 'made from the death of roses' ('faite avec la mort des roses'), as an early (April 1868) manuscript draft reveals.

35–7   *these hairs of mine . . . are not flowers . . . but gold*: not soft and living, but hard and inanimate.

86   *for myself alone I bloom*: Herodias's quest for self-sufficiency is a prototype of the poet's.

96   *Sibylline*: arcane or esoteric.

125   *Venus*: (*a*) the evening star, (*b*) the Roman goddess of love, to whom virginity is hateful.

129   *You are speaking a lie*: the Nurse has now departed, and Herodias, left alone, addresses the final lines to her own lips.

A Faun in the Afternoon

Written June–July 1865; after radical revision, published April 1876 in booklet form. It was originally part of a longer poem-cycle in dialogue form, but as in the case of *Herodias*, only one of the projected poems finally met its author's approval and was published. The faun of late Graeco-Roman mythology is both perennially lustful (especially in pursuit of nymphs) and a quintessential artist (since he plays the panpipe); in the former respect he contrasts with Herodias, in the latter he resembles her (she too is a dreamer). Mallarmé's use of 'v' for 'u' in the printed title gives it the look of an ancient Latin inscription.

1   *those nymphs*: their identity is revealed gradually as the poem progresses. The nymphs were disturbed by the faun's flute-playing (ll. 26–32); he caught two of them asleep and tried to make love to them, but they slipped away (ll. 63–92); the whole episode may have been merely his own fantasy (ll. 3–9).

2   *incarnate*: both 'flesh colour' and 'carnality'.

4   *My doubt . . . ends*: 'ends' is ambiguous; perhaps the doubt is dispelled, yet perhaps it is completed. The faun believes that he met the nymphs in

these forests, and the forests are 'true' (l. 5), which may support the reality of the whole story—or else may show by contrast that the rest of the story was *not* true. What the faun took for nymphs, for instance, may have been merely 'roses' (l. 7).

7   *failing*: both 'guilt' and 'failure to exist'.

11–12   *the chaster one . . . the other*: here and elsewhere in the poem, one of the nymphs pursued by the faun seems to be more 'spiritual' (associated with whiteness, intangibility, and innocence), the other more 'carnal' (associated with darkness, passion, and cruelty).

15–17   *sound of water . . . stir of air*: i.e. the only sounds and breezes are those produced by the faun's own flute. Perhaps the 'chaster' nymph was an 'illusion' generated by the watery sound, and the 'other' by the breeze—in which case neither would have any existence outside his art.

21   *artificial*: both 'unnatural' and 'created by art'.

23   *mere in Sicily*: Sicilian swamps are a traditional home of fauns.

26–7   *made tame by talent*: the reeds are 'tamed' by the artisan's talent when they are shaped into a panpipe.

31   *naiads*: water-nymphs.

32   *fulvid*: both 'tawny' and 'wild'.

34   *nuptial excess*: 'excess', apparently, because of the faun's desire to possess both nymphs.

34–5   *A natural*: the note customarily played to tune orchestral instruments.

37   *lilies*: both a phallic symbol and a traditional emblem of chastity; the faun is 'one among' the lilies, because the failure to consummate his passion has left him 'erect, alone' (l. 36).

38   *sweet nothing*: the kiss is 'nothing' (*a*) because it is not the consummation the faun seeks, and (*b*) because it may be imaginary.

44   *diverting . . . for its own end*: the panpipe transforms the artist's 'disturbances' into art.

45   *it dreams*: two different syntactic constructions hang from this one verb: the panpipe 'dreams . . . that we have seduced the beauties round about us' (ll. 45–7), and it 'dreams of . . . evacuating . . . a sonorous, monotonous and empty line' (ll. 48–51) from the 'commonplace illusion' of the faun's sexual fantasies.

52   *flights*: a triple allusion: (*a*) the flight of the nymph Syrinx, who was transformed into a reed to escape the pursuit of Pan; (*b*) the recent nymphs' flight from the speaker; (*c*) the flights of artistic fancy involved in playing the instrument.

53   *syrinx*: panpipe made from a series of hollow reeds cut to various lengths.

57   *the gleam*: both the glossy substance of the grapes, and the drunken illumination induced by them.

62   *expand*: the previous italicized narrative (ll. 26–32) was offered as a mere retelling ('proclaim . . .'); here an element of artistic elaboration becomes explicit.

64   *immortal throats*: the throats of the nymphs, as they cool themselves in the water.

69   *this pain of being two*: the nymphs, though 'linked', suffer because they are two separate creatures, as the faun himself suffers because he is separated from them.

70   *careless*: both 'heedless' and 'haphazard'.

72   *hated by the frivolous shade*: the thicket is in full sunlight, shunned by the 'frivolous' (unstable as well as unserious) shadows.

74   *squandered like the light*: their love-play is to run parallel with the afternoon sunlight.

77–8 *as a lightning-sheet quivers*: the syntax is ambiguous; the quivering sheet of lightning is placed in apposition both to the faun's 'burning lips' and to the 'secret terror' of the nymphs' (and the faun's?) flesh.

90   *untwined by some vague perishings*: the faun, involved with the more 'carnal' nymph, is too weak to retain his hold on the more 'spiritual' one.

99–100 *at times when the forest glows with gold and ashen tints*: at evening (now approaching).

101   *Etna*: Sicilian volcano, where Venus went in the evening to visit her husband Vulcan.

103   *when sad slumbers are sounding*: Venus arrives, not during the eruption ('the flame'), but in the melancholy quiescence afterwards.

104   *the queen*: Venus, whom the faun sees as already in his possession.

110   *the shadow*: both 'the illusion' and 'the mystery' (with a reference back to l. 56, where the female genitals were seen as a realm of 'shadows').

['The hair flight of a flame . . .']

Written by July 1887; published 12 August 1887 (embedded in the prose poem 'The Announcement at the Fair', p. 109) in *L'Art et la mode*. The speaker contemplates 'the fire ever within' a woman's flame-coloured hair, even when it is settled and tidied rather than unlaced and flying; physical contact with a lover could only 'degrade' the beauty of the Ideal.

The woman is presumably based on Méry Laurent (1849–1900), with whom Mallarmé shared a relationship too complex and individual to be labelled by any English word ('friendship' desexualizes it, 'love affair' oversexualizes it); she is thus making her first appearance in the collected *Poésies*, and will be met again in 'The fine suicide fled victoriously . . .', and perhaps 'To introduce myself into your tale . . .' and the 1880s revision of 'What silk with balm from advancing days . . .', as well as various uncollected pieces. Pierre Citron, in the Imprimerie Nationale edition of Mallarmé's *Poésies*

(Paris, 1986), 12, 262, sees the reality of the relationship as being particularly close to the situation described in 'The hair flight of a flame . . .': it clearly involved a strong erotic attraction, yet it was not expressed in overt sexual activity. (As Citron points out, Méry later denied that she had ever been Mallarmé's mistress; since she made no secret of her liaisons with other public figures, there is no reason to doubt this statement—which fits well with everything that we know of the poet's complex psychology.) Similarly rich and subtle tensions may be detected in several of Mallarmé's other poems addressed to her. Nevertheless, 'The hair flight of a flame . . .' is a poem, not a piece of autobiography; Mallarmé designed it to be read in its own right, without recourse to private biographical data, and he would no doubt have rewritten the 'facts' of everyday life or jettisoned them altogether, if the needs of the poem had demanded it. His Méry, like his Herodias, need not greatly resemble the historical person of the same name.

13   *scorch*: (*a*) scratch (a rare sense in English, but the usual meaning of *écorche* in French); (*b*) burn (an Anglicism, suggested here by 'torch' in the next line).

Saint

Written December 1865; published 24 November 1883 in Verlaine's essay on Mallarmé in *Lutèce*. Cecilia, the patron saint of music, is seen in an emphatically ancient stained-glass window. The earliest surviving draft has the fuller title 'Saint Cecilia Playing on a Cherub's Wing'.

2   *viol voiding gold*: either the gilt of the viol (an aptly antiquated musical instrument, and imagined rather than seen, since the window 'veils' it) is peeling with age, or the golden sunset (which used to illuminate it) is now fading.

6   *the Magnificat*: Mary's hymn 'My soul doth magnify the Lord . . .', as sung in the Roman Catholic liturgy.

7–8   *compline or vespersong*: religious rites of evening; in nineteenth-century Roman Catholic ritual, the Magnificat was traditionally sung at vespers.

9   *this ostensory pane*: the illuminated window is compared to a monstrance or ostensory (a vessel for displaying holy relics).

10   *a harp*: the angel's flight makes his wing look like a harp, and from the viewer's perspective, the saint's fingertips appear to be almost in contact with it.

13   *she*: the saint, not the angel (who is male).

Funerary Toast

Written by September 1873; published December 1873 in the memorial volume *Le Tombeau de Théophile Gautier*. Théophile Gautier (1811–72), poet, novelist, critic, and journalist, had been a tireless supporter of his fellow writers, and his death elicited commemorative tributes from many of them. At the start of 1873, in a letter to François Coppée, Mallarmé described the plan of his poem as follows: 'I want to praise one of Gautier's most glorious

strengths: "The mystic gift of seeing with the eyes" (delete "mystic"). I shall praise the *seer* who, set down in this world, looked at it—which people simply don't do.' The dead Gautier is not to be mourned ('I scorn the lucid horror of a tear'); he is an emblem of the 'happiness' that awaits all poets: the happiness of 'enduring', even after death, by means of 'radiant eternal genius'.

51   *when he rests in pride*: 'he' is perhaps death, perhaps the poet.

Prose

Written probably by 1876; published January 1885 in *La Revue indépendante*, when the dedication to des Esseintes (the fictitious protagonist of Huysmans' 1884 novel *A rebours*, which had paid generous tribute to Mallarmé) was added. The title is of course an act of playful self-deprecation after the composition of a particularly ambitious poem (compare 'A Few Sonnets'), but it also reflects the specialized use of the term 'prose' for liturgical compositions in rhymed verse (a use employed by Mallarmé himself in 'Autumn Lament'). The speaker remembers a summer walk with his 'sister' on an island rich in flowers. The island, like so many other entities in Mallarmé poems, is situated in a no-man's-land between fact or fantasy: ll. 37–44 can be read as asserting either its reality, 'the truth is not (as the shore fraudulently weeps) that there was never such a land', or its unreality, 'the truth is not as the shore fraudulently weeps; there was never such a land'. The identity of the 'sister' is one of the most disputed points in Mallarmé studies; she has been interpreted as the poet's beloved sister Maria (who died in 1857), his wife, his daughter Geneviève, one of his friends (e.g. Méry Laurent or Harriet Smyth), an archetypal lover (the beloved is addressed as 'sister' in the Song of Songs and in Baudelaire's 'L'Invitation au voyage'), the Eternal Feminine, his Muse, his disciple, his reader, a fictional heroine, his childhood self, knowledge, reason, inspiration, memory, and the technique of 'hyperbole' that is invoked at the start of the poem. Thus the speaker may be recalling his past relations with a specific individual, or probing an abstract concept (art or beauty or the existence of the Ideal), or working out a poetic strategy to be employed in the future. The playful title, jaunty manner, and virtuoso rhymes have also led to suggestions that the poem is largely a game—that its sense is determined partly by its choice of rhymes (as in the lighter works of many poets; we might compare Rimbaud's 'Ce qu'on dit au Poète à propos des fleurs') and should not be analysed too minutely. This, however, is doubtful: Mallarmé is never more playful than when he is most in earnest.

24   *at no word that we could recite*: (*a*) the outspread flowers were not merely invented by our utterance; (*b*) the outspread flowers struck us dumb.

31   *the irid family*: the Iridaceae, the family that includes irises (l. 18) and gladioli (l. 56); sometimes placed in the same family as lilies (l. 39) by nineteenth-century botanists.

41   *the shore*: the people who have been left behind on the shore, and have failed to reach the island.

51   *'Anastasius!'*: 'Resurrection' (Greek).

55   *'Pulcheria!'*: 'Beauty' (Greek).

Fan (Belonging to Madame Mallarmé)

Written December 1890, and inscribed on a fan as a New Year's gift to the poet's wife; published 1 June 1891 in *La Conque*. The fluttering of the fan is a creative act, like the composition of a poem.

4   *its precious dwelling-place*: the owner's hand.

11   *scattered dust*: the specks of matter that necessarily contaminate the ideal beauty of any creative act.

13   *like this*: with 'its wing low'.

Another Fan (Belonging to Mademoiselle Mallarmé)

Written early 1884, and inscribed on a fan presented to the poet's daughter Geneviève; published 6 April 1884 in *La Revue critique*. The speaker is the fan itself, addressing its owner; in the initial stanzas she is beating it, in the final stanzas she has closed it. As in the preceding poem, the wielding of the fan parallels the composition of a poem; the addressee, like the poet, is a 'dreamer'.

Album Leaf

Written July 1890 for the album of Thérèse Roumanille, the daughter of a Provençal poet; published first in an unidentified magazine, then (September–December 1892) in *La Wallonie*. The speaker presents himself as an ancient faun who has been asked to play the flute; the true value of his performance comes only at its end, when he looks up and sees the beauty of his addressee, which his own art is unable to match.

Remembering Belgian Friends

Written early 1893; published July 1893 in *Excelsior 1883–1893*, an anniversary volume compiled by the Excelsior Club, a literary group at Bruges. The poet recalls his visit to Belgium in February 1890, when he lectured to the Excelsior Club on the subject of the recently deceased writer Villiers de l'Isle-Adam.

3–4   *as I feel . . . visibly*: the two lines form a dependent clause; the principal clause of the sentence runs 'all the almost incense-hued antiquity . . . floats or seems . . .'.

8   *we immemorial few who feel so calm*: this clause is placed in parentheses in the 1893 edition.

Cheap Songs

Written 1888, to accompany an illustration by Jean-François Raffaëlli; published March 1889 in *Les Types de Paris*. In 'The Cobbler', the speaker complains that his shoes are being repaired only too well: his 'urge to be passing through' with 'heels unclad' is suppressed by the cobbler's nails. In 'The

Seller of Scented Herbs', the speaker comments that, instead of being used to embellish some purchaser's lavatory and disguise the existence of his bowels, the lavender should be used to embellish its seller and disguise the existence of her lice.

['The Cobbler']

6   *places most convenient*: the poet slyly embroiders the standard euphemism 'conveniences' (*lieux d'aisance*).

14   *firstfruits*: under the law of Moses, the Israelites were commanded to bring the Lord an offering from the firstfruits of their harvest (Leviticus 23: 10).

Note

Written early November 1890; published 15 November 1890 in *The Whirlwind*. What kind of a whirlwind is this magazine? Not a gale blowing hats in the 'broad highway', says the poet, but the breeze stirred up by a ballerina dancing in defiance of 'every well-trodden thing'. The poem was written in response to a request from the American painter and wit James McNeill Whistler (1834–1903), a personal friend; in a letter to him, Mallarmé described it as 'a little sonnet of good wishes, rhyming on your name—Ha, ha, ha!'

2   *the broad highway*: the *rue* in nineteenth-century French poetry is the public realm, the sphere of common social and political action.

9   *(enraptured, witty, yet inert)*: the adjectives describe the girl.

11   *beyond it*: beyond (*a*) the skirt, (*b*) the whirlwind.

13   *in gay dismissal*: perhaps an unacceptably free rendering of the French *rieur* ('laughingly'); but we felt that the Whistlerian outrageousness of the final rhyme (*puisse l'air—Whistler* in the original) was too central to the poem's effect to be ignored.

Little Ditty I

Written 1894; published November 1894 in *L'Épreuve*. The speaker, contemplating an unfrequented lake or stream at sunset, sees (at least in imagination) a woman undress and dive into the water. The wording of ll. 9–14 is highly ambiguous; some commentators take the 'bird' as a metaphorical description of the woman's discarded clothes or her body, others as a waterbird startled by her dive.

9   *skirt*: the subject of this verb could be the solitude of l. 1 or the bird of l. 11; or else it could be an exhortation addressed to the woman. An English translation must, to some extent, choose between these possibilities; we have arbitrarily opted for the third, but by way of compensation, we have used a verb that could easily be read as a noun (especially with 'drapery' in the next line: Mallarmé clearly chose *longe* in part because it would echo *linge*).

Little Ditty II

Written by 1894; published 1899 in the Deman edition of Mallarmé's *Poésies*. A swan, according to legend, sings only once in its life, when it is dying; but does the poet face an even worse fate?

9   *haggard*: (*a*) distraught, (*b*) untamed.

14   *whole*: the word goes primarily with *Rester* ('stay whole'), but the lineation associates it also with *Déchiré* ('wholly torn apart'): the poem's concluding lines therefore suggest both the completeness of the destruction and the completeness of the hoped-for persistence.

A Few Sonnets

The casualness of the title ('Four Sonnets', or simply 'Sonnets', would have been more usual) contrasts slyly with the abstruseness of the poems themselves, which were written separately and not grouped together till the Deman collected edition—where they stand at the centre, as the volume's 'holy of holies' (Yves-Alain Favre's term). The ambiguous visual presentation invites readers to view the 'Few Sonnets' almost as a single poem, with major stanza-breaks after every fourteenth line and minor stanza-breaks after every quatrain and tercet.

['When the shade threatened with the fatal decree . . .']

Date of composition unknown; published 24 November 1883 in Verlaine's essay on Mallarmé in *Lutèce*. The setting is a night sky ('shade', 'funereal height', 'ebony hall', 'gloom') where 'trivial fires' are vanishing ('illustrious wreaths writhe in their doom') in the sight of the poet ('the faith-dazzled Solitary').

Some commentators regard the 'trivial fires' as the doomed glimmers of sunset, and the 'festive star' of l. 14 as the sun whose light has kindled the poet's genius. On this interpretation, the apparent 'splendour' of sunset is deceptive (ll. 5–7) because the earth's rotation has 'cast' the 'sheer dazzling-ness' of the sun below the horizon and into the 'night' (ll. 9–10). Nevertheless, as the sun submits to its fate, its flight is absorbed into the poet's thought ('it bowed its doubt-less plumage deep in me'); therefore, the 'dread aeons' darken it less than would otherwise be the case, and the 'trivial fires' of sunset 'show' (not only illuminate, but also act as a foil to) a continuing light—the light of the poet's kindled imagination. Compare the progression of thought in the other sunset-poem of this group ('The fine suicide fled victoriously . . .'), where we are told: 'Out of all that brilliance not one shred stays . . . except the arrogant treasure of a head.'

Other commentators take the 'illustrious wreaths' of l. 6 as the stars, which are doomed ultimately to run out of energy. The 'sheer dazzlingness' of l. 10 would then be the poet's genius sent out through the darkness from the earth, and the 'festive star' of l. 14 would be not the sun, but the earth on which the poet lives.

Nevertheless, the basic drift of the poem is the same on either reading. Material things are 'trivial', never escaping from their own nature even when

they seem to increase or decrease ('fail or grow', l. 12), and ultimately passing away; yet the immaterial things kindled by them may endure. 'The light that triumphs in this sonnet is both essential and internal, spiritual' (Rosemary Lloyd, *Mallarmé: Poésies* (London, 1984), 44).

['This virginal long-living lovely day . . .']

Date of composition unknown; first published March 1885 in *La Revue indépendante*. The slow movement of the sequence. The other three sonnets are night-pieces, beginning with sunset, darkness, annihilation, yet struggling through to hint at something triumphant and enduring. This one is a day-piece in contrary motion: it begins with what is 'long-living' and 'lovely', yet ends with what is 'dismissed to futile things'.

Whiteness is everywhere, in this poem: the white swan is trapped in a white universe. And once we go beyond the opening line, the whiteness is presented almost entirely in negative terms: 'hard', 'sterile', 'frigid', 'white throe'. The poem is full of attempts to escape—yet all such attempts are either doubtful ('will it tear . . .') or instantly and decisively opposed ('flights that never flew away', 'strives to break free woebegone', 'will shake off this white throe . . . but not the horror of earth'). No significant escape ever occurs; from the glacial realm of this poem, no 'territory to live' can be reached.

The swan is a familiar symbol of the poet. Nothing here limits the symbol to one particular poet or type of poet; there is nothing to suggest, for instance, that the sonnet is a lament for Mallarmé's own individual artistic sterility, or a criticism of the sterility of certain inferior verse-writers. On the contrary, the poem operates in general rather than specific terms; if anything, it moves away from the individual ('a swan of old') to the universal ('the Swan').

['The fine suicide fled victoriously . . .']

Written November 1885; published February 1887 in Verlaine's *Les Hommes d'aujourd'hui*. The scherzo of the sequence: the night- and sunset-themes of the first and fourth sonnets are taken up, but in a more playful, light-hearted mode; here, the 'triumph' remains at a relatively 'childish' level.

The characters are general, archetypal figures: the speaker is 'poet' (in the 1887 draft) and also sun (he sees the regal purple of sunset as being laid out for his own tomb); the listener is the stereotypical 'caressed' female, both child and empress, with the stereotypical associations of blonde hair as Mallarmé defined them in 1862: 'gold, light, richness, reverie, nimbus.' The sun has set, and the scene now abounds with hard-won military and imperial glory ('blaze of fame, blood in foam', 'regal purple', 'triumph'). But if 'regal purple' is being lavished on the speaker's tomb, it is being lavished to no purpose, since the speaker's tomb is 'absent'; funeral rites are a little premature. The glorious spectacle passes, 'the heavens . . . have gone', yet one trace of them is retained: the gold ('treasure') of the listener's otherwise unlit hair. In its limited ('childish') way, the hair has the imperial arrogance and triumph of a war-helmet ('morion'); when the glory of sky and war and empire has passed, part of it

lingers ('stays', remains 'constant') in the admittedly childish head of the listener.

13   *war-morion*: a visorless helmet.

14   *showers roses*: an image ('likeness') of the listener herself, pictured as showering down beneath her helmet of hair.

['With her pure nails offering their onyx high . . .']

Written mid-1868; after substantial revision, published October 1887 in the *Revue indépendante* edition of Mallarmé's *Poésies*. A letter of 18 July 1868 contains an early draft with some significant variants, particularly in the opening quatrain:

> La Nuit approbatrice allume les onyx
> De ses ongles au pur Crime, lampadophore,
> Du Soir aboli par le vespéral Phœnix
> De qui la cendre n'a de cinéraire amphore

> [Approving Night brightly begins to burn
> her onyx nails at pure lampbearing Crime
> of Dusk abolished by the vesper-time
> Phoenix whose ashes have no funerary urn . . .]

In the same letter Mallarmé describes the scene as follows: 'A window open at night, with both shutters fastened back; a room with nobody in it, despite the impression of stability given by the fastened shutters; and hung at the rear—in a night composed of absence and enquiry, with no furniture except the plausible outline of indistinct console-tables—a warlike mirror-frame in its death agony, containing the stellar and incomprehensible reflection of the Great Bear, which alone links this world-forsaken dwelling-place to the heavens.'

Thus the sonnet is another night-piece. The Phoenix, the mythical bird repeatedly dying and being reborn from its ashes, has burned its 'vesperal' (both evening and ritual) fantasies and gone down to the underworld, to the River Styx. The gold decorations in the room—a scene of struggle between a naked water-nymph and unicorns (which could be overcome only by virginity)—are themselves dying or dead. Not even a funerary urn remains in the room to contain the ashes (compare the absence of the sun-poet's tomb in the preceding poem); and this is a still greater loss, because a funerary urn, 'bauble' and 'inanity' though it is, would at least be 'sonorous' (both hollow and—like a poem—resonant) and would therefore be the one thing in which the Void could take any pride. But alas! the urn is a mere 'ptyx', a MacGuffin, something with no meaning and no existence (Mallarmé explained that he chose the word purely for the rhyme, although some of his commentators have ingeniously tried to discern a connection with its Greek meaning, 'fold, crease', or with Hugo's use of it to denote the home of a faun).

Yet the mirror in the room reflects something 'incomprehensible' beyond itself, something which 'links' it 'to the heavens' (see Mallarmé's letter) and

which 'sustains' the now-absent poet's burned and seemingly annihilated fantasies. Night (in the 1868 draft) or Agony (in the final draft) is lighting up her onyx nails (the stars) after the 'Crime of Dusk' (1868 draft) has occurred; and seven of those stars—the seven principal stars of the Great Bear—are reflected in the empty room's mirror, as a 'fixed septet of scintillations'.

5   *credences*: console tables, but carrying also a suggestion of 'beliefs' (compare the 'doubt-less plumage' and 'faith-dazzled Solitary' of 'When the shade threatened . . .').

The Tomb of Edgar Allan Poe

Written mid-1876, to commemorate the erection of a monument at Poe's grave in Baltimore (Mallarmé was invited to contribute at the suggestion of the poet Swinburne); published December 1876 in *E. A. Poe: A Memorial Volume*. Mallarmé prepared a primitive annotated English rendering for the guidance of his American translators; many of its explanations are cited below.

1   *Changed to Himself at last*: it is only after death that the poet's true identity emerges. 'In death the words take on their absolute value' (Mallarmé's English comment), so that the 'sword' is bared.

2, 4 *a bare sword . . . that strange word*: both phrases are descriptions of Poe's writings (in his English rendering, Mallarmé substituted 'hymn' for 'sword').

6   *as vile freaks writhe*: in his draft translation, Mallarmé himself rendered *sursaut* as 'writhing'. The freak is a hydra—a many-headed monster, a traditional symbol for the populace.

   seraphim: the particular seraph under consideration is Poe himself (Mallarmé's explanation).

8   *in some . . . dishonourable flow*: 'in plain prose: [they] charged him with always being drunk' (Mallarmé's English explanation).

10 *hostile clod and cloud*: the heavenly ('cloud') and the earthly ('clod') are irreconcilable antagonists.

   struggling grief: the French is *grief*, but Mallarmé rendered it 'struggle' in his English version. 'Actually, the poetic effect is of [both] that and grief at the poet's tragic life and death' (R. G. Cohn, *Toward the Poems of Mallarmé* (Berkeley, 1965), 155); therefore the present·translation combines both.

12 *dropped by an occult doom*: the granite block is depicted as having fallen as a result of some obscure catastrophe.

14 *Blasphemy-flights*: 'blasphemy means against poets, such as the charge of Poe being drunk' (Mallarmé's English explanation).

   dispersed: a characteristic ambiguity: will the 'Blasphemy-flights' be eradicated or spread more widely? In either case, the Baltimore memorial ('this block . . . this calm granite') may help to 'limit' them.

The Tomb of Charles Baudelaire

Written March 1893–April 1894; published 1 January 1895 in *La Plume*, and reprinted 1896 in the commemorative volume *Le Tombeau de Charles Baudelaire*, for which it had been designed.

1–3   *The buried shrine disgorges . . . some Anubis-god*: Baudelaire's poetry is compared to an underground temple containing an image of the jackal-headed Egyptian god Anubis.

2–3   *sod and ruby*: the constituents of Baudelaire's writings.

5–7   *new gas . . . lights eternal loins*: whereas older forms of literature, like the older and dimmer forms of street lighting, used to conceal the 'eternal loins' of the prostitute, Baudelaire's poetry, like the recently invented gaslight, exposes them.

     gas wrings the wicks that erase shiftily insults suffered: two main readings are possible: (*a*) the gaslight, as it flickers ('wrings the wicks . . . shiftily'), dispels the shameful activities that are 'suffered' (painfully endured, yet tolerated) in city streets; or (*b*) the gaslight does away with ('wrings') the older wick-bearing lamps which used to 'erase' such activities 'shiftily' by hiding them from view.

8   *whose flight beds out according to its rays*: the prostitute's fugitive street-walking ('flight') takes place by gaslight and in an alien or outlawed situation (it 'beds out').

9–10   *What foliage . . . could consecrate as she can do*: the prostitute is a more appropriate ornament for Baudelaire's tomb than any conventional tribute of laurel leaves.

10   *any nightless town*: modern towns have become 'nightless' since the invention of gaslight.

12–13   *the veils that form her gown with shimmers*: the flickering gaslight—and the work of Baudelaire.

13   *she, his Shade, a guardian bane*: the prostitute is now seen as Baudelaire's very ghost or spirit, both poisonous ('bane') and edifying ('guardian'). 'Departed' in l. 12 thus refers both to the prostitute's departure from the gaslight and Baudelaire's departure (through death) from his work.

Homage ['Already mourning . . .']

Written late 1885; published 8 January 1886 in *La Revue wagnérienne* (Verlaine's 'Parsifal' made its first appearance in the same issue). Like many young French writers of his era, Mallarmé was intensely interested in the music-dramas of Richard Wagner (1813–83); he published an essay on the composer in August 1885, and during the months before the composition of his poem he frequently attended orchestral concerts of Wagner's music. Nevertheless, as both essay and poem show, he was uneasy. Discussing the poem in a letter on 17 February 1886, he wrote: 'The homage is a bit sulky; as you'll see, it's the grief of a poet who sees the old poetic confrontation

collapse, and the opulence of words fade, before the sunrise of contemporary Music, whose latest god is Wagner.'

3   *the central pillar's collapse*: the failure of poetry ('our magic scrawl'), at least as hitherto practised, when faced with the success of the new music.

10   *has gushed*: Wagner (the subject of the sentence, l. 13) has emitted a flood of new light, like a rising sun. The syntax is ambiguous—either (*a*) Wagner has gushed from the noisy crowd that is hated by the master lights, or (*b*) Wagner has gushed from the master lights that are hated by the noisy crowd—and the 'noisy crowd' may be either the proponents of pre-Wagnerian music or the notes of Wagner's own music.

11   *a shrine born for their representation*: the 1876 theatre at Bayreuth, designed by Wagner specifically for the performance of his music-dramas.

14   *the ink's Sibylline tears*: the tears of the arcane ('magic', 'Sibylline') art of poetry, sadly contemplating the triumph of its competitor.

I ['Does every Pride in the evening smoke . . .']

Date of composition unknown (in a letter of May 1866 Mallarmé stated that he was writing 'three short poems . . . all three glorifying Beauty', but those poems cannot be identified with certainty); published January 1887 in *La Revue indépendante*. The first in a series of three numbered sonnets (headed 'Suite de Sonnets' ('Sonnet-Cycle') in the *Revue indépendante* edition of Mallarmé's *Poésies*), which evoke states of nihilism scarcely (if at all) modified by a suggestion of something faintly positive in the final lines of each poem: at evening, absence of any fire 'except the console's lightning glow' (I); at night, absence of any flowers except perhaps the prospect of 'some rose' (II); at dawn, absence of any bed except perhaps for the birth of someone 'filial' (III). In each case the positive image is hedged with cautions: it is envisageable, but that does not necessarily make it possible.

  Beyond this point, published interpretations of the sonnet-cycle differ considerably, and none of them has yet gained general acceptance. The cycle has been read as depicting the bleak situation of the human race in general, or of artists, or of Mallarmé in particular—either as a poet mourning his personal inability to create, or as a father mourning the loss of his son (Anatole, who died in 1879 at the age of 8). Nor is there agreement that the three sonnets share a common theme: as with the tetralogy 'A Few Sonnets', poems written on different subjects at different times may subsequently have been grouped together for purposes of comparison and contrast. (Nevertheless, it should be noted that Mallarmé always presented them together, in the same order and with the same numbering.)

6   *outmoded ware*: the words *hoir* and *chu* were obsolete by Mallarmé's time.

II ['Arisen from the rump and bound . . .']

Date of composition unknown; published January 1887 in *La Revue indépendante*. The second component of the sonnet-cycle.

13   *breathe out . . . final*: French *expirer* suggests both 'breathe out' and 'die'.

III ['A lace vanishes utterly . . .']

Date of composition unknown; published January 1887 in *La Revue indépendante*. The third and last component of the sonnet-cycle.

['What silk with balm from advancing days . . .']

Written by July 1868; after radical revision, published March 1885 in *La Revue indépendante*. As usual in Mallarmé, the woman addressed is a representative, archetypal figure, without any individual characteristics (it is unknown for whom—if for any real woman—this sonnet was originally written). The silken banners of creative thought, embroidered with struggling and perishing chimeras, cannot match her rich and tangled tresses; the speaker is tempted to stifle the 'glories' of the former by plunging his face into the latter. In at least one early draft, the 'No!' at the start of l. 9 rejects the temptation presented in ll. 1–8. The final text is ambivalent, exquisitely poised between acceptance and rejection; in ll. 9–16, the speaker may either be succumbing to the temptation ('No, I will taste your hair and stifle the glories of artistic creation!') or explaining why he refuses to succumb ('No! I can taste your hair only if I stifle the glories of artistic creation!').

The earliest surviving draft (July 1868) reads as follows:

> De l'orient passé des Temps
> Nulle étoffe jadis venue
> Ne vaut la chevelure nue
> Que loin des bijoux tu détends.
>
> Moi, qui vis parmi les tentures
> Pour ne pas voir le Néant seul,
> Mes yeux, las de ces sépultures,
> Aimeraient ce divin linceul.
>
> Mais tandis que les rideaux vagues
> Cachent des ténèbres les vagues
> Mortes, hélas! ces beaux cheveux
>
> Lumineux en l'esprit font naître
> D'atroces étincelles d'Être,
> Mon horreur et mes désaveux.
>
> [No fabric that came in the past
> from the east of some bygone Day

can match the naked tresses you cast
beyond all jewels far away.

Living with banners, I decline
solely to see Nonentity.
Tired of such tombs, my eyes would be
charmed with a gravecloth so divine.

But while dead waves of darkness lie
hidden within the ill-defined
curtains, alas! those locks of hair,

lovely and luminescent, bear
cruel sparks of Being in the mind
which I dread and deny.]

2   *Chimeras*: (*a*) mythical monsters, (*b*) fantasies.

6   *in our avenue*: an early (1868–70?) draft is more explicit: 'en mon rêve,
     antique avenue de tentures' ('in my dream, that ancient avenue of
     banners').

['To introduce myself into your tale . . .']

Date of composition unknown; published 13 June 1886 in *La Vogue*. As in
the preceding poem, the speaker addresses an archetypal female figure and
hesitantly ('afraid') contemplates the possibility of sexual contact (assaulting
glaciers, setting his bare foot on a grassy dale). Again the phrasing is poised
between acceptance and rejection of the possibility. Lines 5–8, for instance,
may be read either as 'you did nothing to prevent a sin, which I cannot
describe' or as 'I do not know any sin that you did nothing to prevent'. On the
first reading, a sin has not been prevented; on the second reading, no sin
has not been prevented. Similarly, the sunset fires of ll. 9–16 may suggest
either the consummation or the dismissal of erotic passion (or indeed both).
Nevertheless the tone is resoundingly positive: the poem triumphantly
celebrates a sexual tension that has not been unambiguously resolved.

1   *into your tale*: into the story of your life (with a pun on 'into your
     genitals').

['Stilled beneath the oppressive cloud . . .']

Written by 1892; published 15 May 1894 in *L'Obole littéraire*. The speaker
ponders whether a 'white and trailing tress' of spray on the surface of the sea
may have been left by the submergence of a ship—or of a mermaid. As in 'Sea
Breeze', but much more radically, the central submergence disrupts the syntax
and word order—to such an extent that Tolstoy, always an attentive reader of
the latest French literature, cited this sonnet in 1898 as an example of a poem
with 'no meaning whatever' (Leo Tolstoy, *What is Art? and Essays on Art*,
trans. Aylmer Maude (Oxford, 1930), 167). Amid the jumble of words, the

submerged object vanishes so completely that it is hard to tell what it used to be, or even whether any significant submergence has taken place at all; the focus of attention is principally on the act or state of obliteration, rather than on the thing that may have been obliterated.

1   *cloud*: in the French, the word (*nue*) suggests the feminine of 'naked' and thus looks ahead, by way of 'stripped bare' in l. 8, to the 'siren's childlike side' of l. 14.

2   *base*: (*a*) a rocky reef (the cause of the apparent wreck); (*b*) the cloud of l. 1, solid and lowering; (*c*) a bass note or instrument (associated with the trumpet of l. 4).

4   *before a trumpet*: the primary syntax is presumably 'stilled . . . before a trumpet': the wreck is 'stilled' because the trumpet has failed to sound. But there is also a hint of 'bowed before a trumpet': the echoes are subservient to the trumpet because they simply follow its lead.

    a trumpet lacking grace: the trumpet is ineffectual (lacking in power), but the phrase also anticipates the suggestion of damnation in ll. 10–11: this instrument is not the biblical trumpet sent by God to announce the Last Judgement.

7   *ultimate*: (*a*) supreme, (*b*) final.

9   *concealed*: most recent commentators have accepted Luigi de Nardis's suggestion that *cela* in this line is the past participle of *celer* ('conceal')—itself fittingly concealed by the syntax, so that it can easily be construed as the pronoun 'that'.

10 *failing*: the word simultaneously confirms and denies the existence of the 'great catastrophe'.

11 *chasm*: (*l'abîme*) (*a*) the sea, (*b*) hell. An early (1892?) draft has *le courroux* ('the wrath') instead.

13 *would have drowned*: in the French, the tense may express either a future action (such as the death of the poet and/or of his poetry) or a probable action.

['My old tomes closed upon the name Paphos . . .']

Written probably in 1886; published 3 January 1887 in *La Revue indépendante*. The *Poésies* end with a characteristically complex valedictory gesture: the speaker shuts his books on the realm of the imagination, but nevertheless finds himself dwelling on it rather than on the 'fruits' and 'love' accessible in the world around him, which is 'cold' and 'bare', inhibiting imaginative creation ('some feigned vista').

1   *Paphos*: an ancient city in Cyprus, famous as a centre of the worship of the spray-born goddess Aphrodite, and thus suggesting the mythology of love (as contrasted with the reality contemplated later in the poem). In the French, the name has to be mispronounced if it is to rhyme with *triomphaux*—a 'negligence' most uncharacteristic of Mallarmé (the English translation imitates this by rhyming it with 'genius'). The

speaker, shutting his 'old volumes' on Paphos, seems to have put away the traditional rules of literature at the same time. Yet the act can also be construed as an affirmation of the importance of Paphos: the word is so crucial that it *has* to be placed in rhyme-position, at whatever cost to literary orthodoxy.

12   *wyvern*: in heraldry, a viper or other serpent; the image is drawn from Genesis 3: 15 and Romans 16: 20, where the serpent (Satan) is crushed underfoot.

14   *Amazon*: in Classical mythology, the Amazons were female warriors who burnt off one breast in order to draw their bows more freely. The speaker is thus pondering on something that has no existence even in the realm of myth.

Anecdotes or Poems

Mallarmé first collected his prose poems in *Pages*, published 5 May 1891 by Deman. When he reprinted them in *Divagations* (*Diversions*, 1897), he retained the 1891 order with only two changes: 'Glory' was now placed after, rather than before, 'The Ecclesiastic', and the newly composed 'Conflict' was added. The 1897 sequence is followed here.

The Future Phenomenon

Written early 1865; published 20 December 1871 in *La République des lettres*. At sunset in a pallid, dying world ('an age that has outlived beauty'), a show-man exhibits a 'Woman of ancient times', whose vitality and nobility are beyond the reach of her onlookers, though science may preserve her and poets may draw inspiration from her. 'Phenomenon': (*a*) an object of perception; (*b*) a prodigy.

Autumn Lament

Written 1863; published 2 July 1864 in *La Semaine de Cusset et de Vichy*. At sunset on an autumn day, the speaker is mourning the loss of an unspecified Maria—a beloved, a relative, or the Virgin revered in Roman Catholicism? (The name was borne both by Mallarmé's sister, who died on 31 August 1857, and by his wife, whom he married on 10 August 1863, but the poet would not have expected his readers to be aware of either fact; its Italianate spelling is thematically relevant.) He is reading poetry from the decline of pagan Latin literature (the early centuries CE), which suits his mood, when he hears outside the equally apt music of a barrel-organ; its French name, *orgue de Barbarie*, recalls the Barbarian invaders of Rome mentioned in the poem's first paragraph.

Winter Shivers

Written 1864; published 20 October 1867 in *La Revue des lettres et des arts*. A companion to the previous piece; in 1873 and 1886 Mallarmé grouped them together under the single title 'Autumn Lament and Winter Shivers'. The

season is now winter, and the speaker is now accompanied by an unnamed living 'sister' (biological relative or beloved? the poem contains suggestions of both), who reads an old almanac silently while he contemplates their out-of-time surroundings and their common love of bygone things. 'Wyverns' are serpents or dragons (a heraldic term).

The Demon of Analogy

Written probably in 1864; published 15 February 1874 in *Revue du monde nouveau*. The poem's title is modelled on that of 'Le Démon de la perversité', Baudelaire's rendering of Poe's tale 'The Imp of the Perverse'. Into the speaker's mind comes the curious sentence 'The Penultimate is dead'; he associates it (especially its syllable *nul*) with the sound of a stringed instrument; and as he roams the streets preoccupied with these things, he finds that he has instinctively come to rest gazing at his reflection in a shop window displaying old lutes.

Poor Pale Child

Written June 1864; published 2 July 1864 in *La Semaine de Cusset et de Vichy*. A lone boy is singing 'for his supper' in the street; the poem's narrator, listening, identifies both with him (artist and potential rebel: 'crimes aren't very hard to commit . . .') and with the social world that is shaping his destiny ('people will make you wicked . . .').

The Pipe

Written 1864; published 12 January 1868 in *La Revue des lettres et des arts*. The speaker, a writer, tries to settle down to work, but is distracted by rediscovering his pipe, which recalls his previous winter in London and his Channel crossings accompanied by a 'poor wandering beloved' (feminine in gender, like his other 'friend' the pipe) who has apparently been through the social ritual of 'saying goodbye to each other for evermore' with him. (Mallarmé and his wife had been in London between November 1862 and August 1863, apart from a brief return to the Continent during spring 1863.)

An Interrupted Performance

Written by 1875; published 20 December 1875 in *La République des lettres*. At a stage performance, a clown is handling (with conventional human superiority) a trained bear, when an accident suddenly cuts short the audience's applause. As the clown is pretending to catch invisible flies, the bear reaches out to hug him, causing the man to panic and toss his head (which is adorned with 'a paper-and-gold fly'). The poem's speaker sees profound significance in this encounter, and marvels that the other onlookers fail to share his view; he pictures the bear's act as an appeal for enlightenment and an attempt at 'reconciliation' with humanity. At last the animal is lured away by a piece of raw meat, and the curtain comes down.

Atta Troll, in Heinrich Heine's poem of that name (1841–7), was a dancing bear that broke its chain but was eventually killed by magic; Martin, in French

legend, was a bear that devoured a priest's (in some accounts St Martin's) donkey and was then compelled to carry the priest's luggage. Both animals defied, but were ultimately quelled by, humanity.

Reminiscence

Written 1864; published 24 November 1867 in *La Revue des lettres et des arts*, with the title 'The Orphan'; retitled and substantially revised in 1888. The speaker, an orphan dressed in mourning, comes into contact with a securely though comically parented circus boy, whose headgear recalls the hood worn by the Italian poet Dante Alighieri (1265–1321), and whose example raises the possibility of an artistic career ('did I perhaps experience the future and that I would be like this').

The Announcement at the Fair

Written by 1887; published 12 August 1887 in *L'Art et la mode*. The speaker recalls a late afternoon carriage ride with a nonspecific female friend ('any woman'). She persuades him to stop at a fairground, where she takes possession of an unoccupied booth, attracts a crowd, and stands on a table to display her beauty, while her companion recites a relevant sonnet ('The hair flight of a flame . . .', discussed on pp. 245–6). The onlookers disperse, and the speaker looks back on the episode, addressing both the 'dear woman' and an equally nonspecific 'you . . . my friend' (masculine in gender).

The White Water Lily

Written June 1885; published 22 August 1885 in *L'Art et la mode*. On a July day the speaker rows along the river, ultimately landing near 'the gardens of Madame . . .', a 'friend of a friend'. He hears a sound, perhaps of footsteps approaching, but they stop, as if the walker is hesitant to destroy the 'mystery'. The speaker too hesitates, and then resolves to depart while he is still in possession of this 'virgin absence' (which he compares to a white water lily 'enveloping nothing').

The Ecclesiastic

Written by 1886; published 4 December 1886 in *Gazetta letteraria*. On a fine spring day a priest responds to the season by rolling auto-erotically on the grass in the Bois de Boulogne, the famous Parisian park (in nineteenth-century French literature, frequently a meeting-place for lovers). The poem's speaker glimpses this scene briefly and then discreetly withdraws, but in his imagination its resonances become all the richer because he saw so little of the reality.

Glory

Written 1886; published February 1887 in Verlaine's *Les Hommes d'aujour-d'hui*. On an autumn day the speaker travels by rail to the Fontainebleau Forest south-east of Paris, where he is tempted to strangle the official who is discordantly shouting the name of the station—or at least to bribe the fellow into silence. To his surprise, he is the only passenger to alight there, and

after the train has vanished, he is able to pass into the glory of the forest undisturbed.

Conflict

Written by 1895; published 1 August 1895 in *La Revue blanche*, as the only prose poem in a series of miscellaneous pieces collectively entitled 'Variations on a Subject'. Each summer the speaker stays at a country retreat in a landscape similar to that sketched in 'The White Water Lily' (most of the details are drawn from Mallarmé's own summer home at Valvins). This time, on his arrival, he finds that the house's ground floor is occupied by some railway workers, who pass the time on Sunday shouting and getting drunk. The speaker contemplates the tensions between himself and them, both in social class (he is 'middle class', they are 'proletarians') and in occupation (he works on intangible things, with 'the head'; they on tangible things, with 'the arm'), yet as night falls and the labourers fall asleep, he recognizes that 'they honourably retain the sacred part of existence', share 'a healthy understanding of the human condition', and slumber at last on their 'mother earth'.

A Dice Throw At Any Time Never Will Abolish Chance

Written 1896; published 17 May 1897 in *Cosmopolis*. The poem is laid out in eleven double-page spreads, with the visual arrangement of the words dramatizing their sense. For publication in *Cosmopolis*, Mallarmé was obliged to prepare a simplified form of the work (with the words realigned so that they could be presented on single pages), which he prefaced with the following 'Comment':

I would prefer this Note not to be read, or to be glanced at and then actually forgotten; it teaches the practised Reader little that is located beyond his perception: yet may cause trouble for the novice who should apply his gaze to the Poem's first words so that the following ones, laid out as they are, lead him to the final ones, the whole without any novelty except in the spacing of the act of reading. The 'blank spaces', in reality, assume importance and catch the eye at once; versification has always demanded them, as a surrounding silence, so that a lyric or a short-lined piece usually occupies only about the central one-third of its page: I am not transgressing against this arrangement, merely dispersing its components. The paper intervenes every time an image ends or withdraws of its own accord, accepting that others will follow it; and as there is no question of the customary regular sound patterns or lines—rather, of prismatic subdivisions of the Idea, at the moment when they appear and as long as they last, in some precise mental context, the result is that the text establishes itself in varying positions, near or far from the implicit leading train of thought, for reasons of verisimilitude. If I may say so, from a literary viewpoint this reproduced distance mentally separating word-groups or words from one another has the advantage of seeming to speed up and slow down the rhythm, scanning it, even intimating it through a simultaneous vision of the Page: the latter being taken as the basic unit, in the way that the Verse or

perfect line is taken in other works. The fiction will brush the surface and dissipate quickly, depending on the motion of the writing, around the fragmentary pauses in a key sentence that is introduced in the title and then continued. Everything takes place in a foreshortened, hypothetical state; narrative is avoided. Let me add that, for anyone who would read it aloud, a musical score results from this stripped-down form of thought (with retreats, prolongations, flights) or from its very layout. The difference in typeface between the principal theme, a secondary one, and adjacent ones, dictates their level of importance when uttered orally, and the position on the stave, intermediate, high, or low on the page, will indicate how the intonation rises or falls. Only some very bold directions, infractions, etc., which act as a counterpoint to this prosody, remain in an elementary state in this unprecedented work: not that I believe first attempts should be timid; but outside my own special pages or personal volume, it would not be appropriate for me to behave too unconventionally in a Periodical, however daring, generous, and receptive to artistic liberties it may be. In any case I shall have displayed, not merely a draft, but a 'state' of the accompanying Poem—a state that does not break with tradition in any way; I shall have developed its presentation in many respects, but not to the extent of offending anyone: just enough to open people's eyes. Today, or without making any assumptions about the future that will arise from this—nothing or a mere approximation to art—let us frankly admit that the attempt participates unexpectedly in certain pursuits that are dear to our time: free verse and prose poetry. They have been brought together by means of a strange influence, that of concert Music; several of its methods will be found here: they seemed to me to belong to Literature, so I am retrieving them. Its genre, if it should gradually become a unity like the symphony, alongside individual song, leaves intact the old form of verse, which I continue to venerate, and to which I ascribe the realms of passion and reverie; while this might be a more suitable way to handle (as may follow) subjects of pure and complex imagination or intellect: which there is no longer any reason to exclude from the unique source—Poetry.

In *Cosmopolis* the 'Comment' was accompanied by the following 'Editorial Note', also derived from material submitted by Mallarmé: 'Wishing to be as eclectic in literature as in politics, and to defend itself from a charge that has been levelled against it—the charge of despising the new school of French poetry—the editorial board of *Cosmopolis* offers its readers a previously unpublished poem by Stéphane Mallarmé, the undisputed master of Symbolist poetry in France. In this work of a totally new kind, the poet has striven to compose music with words. A kind of general leitmotif is developed, and constitutes the unity of the poem: various accompanying themes are grouped around it. The various typefaces and blank spaces take the place of musical notes and pauses. This attempt may have its gainsayers: no one will fail to recognize and be interested in the author's extraordinary artistic exertions.' Both the 'Comment' and the 'Editorial Note' were omitted from the definitive text of the poem, which was already in proof when Mallarmé died (though it was not published until 1913).

Bold capitals single out the title sentence; note its physical fall and (partial) rise: '**A DICE THROW**' is set high on the page, '**AT ANY TIME**' partway down, '**NEVER WILL ABOLISH**' at the foot, and '**CHANCE**' partway up again. Smaller capitals identify a subsidiary sentence: 'EVEN WHEN CAST IN EVERLASTING CIRCUMSTANCES FROM THE DEPTH OF A SHIPWRECK, WHETHER THE MASTER MIGHT HAVE EXISTED, MIGHT HAVE BEGUN AND ENDED, MIGHT HAVE BEEN RECKONED, MIGHT HAVE ENLIGHTENED, NOTHING WILL HAVE TAKEN PLACE OTHER THAN THE PLACE, EXCEPT PERHAPS A CONSTELLATION'. But each phrase of these sentences also participates in many other, visually subordinate sentences, which intersect with each other—sometimes supporting, sometimes challenging, and sometimes operating independently of each other. '*If it was the number, it would be* **CHANCE**' and 'THE MASTER hesitates ancestrally not to open his hand to the ulterior immaterial demon' are two examples, chosen almost at random. It will be clear that the possible readings of the poem are almost infinite. Of many published summaries, we quote here that offered by Yves-Alain Favre (Mallarmé, *Œuvres* (Paris, 1986), 417–18): 'Within a grand cosmic frame—surging sea, clouded or starlit sky—we see a wrecked ship. The captain knows that all his nautical skills are now useless; he can only allow himself to be engulfed by the waves and thus submit to fate, or else commit an act of Promethean defiance by throwing dice. But ultimately, even if he chooses the latter option, chance will not have been overcome. The sea once again covers everything; nothing seems to have happened, and the spots on the dice merge into the stars of the Great Bear, above an indifferent ocean.' The poem's general content has often been compared with that of the sonnet 'With her pure nails offering their onyx high . . .': both works contemplate a position of almost complete nihilism with the possible exception, tentatively but affirmatively offered at the very end, of a constellation—the seven principal stars of the Great Bear. Nevertheless, any attempt at summary is not only inaccurate; it also absolutely contradicts the poem itself, which depends intrinsically on an openness to possible alternatives and a refusal to shut out options. (For numbering of the following notes, see headnote, p. 233).

3:8   *desperately*: (*a*) in desperation; (*b*) in despair.

3:15   *the deep*: the *Cosmopolis* text reads *la transparence* ('the clarity').

3:15   *veiled . . . sail*: French *voile* has both meanings.

4:1   THE MASTER: (*a*) the captain of the sunken ship; (*b*) the artist.

4:10   *as you threaten some destiny*: the clenched hand is ambiguous: it may simply be holding the dice, but it may also be shaking its fist at fate.

4:12   *Spirit*: (*a*) the Master; (*b*) the Number.

4:15   *the division*: the *Cosmopolis* text reads *l'âpre division* ('the bitter division'). The adjective 'bitter' is traditionally used in French to describe the saltiness of the sea.

5:19–20   *the sea attempting via the old man or the latter versus the sea | an idle chance*: (*a*) the old man defies the very sea that has chanced to bring

him to (rebirth); (*b*) either the sea seizes its chance to engulf the old man before he has cast the dice, or else the man defies the sea and casts the dice first.

6:2–3   *A simple insinuation | . . . inrolled ironically*: the *Cosmopolis* text reads *Une simple insinuation | d'ironie | enroulée à tout le silence* ('A simple insinuation | of irony | inrolled in the whole of the silence').

7:1   *an utterly lost and lonely quill*: (*a*) the pen writing in the dark; (*b*) the featherlike white crest on the dark sea; (*c*) the white constellation of the Great Bear at the zenith of the midnight sky; (*d*) the white feather in the cap of the black-suited 'bitter prince' Hamlet.

8:7–21   *The lucid and lordly plume . . . on the infinite*: this passage is placed in parentheses in the *Cosmopolis* text.

8:15   *with forked and impatient terminal scales*: the siren is a mermaid, with the tail of a fish.

8:16–19   *some rock | a false mansion | suddenly | dispelled in mists*: the *Cosmopolis* text reads *un mystère | faux roc évaporé en brume* ('something unknown | some false rock dispelled in mist').

9:17–24   *Down falls . . . the abyss*: this passage is placed in parentheses in the *Cosmopolis* text.

9:22   *whose frenzy*: in the *Cosmopolis* text, the pronoun is *leur* (i.e. the frenzy is that of the spray); in the definitive text, the pronoun is *son* (i.e. the frenzy is that of the disaster or the quill).

10:14–15   *indefinite . . . swell*: French *vague* has both meanings.

11:21–7   *keeping watch . . . a Dice Throw*: the poem's last seven lines outline the shape of Septentrion (the seven principal stars of the Great Bear). Successive approximations toward that shape may be seen in the upper parts of the page; indeed the basic pattern may be felt to underlie the visual presentation of the poem as a whole and of many of its subsections—which often move obliquely down from isolated fragments at upper left to a block of text at lower right.

Appendix 1: Poems Uncollected by Mallarmé

Although these pieces are grouped together for convenience, they do not belong to a single category, as their varied publication histories show. Two of them—the *Herodias* Overture and Prelude (the latter of which was to include the 'Canticle of John the Baptist')—were never completed. Ten—'The Prodigal Son', '. . . In the Mystical Shadows', 'Hatred of the Poor', 'Because a bit of roast . . .', 'The Castle of Hope', 'In the Garden', 'When sombre winter . . .', 'O so dear from afar . . .', 'The Glazier', and 'Fan (Belonging to Méry Laurent)'—were completed but never published (some were rejected by the publishers to whom they were initially submitted; others may never have been submitted by Mallarmé to any publisher). Nine—'Winter Sun', 'Often the Poet catches my gaze . . .', 'Nothing on waking . . .', 'Lady without too much

passion . . .', 'If you wish we shall make love . . .', 'The Seller of Garlic and Onions', 'The Roadmender', 'The Quarryman's Wife', and 'The Old Clothes Woman'—were published, but never reprinted in Mallarmé's collected *Poésies*. One—'A negress aroused by the devil . . .'—was reprinted in the 1887 edition of his *Poésies*, but omitted from the final edition. 'All the soul that we evoke . . .', the 'Tomb' for Verlaine ('The black rock, cross . . .'), 'For the sole task of travelling . . .', and perhaps 'Little Ditty (Warlike)' and the 'Homage' to Puvis de Chavannes ('Every Dawn however numb . . .') were completed too late for Mallarmé to include them in either collection of his *Poésies*, even if he had wished to do so. Most of these items, whatever their provenance, were interpolated by Mallarmé's literary executors in the 1899 and 1913 editions of his *Poésies*. In the present volume they are arranged in approximate order of composition.

Winter Sun

Written early 1862; published 13 July 1862 in the Dieppe *Journal des baigneurs*. Éliacim Jourdain was the pen-name of Étienne Pellican, poet and secretary of the Dieppe town council.

1   *Apollo*: the sun-god in Greek mythology.

9   *Guritan*: the duel-prone (hence 'challenges' in l. 14) old Spanish grandee in Victor Hugo's drama *Ruy Blas* (1838; Mallarmé had reviewed a performance of it in December 1861).

13   *aglet*: the metal tag at the end of a lace.

The Prodigal Son

Written 1862; published 1926 in *Le Manuscrit autographe*. The poem is markedly influenced by Baudelaire; there are particularly close reminiscences of the older writer's 'Au Lecteur', 'Femmes damnées', and 'Duellum'.

. . . In the Mystical Shadows

Written 1862; published in the 1945 Pléiade edition of Mallarmé's *Œuvres complètes*. The title is a quotation (given by Mallarmé in Latin) from the Office for the Feast of Fools, originally referring to the virgin birth of Christ: 'In mystical shadows in former days was prefigured . . . that which has been revealed in our own age, in order that we may rejoice.'

Sonnet ['Often the Poet catches my gaze . . .']

Written 1862; published 6 July 1862 in the Dieppe *Journal des baigneurs*. The schoolteacher Emmanuel des Essarts (1839–1909) was an early friend of Mallarmé; shortly before the composition of this poem they had collaborated in a little verse skit, *Le Carrefour des demoiselles*. The sonnet was originally entitled 'Against a Parisian Poet' (in 1861 des Essarts had published a volume of *Poésies parisiennes*), but Mallarmé later preferred a more general and less privately allusive title.

5   *Dante*: Dante Alighieri (1265–1321), Italian poet, whose *Divine Comedy* contemplates (among other things) the fate of the soul after death (hence

'funereal drapes'); in art, he is commonly portrayed with the laurel wreath traditionally worn by eminent poets.

7   *Anacreon*: Greek lyric poet (sixth century BCE), whose verses celebrating love and wine were frequently imitated by later writers.

13   *ostensory*: a vessel for the display of holy relics.

Hatred of the Poor

Written 1862; published 1930 in *La Revue de France*. The subject is closely akin to that of 'Alms' (p. 25), written in the same year.

['Because a bit of roast was done to a turn . . .']

Letters from several of Mallarmé's friends indicate that he wrote a sonnet on 'the birth of the poet' or 'the bourgeois who begets a poet' by November 1862 at the latest. The present sonnet was published in 1880 as the work of Clément Privé (d. 1883). Later still (1885–90) Mallarmé made a manuscript copy of the 'Privé' poem. Two explanations of these facts have been offered: (1) The existing sonnet is Mallarmé's, and the ascription to Privé is an error. (2) Both Mallarmé and Privé wrote sonnets on this subject (Privé was in contact with several of Mallarmé's friends and might easily have got the idea for his own poem from seeing a copy of Mallarmé's); the existing sonnet is Privé's, but Mallarmé, seeing it after its publication, took a natural interest in it and copied it out for reference (just as he copied poems by Baudelaire and other writers).

The Castle of Hope

Written early 1863, and sent to Cazalis on 3 June with the commentary: 'Starting from a lock of hair that has engendered in my mind the idea of a flag, my heart, filled with military enthusiasm, leaps over dreadful landscapes and lays siege to the fortified castle of Hope, in order to plant that banner of fine gold there. But after this brief spell of madness, the rash creature catches sight of Hope, who is merely a kind of veiled and sterile wraith.' The poem's author submitted it for publication at least twice, in *Le Parnasse contemporain* (1866) and in Verlaine's *Lutèce* essay on Mallarmé (1883), but on both occasions it was ultimately rejected. It finally appeared in print in 1919 in *Littérature*.

['A negress aroused by the devil . . .']

Written late 1864; published 1866 in *Le Nouveau Parnasse satyrique du XIXe siècle*. A lesbian scene of the type made fashionable by Baudelaire's *Les Fleurs du mal* (1857); compare Verlaine's sonnet-cycle *Les Amies*, also published in 1866. Mallarmé has combined this subject with another from *Les Fleurs du mal*, the exotic sexuality of the African woman.

Herodias: Overture

Written 1866; published 1926 in *La Nouvelle Revue française*. This mono-logue, never completed to Mallarmé's satisfaction, and finally abandoned, was intended to introduce his Herodias cycle; it would have immediately preceded the 'Scene' published in his collected *Poésies* (p. 29). During the 1890s Mal-

larmé began preparing a new 'Prelude' to replace the rejected 'Overture', but little of it was completed; see the notes to 'Canticle of John the Baptist' (p. 271).

This volume presents the 'Overture' in its final state, as it stood when it was abandoned. Where Mallarmé's final revisions were left incomplete, we have printed the last grammatically complete text; where he had not decided between two or more variant readings, we have printed the reading chosen by Edmond Bonniot for the 1926 edition, except in l. 3 (where the text printed by Bonniot does not correspond exactly to anything written by Mallarmé) and l. 27 (Bonniot chose the third-person variant in l. 26 but the first-person variant in l. 27).

A bed stands empty in a now-tarnished antiquated room against a backdrop of absence and bereavement; the Nurse's incantation is an attempt to summon up its vanished (or nonexistent) occupant, who does not appear, but who begins to take shape in the monologue's closing stages: she is a 'cold little girl', a king's daughter.

24–5 *Sibyls . . . Magi*: both terms recall the historical context of the poem. The Sibyls were pagan priestesses, who were popularly supposed to have foretold the coming of Christ; the Magi were the wise men from the East who brought gifts to him.

26 *woven past*: French *passé* means both 'past' and 'embroidery'.

48 *rise*: the subject of this verb is 'A voice' (l. 39). Various ingenious numerological theories have been based on the fact that l. 48 is the monologue's central line, but this is merely an accident of the poem's unfinished state; the final 'And' shows plainly that Mallarmé did not mean it to end at l. 96.

59 *a lamentable sign*: in legend, a swan is reputed to sing only when it is about to die.

68 *Lucifer*: 'light-bringer', the morning star (the planet Venus); the name was applied to the Devil in medieval theology.

80 *the Cisalpine lands*: Italy, the heart of the Roman Empire.

In the Garden

Written August 1871; published 1975 in *French Studies*. A young bride reverently surrounded by summer flowers and fruits rejects the assurances of Death, who is seeking to lure away her husband ('her Poet'). The Provençal poet William Charles Bonaparte-Wyse (1826–92) had been very seriously ill in 1869; this sonnet was written in the album of his wife Ellen (1840–1925). Mallarmé never included it in the collected editions of his *Poésies*, even though W. C. Bonaparte-Wyse offered to send him a copy for that purpose.

Sonnet ['When sombre winter sweeps over the forgotten woods . . .']

Written 1877; published in the 1913 Gallimard edition of Mallarmé's *Poésies*. An unidentified dead woman speaks to her still-living beloved, who is sitting alone in front of a dying fire at midnight in winter, and assures him that the

utterance of her name will revive her. In Roman Catholicism, 2 November is All Souls' Day, when the faithful dead are remembered. The sole extant manuscript of the poem is subscribed 'Pour votre chère morte, son ami' ('For your dear departed, from her friend'). It is often suggested that the 'dear departed' was Ettie Yapp, the wife of the Egyptologist Gaston Maspero; but that hypothesis is not supported by anything specific in the poem itself—or by the dates (Ettie had died on 10 September 1873).

['Nothing on waking . . .']

Written at the beginning of 1885, and sent to Méry Laurent on 31 January with the title 'Rondel'; published June 1896 in *La Coupe*. Like many other medieval verse-forms, the rondel was revived by many nineteenth-century poets; Mallarmé had experimented with the genre since his teens. The present example is an orthodox 13-line rondel, repeating l. 1 (with different meanings) as ll. 7 and 13, and l. 2 as l. 8.

Sonnet ['O so dear from afar . . .']

Written about 1886; published 1908 in *La Phalange*. The sonnet is addressed to Méry Laurent. The speaker 'rejoices that their wonderful relationship remains ideal—wherein he may address her not as Lover, but as "Sister"—a term both lofty and tender, and which denotes her as equal . . . Yet, when he kisses her hair, something more erotic than aesthetic loftiness is present' (Daisy Aldan, *To Purify the Words of the Tribe* (Huntington Woods, Mich., 1999), 188).

['Lady Without too much passion . . .']

Written 1887; published 10 February 1896 in *Le Figaro*. Another sonnet of muted passion originally addressed to Méry Laurent (who is named in the first draft); in a letter dated 15 February 1896, Mallarmé wrote that it was intended to convey 'a need for calm friendship without passionate crises or too intense a flame consuming the flower of sentiment, which is a rose'.

['If you wish we shall make love . . .']

Written possibly late 1888 (according to Robert de Montesquiou, it was sent to Méry Laurent on 1 January 1889); published 15 March 1896 in *La Plume*. The earliest manuscript is headed 'Song (on a Line Composed by Méry)'; the line in question is presumably the first one. The poem is a 13-line rondel of the same form as 'Nothing on waking . . .'.

Street Folk

Written 1888, to accompany illustrations by Jean-François Raffaëlli; published 1889 in *Les Types de Paris*, except for 'The Glazier', which was deleted from that volume in proof and first appeared in print in the 1913 Gallimard edition of Mallarmé's *Poésies*. Unlike the two longer poems from *Les Types de Paris* ('The Cobbler' and 'The Seller of Scented Herbs'), these quatrains were not included in Mallarmé's final collected edition; presumably their author regarded them as too insubstantial to appear in such a publication.

Fan (Belonging to Méry Laurent)

Written 1890; published in the 1945 Pléiade edition of Mallarmé's *Œuvres complètes*. Méry is addressed in ll. 1–8 by the fan, in ll. 9–14 by the poet himself.

10   *phial*: a phial of perfume.

Homage ['Every Dawn however numb . . .']

Written 1894; published 15 January 1895 in *La Plume*. The painter Pierre Puvis de Chavannes (1824–98) is compared to one of the shepherds in his own paintings, leading his contemporaries ('our time') to drink from the spring of the pure Ideal ('the nymph without a shroud').

6   *the rod struck forcibly*: like Moses (Exodus 17: 5–6), the shepherd causes water to spring forth by striking the ground just ahead of his feet ('where his future steps will be') with his rod.

9   *facing the brink*: the artist is forward-looking, ahead of his time.

Little Ditty (Warlike)

Written about 1894; published 1 February 1895 in *La Revue blanche*, where it introduced an essay rejecting the notion that poets should produce politically committed verse. The speaker, relaxing at his fireside, sees his legs tinged with red like a soldier's trousers; like a white-gloved military drummer, he prepares to fend off the attacks of the enemy—which is not Germany (France's stereotypical foe after the Franco-Prussian War of 1870) but the army of those who urge him to write committed literature.

4   *it (not to keep my peace) suits me*: the French 'hormis l'y taire' ('apart from keeping silent about it') contains a play on *hors militaire* ('outside the militia'); several previous English translators have offered puns on 'suit' and/or 'peace' in this line.

['All the soul that we evoke . . .']

Written 1895; published 3 August 1895 in the literary supplement of *Le Figaro*, where it accompanied Mallarmé's response to a survey of poets' opinions about free verse.

Tomb ['The black rock, cross . . .']

Written late 1896; published 1 January 1897 in *La Plume*. Paul Verlaine (1844–96) had been the poet of his generation most closely associated with Mallarmé, and had done much to promote Mallarmé's work, especially in his influential series of essays *Les Poètes maudits* (1883–8).

1   *The black rock*: probably Verlaine's work, now beyond the reach of 'pious throngs'.

3   *handling its parity with human wrongs*: the 'pious throngs' think that, by detecting some resemblance between Verlaine's activities and 'human wrongs', they may be able to assign him to some comfortable pigeonhole. Compare the thought in ll. 5–8 of 'The Tomb of Edgar Allan Poe'.

5   *the dove*: a conventional symbol of conventional mourning.

7   *the ripe star of that tomorrow*: Verlaine's future glory, already 'ripe' and hence ready to shed the folds of conventional mourning which are currently obscuring it. The folds are 'nubile' (l. 6), and thus are ready to be discarded like a bride's garments.

9–10   *our vagabond's withdrawn leap*: Verlaine's 'withdrawn' (both isolated and isolating) departure from life.

11–14   *Verlaine is hidden ... to catch ... death*: he has departed purely to experience death, which he accepts with childlike simplicity ('in plain harmony') even before he has tasted it.

['For the sole task of travelling . . .']

Written October 1897–January 1898; published April 1898 in *Album commemoratif: A Vasco da Gama*. (The 1899 Deman edition of Mallarmé's *Poésies* printed a slightly different text, which is believed by most contemporary scholars to be a preliminary draft.) The Portuguese navigator Vasco da Gama (d. 1524) set out from Lisbon in July 1497, rounded the Cape of Good Hope four months later, and reached India in May 1498. Mallarmé envisages him travelling even further, like the artist of 'Toast'.

8   *intoxication*: the 1899 Deman edition reads *annonce* ('annunciation').

Herodias: Canticle of John the Baptist

Date of composition unknown (certainly after 1886, and possibly as late as 1898; in November 1894 Mallarmé already listed it among the components of *Herodias*, but most of the other listed items had not been written by that date); published in the 1913 Gallimard edition of his *Poésies*. In Mallarmé's manuscripts this is the middle (and only completed) section of the projected 'Prelude' to *Herodias*, being preceded and followed by fragmentary monologues uttered by Herodias's Nurse (in both monologues John is apparently still alive: this poetry is not constrained by any earthly time-scale). But it may originally have been designed to occupy a different place in the Herodias cycle.

The prophet John the Baptist was beheaded at the request of the girl (called Herodias in Mallarmé's poems) who danced before Herod the tetrarch; see the notes to the *Herodias* 'Scene' on p. 242 above. Paul Valéry, who knew Mallarmé well during the years when he was working on the 'Prelude', described the 'Canticle' as 'the song of the severed head, flying from the blow toward the divine light'. John rejoices that the severance of his head cuts it away from 'the immemorial war' against the body; as it falls, it bows in humble acceptance of its fate—which is akin to the baptism that had saved him during his life—rather than striving to ascend to lofty realms of icy remoteness (like those sought by Herodias in the 'Scene').

12   *the scythe's blade*: the executioner's sword is assimilated to the scythe traditionally carried by Death.

Appendix 2: Occasional Verses

On 8 September 1898 (the day before his death), Mallarmé authorized his family to publish what he called his *vers de circonstances* ('occasional verses'). His daughter and her husband issued a volume entitled *Vers de circonstance* (*Occasional Verse*) in 1920; but there is no reason to suppose that its contents (rhymed addresses to letters; inscriptions on photographs, fans, and Easter eggs; verse dedications accompanying presents; and so on) are necessarily what Mallarmé would have wished to include. In this volume we reprint only the items that he himself released for publication. Even this selection must be treated with caution. In particular, it is doubtful whether he would have reckoned the 1895 'Toast' among his *vers de circonstances*; it is clearly akin to the 1893 'Toast', which he placed in his *Poésies*.

Postal Recreations

Written at various dates between about 1886 and 1893; published 15 December 1894 in *The Chap Book*. Quatrains addressed to personal friends, most (but not necessarily all) of which had been inscribed on the envelopes of letters sent to them by Mallarmé; about 120 further quatrains of the same type are known to survive. The introductory paragraphs signed by 'The Editor' were drafted by Mallarmé himself.

'Their laughter will resound . . .'

Written 1893; addressed to the American painter James McNeill Whistler (1834–1903) and his wife Beatrix (1857–96).

'23 Rue Ballu . . .'

Addressed to the painter Edgar Degas (1834–1917).

'Monsieur Monet, whose vision . . .'

Written 1890–2; addressed to the painter Claude Monet (1840–1926).

'At the Villa des Arts . . .'

Addressed to the painter Pierre-Auguste Renoir (1841–1919).

'Paris, the home of Madame Méry . . .'

Addressed to Méry Laurent (1849–1900).

'Amusing herself by fattening up . . .'

Written August 1890 (the original is postmarked 29 August). Évian-les-Bains is a popular spa resort in Savoy, on the southern shore of Lake Geneva.

'Envied by no draught . . .'

Addressed to the poet François Coppée (1842–1908).

'Monsieur Mendès . . .'

Written May–June 1893 (the original is postmarked 2 June); addressed to the poet Catulle Mendès (1841–1909).

'Farewell to the elm and chestnut . . .'

Written October 1892 (the original is postmarked 14 October); addressed to the poet Henri de Régnier (1864–1936), who had just returned to Paris after a holiday 380 kilometres to the south-east, at the rural town of Paray-le-Monial (where he had written 'The autumn is quite pretty here and the trees are turning yellow nicely').

'Our friend Vielé-Griffin . . .'

Written December 1892–January 1893 (the original is postmarked 2 January); addressed to the poet Francis Vielé-Griffin (1863–1937).

'Never inclined to buck . . .'

Written February 1893 (the original is postmarked 25 February); addressed to the poet José-Maria de Heredia (1842–1905; Mallarmé's misspelling of his surname is common).

'Bear this book . . .'

Written 1887; addressed to the painter Berthe Morisot (1841–95), the wife of Manet's brother Eugène.

'Without taking a tumble in the grass . . .'

Written July 1890 (the original is postmarked 8 July); again addressed to Berthe Morisot.

'Mademoiselle Ponsot . . .'

Addressed to Éva Ponsot, a friend of Mallarmé's daughter Geneviève.

'8 and Rue de la Barouillère . . .'

Addressed to Gabrielle Wrotnowska, daughter of the physician Félix Wrotnowski.

'If you are seeking a medico . . .'

Addressed to the pathologist Victor-Henri Hutinel (1849–1933).

'Take your walking-stick . . .'

Addressed to the fashionable medical practitioner Albert Robin (1847–1928).

'In the depths of Saint-James . . .'

Addressed to Méry Laurent's lover Edmond Fournier (1864–1938), a venereologist.

'Augusta Holmès sought after . . .'

Addressed to the Irish-born composer Augusta Holmès (1847–1903).

'Halt, postman, at the sound . . .'

Addressed to the composer Ernest Chausson (1855–99).

'22 Rue, hear ye! Lavoisier . . .'

Addressed to Marie Degrandi, the wife of the photographer Paul Nadar.

'At 137 Avenue . . .'

Addressed to the writer Tola Dorian (Princess Metschersky, 1850–1918).

'Age is helping to weigh me down . . .'

Addressed to the philosopher Gabriel Séailles (1852–1922).

'At Montigny, Monsieur Grosclaude . . .'

Addressed to the journalist Étienne Grosclaude (1858–1932).

'Monsieur Mirbeau . . .'

Written 1889–92; addressed to the poet Octave Mirbeau (1848–1917).

'Unless he is haunting the clouds . . .'

Addressed to the poet Léon Dierx (1838–1912), born on the island of Réunion, where the litchi tree (native to China) is cultivated.

'Ensconced in your warm Inverness cape . . .'

Written December 1885 (the original is postmarked 24 December); addressed to the poet Paul Verlaine (1844–96), who replied on 25 December: 'Dear Mallarmé, your letter reached me, which proves that with the help of a good rhyme [*rime riche*]—and what a rhyme, *ferlane*, Verlaine!—one can accomplish anything.'

Fans

Written at unidentified dates; published March 1896 in *Au Quartier latin*. Quatrains inscribed on fans belonging to various friends; Mallarmé included two longer poems of the same type in his collected *Poésies*, and a third was added by his posthumous editors (see pp. 57 and 207 above). About a dozen other fan-inscriptions by Mallarmé are known to survive.

'Simple, soft, blending with the fields . . .'

Dedicated to Madeleine Roujon, the sister of Nelly Marras and wife of the writer Henry Roujon.

'Formerly brushing vibrantly . . .'

In *Au Quartier latin* this quatrain was dedicated to 'Mlle G. M.' (Geneviève Mallarmé), but Mallarmé deleted the inscription in at least one copy of the magazine. Possibly the dedications of this quatrain and 'From some far-flung dawn in a far-off land . . .' had been transposed (in which case the present piece should have been inscribed to 'Mme M. L.'); or possibly Mallarmé had

inadvertently selected two quatrains addressed to the same person, and did not discover his mistake until the texts were in print.

'Amid the marbles a lily grows . . .'

Dedicated to Nelly Marras, whose husband Jean was Curator of the Dépôt des Marbres at Paris.

'From some far-flung dawn in a far-off land . . .'

In *Au Quartier latin* this quatrain was dedicated to 'Mme M. L.' (no doubt Méry Laurent), but Mallarmé deleted the inscription in at least one copy of the magazine. In fact the quatrain was addressed to his daughter Geneviève (as the dedication of a manuscript copy in her own handwriting confirms).

'Shut, I am the fingers' sceptre . . .'

Probably dedicated to the writer Marie Letizia de Rute (1831–1902), the half-sister of W. C. Bonaparte-Wyse (see p. 268).

Presenting the *Faun* to Various People

Written 1876 and 1887; published 1898 in *Au Quartier latin*. Quatrains written in presentation copies of early editions of Mallarmé's *L'Après-midi d'un faune*; about twenty further inscriptions of the same type are known to survive.

'Had he sat you down in a grove . . .'

Written 1876; addressee unknown.

'O Faun, as you steal through a clearing . . .'

Written 1887; addressed to Édouard Dujardin (1861–1949), the publisher of the 1887 edition of the *Faun*.

'Faun, if you should wear a garb . . .'

Written 1887; again addressed to Dujardin. The 1887 edition of the *Faun* was issued in a cheaper and simpler format than the 1876 first edition.

'Rightly did you have a little doze . . .'

Written 1887; addressed to the engineer Michel Baronet, a personal friend of Mallarmé.

'With his flute a bit askance . . .'

Written 1876 or 1887; addressee unknown.

'Must you hoot like a passing train in the thickets . . .'

Written 1876; addressed to Suzanne Manet (1830–1906), the wife of the painter.

'O Satyr pursuing not only the brunette . . .'

Written 1876 or 1887; addressee unknown.

Invitation to the Inaugural Soirée of the *Revue indépendante*

Written November 1887–February 1888; published April 1888 in *La Revue indépendante*, a monthly magazine revived by the publisher and novelist Édouard Dujardin in November 1886. Mallarmé was closely associated with it: he wrote a theatre chronicle for its first seven issues, and in January 1887 four of his sonnets also appeared there. Late in 1887 the magazine acquired a new home at 11 Chaussée-d'Antin, and Dujardin wrote to Mallarmé, asking him to provide a versified invitation for a housewarming to be held there on 26 November. Mallarmé promptly set to work; but the banquet was ultimately postponed until 3 March 1888, and the verses had to be revised accordingly.

Toast ('As a man sought from his own province . . .')

Written January 1895; recited by Mallarmé at a banquet on 2 February, and published in *La Revue scolaire* on 7 February. The toast is addressed to Rousselot, headmaster of the Collège Rollin, the school where Mallarmé had taught between 1885 and 1893.

INDEX OF TITLES AND FIRST LINES